Beethoven's Piano Sonatas

Beethoven's Piano Sonatas

A Short Companion

Charles Rosen

Yale University Press
New Haven and London

For information about this and other Yale University Press publications, please contact:
U.S. Office: sales.press@yale.edu   www.yale.edu/yup
Europe Office: sales@yaleup.co.uk www.yaleup.co.uk

Set in Ehrhardt by Fakenham Photosetting Ltd, Norfolk
Printed in Great Britain by St Edmundsbury Press, Suffolk

ISBN 0–300–09070–6

Library of Congress Control Number 2001093745

A catalogue record for this book is available from the British Library.

10 9 8 7 6 5 4 3 2 1

*To the piano students in the summer school
at the Pontina Festival at Sermoneta*

Contents

List of tracks on accompanying CD   ix

Preface   xi

PART I: THE TRADITION   1

Introduction   3

Formal principles   9

Phrasing   13

Tempo   43

Pedal, trills, extending the keyboard   107

PART II: THE SONATAS   121

The eighteenth-century sonatas   123

Youthful popularity   150

The years of mastery   164

The years of stress   208

The last sonatas   229

Endnotes   251

Index   253

List of tracks on accompanying CD

Tracks 1 to 5 are a few selected examples of composers' alterations of phrasing at different points of a movement. Example 6 shows the use of the notation of detached touch and tone colour to indicate a *rubato*.

The recorded examples 7–32 largely demonstrate the relative consistency of tempo indications from Mozart to Beethoven. They should not be taken to imply that deviation from these tempi would be wrong or unjustified, but only to show the existence of a fairly coherent tradition from which deviation could be expected. Composers as well as performers change their minds about tempi, and Beethoven insisted on a considerable freedom for expressive purposes. But it was a freedom defined by the tradition in which it would be exercised. Since there is a discussion of the place of op. 54 in this tradition, I have recorded the whole of this short sonata.

Track 37 is an example of indications of an ending probably intended, and most suited, for a performance in private or for a small group of listeners.

1. Opening of the finale of the Pathétique sonata op. 13
2. End of the finale of the Pathétique sonata op. 13
3. Opening of the Scherzo of the Sonata in A flat major op. 26
4. Opening theme of Mozart's Sonata in B flat major K. 570
5. A later appearance of the same theme with altered phrasing
6. Bars 9–10 of the Adagio variation from Mozart's Sonata in A major K. 331
7. Finale of Mozart's Concerto for piano in G Major K. 453
    Theme in the orchestra
    Variation I
    Variation II
8.   Variation III
9. Opening of the slow movement, *Allegretto*, from Beethoven's Symphony no. 7, arranged by Liszt
10. Opening of the *Allegretto* finale of Mozart's Sonata for violin and piano in B flat major K. 454 (absent-mindedly announced as 451)
11. Ending of this finale
12. Theme of the finale of Mozart's Sonata for piano and violin in E flat major K. 481
13. Variation V of this finale
14. Opening of the finale of Mozart's Sonata for violin and piano in D major K. 306
15. Bars 1–12 of Mozart's Rondo in F major K. 496
16. Opening of the finale of Mozart's Sonata for piano in B flat major K. 333
17. A late passage from the same finale
18. Orchestral theme and variations I–II of the finale of Mozart's Concerto in C minor K. 491
19. Orchestral opening of the rondo finale of Mozart's Concerto in C major K. 503

20. Bars 153–170 of this finale
21. Bars 344–374 of this finale
22. Opening of the finale of Mozart's Sonata in D major K. 576
23. Bars 24–36 of the Adagio of K. 576
24. *Allegretto* movement of Haydn's "Military" Symphony no. 100 in G major
25. Opening of the rondo finale of Beethoven's Sonata for piano in B flat major op. 22
26. Opening of the rondo finale of Beethoven's Sonata for piano in G major op. 31 no. 1
27. Opening of the rondo finale of Schubert's posthumous Sonata in A major
28. Bars 19–16 of the *Allegretto con variazioni* from Beethoven's Sonata for violin and piano in A major op. 12 no. 2
29. Opening of the first movement *Allegretto* of Beethoven's String Quartet in F major op. 135
30. Bars 41–52 of the scherzo from Beethoven's Sonata for piano in E flat major op. 31 no. 3
31. Opening of the finale of Beethoven's Sonata for piano in E minor op. 90
32. Opening *Maestoso* and *Allegro con brio* from Beethoven's Sonata in C minor op. 111
33. End of the development of Beethoven's Sonata in G major op. 31 no. 1
34. Beethoven's Sonata in F major op. 54: *Tempo di Minuetto*
35, 36.   *Allegretto* and *Più Allegro*
37. End of the Sonata in E minor op. 90

Recorded by Giulio Cesare Ricci at the Villa Caetani, Ninfa, Italy, 2001.

Preface

This book was inspired by the invitation to perform all the Beethoven piano sonatas at the Pontina Festival and to give a seminar on them for the piano students at the summer school in the Caetani castle at Sermoneta. It is frustrating to talk or write about the important subject of tempo without being able to demonstrate some of the examples; the administration of the Pontina Festival at the Istituto Musicale "Goffredo Petrassi" and at the Campus Internazionale di Musica in Latina proposed that I record these examples on the fine instrument still in the Caetani villa in the exquisite gardens of Ninfa, a Bechstein of 1879 that Liszt had admired, and of which the sounding-board still produced a lovely tone with a remarkably long decay of sound that every piano ideally should have. The sonority was closer to a piano of 1810 than most modern pianos, and I have always felt that the instruments inspired by changes of style were often better suited to the music that stimulated their construction than the less adequate ones available to the composer. (This does not mean that I find any instrument absolutely adequate to the music of Beethoven.)

This is a practical book, meant as a guide for listeners and performers to many aspects of the Beethoven piano sonatas not always well understood today. It is not an attempt to tell anyone how the sonatas must be played. I have emphasized, and emphasize here again, the freedom necessary for interpretation, a freedom that Beethoven himself expected, although he might be surprised at some of its manifestations today, just as he was surprised by performances during his lifetime. There are frequently good reasons for disregarding a composer's intentions. But there is no reason for not trying to find out what they were, or for not attempting to ascertain what the marks he made on paper signified for him – even if he was not always completely consistent, and even if he was on occasion prone to error like everybody else. It is inevitable, I suppose, that my own prejudices will intrude upon my account.

Above all, this book is not an attempt to coerce listeners and performers into the kind of appreciation of the sonatas that ought rather to come directly from the music itself. I have always despised the writing about music that tries to substitute for the music a kind of pseudo-poetry or, even worse, the sort of facile philosophical speculation that leads readers to believe that they will be engaged in an exalted activity when listening to Beethoven – or are already so exalted merely by reading about it. There is no question, of course, that the music of Beethoven often made a claim to reach the sublime, and that he believed that the experience of great music transcended the day-to-day experience of our ordinary lives. Translating this transcendence into words does not, however, make it more accessible, only more commonplace. The ecstasy provided by music arrives above all through the kind of unselfconscious attention to listening and playing that makes us, for a moment, lose ourselves in the work. Beethoven's music imperiously demanded, and still demands, more intense attention than other composers had dared to require, although his predecessors and his successors have all drawn a benefit from his intransigence. In these pages, I have essentially tried to make that kind of attention attainable with greater ease.

The majority of the printed music examples have been reproduced from editions published during Beethoven's lifetime and are therefore unavoidably irregular in layout. Simple references are printed as numbered endnotes. Any bibliographical reference that required commentary appears in the footnotes.

I am grateful above all for the help of Professor Raffaele Pozzi of the Istituto Musicale di Latina "Goffredo Petrassi" and of Arch. Riccardo Cerocchi, and for the help and encouragement of Robert Baldock, Malcolm Gerratt and Kevin Brown of Yale University Press. Signor Giulio Cesare Ricci of the Fone recording company was extraordinarily helpful. There are too many friends and colleagues to list here who have helped me over the years to understand the Beethoven piano sonatas, but I should mention conversations with Sir Charles Mackerras about eighteenth-century performance practice which were invaluable. I must also thank Professor Kristina Muxfeldt of Yale University for all her help, and am grateful for the aid of Professor Walter Frisch of Columbia University and the incomparable kindness and advice of Professor Lewis Lockwood of Harvard.

PART I
The Tradition

Introduction

Proust's grandmother was a woman of extremely modest, unpretentious demeanour, who never ventured to contradict anyone's literary judgement:

> But on matters of which the rules and principles had been taught her by her mother, on the way to cook certain dishes, to play the sonatas of Beethoven, and to receive guests graciously, she was certain of having a just idea of perfection and of discerning whether others approached closely or not. For all three things, besides, the perfection was almost the same: it was a sort of simplicity of means, of sobriety and of charm. She reacted with horror at putting spices in a dish where they were not absolutely needed, playing with affectation and too much pedal, or going beyond the bounds of what was perfectly natural when "receiving" and speaking of oneself with exaggeration. From the first mouthful, the first notes, a simple letter, she claimed to know if she was dealing with a good cook, a real musician, a well-bred woman. "She might have much more technique than I do, but she lacks taste, playing so simple an andante in such a grandiloquent manner." . . . "She might be a learned cook, but she does not know how to make a steak with potatoes." Steak with potatoes! the ideal competition piece, difficult because of its simplicity, a sort of Sonata Pathétique of cuisine. . . .

> Mais sur les choses dont les règles et les principes lui avaient été enseignés par sa mère, sur la manière de faire certains plats, de jouer les sonates de Beethoven et de recevoir avec amabilité, elle était certaine d"avoir une idée juste de la perfection et de discerner si les autres s'en rapprochaient plus ou moins. Pour les trois choses, d'ailleurs, la perfection était presque la même: c'était une sorte de simplicité dans les moyens, de sobriété et de charme. Elle repoussait avec horreur qu'on mît des épices dans les plats qui n'en exigent pas absolument, qu'on jouât avec affectation et abus de pédales, qu'en "recevant" on sortît d'un naturel parfait et parlât de soi avec exagération. Dès la première bouchée, aux premières notes, sur un simple billet, elle avait la prétention de savoir si elle avait affaire à une bonne cuisinière, a un vrai musicien, à une femme bien élevée. "Elle peut avoir beaucoup plus de doigts que moi, mais elle manque de

goût en jouant avec tant d'emphase cet andante si simple".... "Ce peut être
une cuisinière très savante, mais elle ne sait pas faire le bifteck aux pommes."
Le bifteck aux pommes! morceau de concours idéal, difficile par sa simplicité
même, sorte de "Sonate Pathétique" de la cuisine. ...[1]

Proust's comedy sets the Beethoven piano sonatas in their proper place as the
great representative of Western culture in the upper middle-class household from
1850 almost to our day, as much a part of civilized life as entertaining guests and
family dinners. Great painting was experienced in museums; reading poetry and
novels were generally individual rather than communal activities within the
family; the theatre and the dance existed only outside the home, like symphonies
and operas. For the children of a moderately privileged class of society, however,
learning to play the piano came second – even if a somewhat distant second –
only to learning to read. Particularly for young women, being able to play the
piano was essential to their self-respect, affirmed their place in society.

For music-making at home, the most prestigious form of serious music was the
Beethoven piano sonata. Except for *The Well-Tempered Clavier,* the works of all
other composers could seem light-weight, and Bach was too academic, too
learned, to sustain the rivalry of the drama and emotion of the Beethoven sonata.
Even more than the string quartet, the sonata was, with a few exceptions, the
province of the amateur musician. We may profitably invert Proust's metaphor:
the Beethoven piano sonatas were the steak and potatoes of art music, the proof
that one had access at home to the greatest masterpieces of music.

They were also the bridge from the music made at home to the music of the
concert hall, the staple of the serious recital programme, the way for the professional concert pianist to demonstrate his pretensions to the highest musical
culture. There was nothing meretricious about the Beethoven sonatas: they were
not used – or should not be used, it was felt – to dazzle the listener with the performer's technique, and they betrayed none of the deplorably morbid and effem-
inate character of the works of the great Romantics, Chopin, Schubert,
Mendelssohn and Schumann. They had gravity as well as passion and humour.
They guaranteed contact with the sublime.

They also reached into the future. For all their classic status, they retained
some of the controversial character that had greeted their initial appearance
before the public. Early in the twentieth century the most famous Viennese
teacher of piano, Theodor Leschetizky (his pupils numbered Artur Schnabel,
Ignaz Paderewski and Ossip Gabrilovich), was still advising his students against
playing the late sonatas. Of all Beethoven's works, only the last quartets were as
disconcerting to the concert audience. Paradoxically, the sonatas remained a
model for the avant-garde even as they became a model for the conservative
critic. In our time, they can still stimulate experiment and individuality, encour-
age intransigence.

The double nature – private and public – of the piano sonatas is the essence of their historical role. They not only submitted to the radical changes in the relations of music and society, they also helped to shape those changes. During Beethoven's lifetime almost none of his piano sonatas were played in Vienna in public. The musical tradition of Vienna may have created the first viable style of pure instrumental public music in Western history, but the city of Vienna was backward in the creation of the institution of the public concert – that is, not band concerts or free performances in the open air, but concerts of instrumental music for which tickets are sold, a commercial institution crucial to the development of music as we know it today, and which replaced the patronage of court and church as a way for musicians to make a living. In the early eighteenth century, London and Paris already had a well-developed and flourishing system of public concerts before Vienna: even New York was more progressive. Just as we tend to find the most antiquated plumbing in countries which invested in plumbing very early, while less advanced countries that could not afford plumbing until much later are often able to display the most modern and up-to-date examples, so Vienna, where the development of public concerts lagged behind other European capitals, with the arrival of Haydn produced the most efficient, effective and modern examples of works created for the new form of making instrumental music available.

What made the Viennese achievement possible, however, was a rich tradition of private and semi-private music-making. *Hausmusik*, or music in the home, was widespread, and so were private concerts of quartets and sonatas and songs for small groups of a dozen or twenty friends and guests in both aristocratic and middle-class households. (This was the nursery in which the Romantic *Lieder* of Schubert were to grow to maturity.) The Esterházy princesses learned to play the Haydn sonatas and piano trios, and Archduke Rudolph of Austria was one of Beethoven's most famous pupils, but the sale of sheet music to the general public was an important and growing source of income for composers in their constant attempt, with only a limited success, to emancipate themselves from patronage and from dependence on the aristocracy.

The Beethoven piano sonatas may have been conceived as basically private or semi-private works, but the composer himself was a virtuoso pianist with a considerable reputation. He followed the example of Mozart by introducing into what was essentially private music the difficulties and the display of public virtuosity: the Mozart piano quartets, which are sometimes like concertos for the piano, are the most splendid examples (the publisher cancelled his original commission of six piano quartets because the first two were too difficult for the amateur musician and could not be sold), along with several of the piano sonatas like the one in C minor. The Sonata in B flat major K. 333, indeed, has a finale which takes the form of a concerto rondo, and imitates the alternation of *tutti* and solo passages. Beethoven showed still less consideration for the amateur than Mozart – in fact, famously less consideration for the concerns and comfort of the professional musician as well. His "easy" sonatas, like op. 79 in G major, tend to challenge even the most accomplished performers, and in his first published mature sonatas he specifically prescribed fingering which makes the music harder to play but more effective than the one that most pianists still choose today and editors recommend (see op. 2 no. 2 in A major, first movement, bars 84 to 85: even his pupil Czerny advised an easier fingering). The fitness of his piano music for the public sphere was quickly recognized. The Beethoven sonatas constituted the first body of substantial serious works for the piano adequate for performance in large concert halls seating hundreds. After Liszt created the piano recital a decade after the death of Beethoven, the sonatas gradually became the basis of the public repertoire for any pianist with pretensions to serious musicianship.

Nevertheless, the foundation of musical culture throughout the nineteenth century remained the private sphere. In his articles written in 1802 in the *Allgemeine Musikalische Zeitung,* "On Touring Virtuosos" [*Über reisende Virtuosen*], the critic Johann Karl Friederich Triest remarked that a public concert by a master performer was useful above all as a stimulus, an inspiration to the many amateurs to rise above their laziness and mediocrity. Triest was the most interesting and brilliant music critic of the time, and his observations about the difficulties experienced by the virtuoso on his travels are exactly contemporary with the composition of Beethoven's Sonatas op. 31. They imply the preponderant importance of the amateur musicians who made up so much of the audience for a public concert. At the beginning of the nineteenth century, the concert in a public hall by the professional musician was relatively rare, an exceptional manifestation of music-making, most of which normally took place in private houses or at home. Even the travelling virtuoso had, according to Triest, to be armed with a list of addresses and a set of recommendations so that he or she could be invited to perform at the matinées or soirées which counted for so much musical activity.

The pianistic repertoire supplied by the Beethoven sonatas was one of the principal causes of the shift of the balance of music-making from the private house to the public hall. Intended for the more intimate surroundings, many of the sonatas were seen to be wonderfully apt for virtuoso performance in large halls. Some of the earliest sonatas already presented difficulties resented by the average amateur, and the technical obstacles became harder to surmount with the "Waldstein", the "Appassionata", and "Les Adieux". Later still, it was the "Hammerklavier", op. 106, which appeared to shut out the amateur completely. There is a lady in Vienna, Czerny told Beethoven, who has been practising your B flat Sonata for a month, and she still can't play the beginning. Nevertheless, most of the sonatas remained just within the grasp of the amateur, who could still make something of them: their difficulties, indeed, gave a sense of contact, however tenuous, with the professional that one could get from almost no other set of serious works. They were a challenge which could be taken on, an ideal to which one could aspire, even if they could not, in the end, be fully mastered – not even, as Artur Schnabel remarked, by the consummate professional: no performance of a Beethoven sonata, he claimed, could be as great as the work itself. The piano music of the greatest Romantics – Chopin and Schumann – never attained the full glory of the serious sublime enjoyed by the Beethoven sonatas. Until the second half of the twentieth century, the average music lover became acquainted with many of the Beethoven sonatas at home, stimulated by the occasional hearing of a great (or not-so-great) public performance, as piano recitals became more and more frequent. Only when recordings finally dislodged the tradition of playing music at home did the Beethoven sonatas lose their special status in which the interests of the amateur and the professional were united.

Formal principles

Almost all the possible readers of this book will think that they know what sonata form is, and they will be right (a minimal education in music or music appreciation will include that information). It is doubtful, however, that Beethoven would have made that claim or even understood it. It was not only that one could write a work called a sonata at that time without a single movement that we would later classify as a sonata form. What Beethoven had was not a definition of a standard form,* generally accepted, but a set of models, which he could follow or from which he could deviate: the deviations were, of course, limited by what might be called the rules of musical grammar, more or less unconsciously understood by all contemporary musicians, rules which Beethoven would expand and stretch considerably to the dismay – and later admiration – of his contemporaries. I shall briefly list here a few of the characteristics of the models with which Beethoven was working that largely slipped into forgetfulness during the nineteenth century.

There were two models for a sonata exposition:

1) A bipartite model with a half cadence on V of V before the second part, which is in the dominant throughout, with several new themes, and a cadential flourish at the end. This form is the one Mozart preferred.
2) A tripartite form, largely due to Haydn as Jens Peter Larsen has pointed out. The opening section in the tonic, which presents the main theme, is relatively

---

* A few contemporary theorists, most prominently Heinrich Christoph Koch, described what they thought the most admirable way to write a symphonic movement; in general, they extrapolated from what they judged to be the best models for imitation. What is largely missing from these theorists are the principles that both gave rise to the forms and, above all, allowed for eccentric surprises. Even a composer of moderate talents hoped to surprise by his originality, but the most extreme deviations from the most accepted models are guided, when competent (we must always allow in history and aesthetics for the possibility of incompetence), by what was felt to be inherent in the nature of music – that is, the musical language as the late eighteenth century conceived it. E. T. A. Hoffmann claimed that Beethoven's superiority came from the fact that everything he did arose from the nature of music itself: for "music" we must substitute "triadic tonality".

short. The movement to the dominant is accomplished in a longer section with considerable motivic development; the main theme or a variant of it may appear in the dominant. A short third section rounds off the exposition with a cadential theme.

Beethoven makes use of both these schemes.

There were various models for opening a development section. Since the tension has been increased by the move to the dominant in the exposition and the development enhances the greater tension by a more rapid harmonic rhythm, it was sometimes felt to be expedient to take a step backwards at the beginning of the development and momentarily reduce the tension. This could be done by a brief return to the tonic, an old-fashioned procedure, largely abandoned after 1770, but Beethoven creates a variant of it in the sonatas op. 31 nos 1 and 3. One could also reduce tension by a turn to the subdominant at the beginning of the development, and Beethoven uses this scheme in the Sonata in D major op. 28 and in the "Waldstein" Sonata, although the latter case is more complex as the exposition goes not to the dominant but to the mediant, III.

There were at least two models for concluding a development section for a sonata movement in the major mode:

1) The development could end with a cadence in the relative minor (vi), followed by a transition back to the tonic. When this came to seem too commonplace, the cadence in the relative minor was often replaced by a half cadence on its dominant (V of vi), a more dramatic and unusual effect. The return to the tonic could be abrupt. Mozart used some version of this scheme part of the time, Haydn almost always.
2) The model more often employed by Mozart ends the development in the tonic minor, with a transition back to the major.

Beethoven preferred the Mozartean scheme, but used the Haydnesque form for many important works (e.g. op. 28 and op. 81a ("Les Adieux")).

The recapitulation generally required some use of the subdominant to offset the earlier polarization of dominant and tonic: the subdominant moved the harmony more firmly back in the direction of the tonic. The formal use of the subdominant as essential to the conception of recapitulation largely disappears in the nineteenth century, where it is unrecognized by theorists, but it was a part of eighteenth-century theory. (The subdominant normally plays an important role in the second half of a fugue by Bach, and its appearance at that point of a work was clearly a well-understood prerequisite of musical grammar at the time.) There were two schemes for sonatas:

1) Subdominant harmony is introduced shortly after the return of the main theme in the tonic. In this case, a cadence on the subdominant is avoided. The

new harmony can be the occasion for a moment of more expressive character or lyricism.

2) The subdominant can appear just before the opening of the recapitulation in the transition back to the tonic (e.g. the Sonata in A flat major Hob. XVI/46 by Haydn, bars 75–6), or the recapitulation can be preceded by the principal theme played in the subdominant (e.g. Haydn's Quartet in E flat major op. 50 no. 3, bar 62, where it appears as a false reprise with humorous intent). A variant of this is simply to start the recapitulation in the subdominant, bypassing the tonic at first, as it will simply return in the normal course of events if the exposition is repeated transposed down a fifth. D. F. Tovey considered this a lazy form, and it certainly saves any time-consuming attempt to rethink the exposition. Mozart used it once in an easy sonata in C major (K. 545), and Schubert several times when he was very young.

Beethoven employs the first scheme consistently. The exceptions are to be found, above all, when the initial theme opens with a subdominant harmony: in these cases (op. 31 no. 3, and op. 81a), Beethoven postpones the subdominant appearance until the coda, where it plays a prominent role: he evidently considered it an indispensable part of the musical language. (He also postpones the subdominant to the coda in op. 10 no. 3.)

Works in the minor mode are less frequent and more eccentric than those in the major. Schemes for the exposition remain the same, with the relative major in place of the dominant. In the development sections, the arrival at the dominant minor with a strong cadence is found in enough works to be a model for Beethoven. Often the development opens with the subdominant minor and the dominant minor holds the principal interest at the end of this section (e.g. Haydn's Sonata in C minor Hob. XVI/20, and Beethoven's Symphony no. 9), but the basic chromaticism of the minor mode makes for a larger variety of procedures than the more diatonic major.

Minuet form is much more cut-and-dried than the various first-movement forms, but its very rigidity allows for the composer to play with it to great effect: deviations from the standard pattern are considerably more noticeable.

The main part of the minuet (without the trio) is traditionally in three phrases: the first phrase is repeated and so, grouped together, are phrases 2 and 3. It ought to make a great difference whether phrase 1 ends on the tonic or the dominant, but in fact this does not affect the form of the whole structure. The three phrases are generally of equal length. When they are not, it is usually clear that the composer has interpolated something, and this interpolation acts ostentatiously as an interruption to the expected form. Haydn was a master at this manipulation of the basic scheme, often suspending the harmony with long interpolations that do nothing but make one wait for the resumption of the standard pattern. In the early sonatas Beethoven adapts Haydn's technique with great adeptness, and he returns to it as late as the Symphony no. 8. The structure of the minuet in this symphony is easy to outline:

> phrase 1, bars 1–10, repeated;
> phrase 2, bars 11–20;
>> suspension of movement on the subdominant, bars 20–4;
> phrase 3 (recapitulation starting on IV and going to I), bars 25–36;
>> coda, bars 36–44
>> repeat of phrases 2 and 3 to the end of the coda

The basic form here is the traditional three phrases of equal length, and the extra bars are perceptible as either an interruption or an extension. This is what is found in the minuets of Beethoven's early piano sonatas.

A ternary slow movement will end its first part with a tonic cadence. Even when Beethoven's slow movements are not ternary, he often rounds off his first theme with a strong cadence on the tonic as late as op. 106, which makes us expect a ternary form: this rounding-off is essential to the relaxed lyricism. The variety of types for Beethoven's slow movements is very grand: there are cavatina forms (i.e. an exposition and a recapitulation without a development), ternary forms, sonata forms, variation sets, and simple but moving introductions to a finale. The combination of slow movement and finale for op. 110 is unclassifiable.

Beethoven's final movements are almost always more sectionally constructed, less tightly organized than his first movements, and in this respect he followed eighteenth-century taste to the end of his life. Rondos not only repeat the opening theme several times, but a rondo theme is almost always loosely laid out and repeats elements within itself. Even finales that are not in rondo form tend to have rondo-like themes (e.g. op. 31 no. 3, op. 81a). The late eighteenth-century tradition that the finale was to be more loosely constructed than the opening movement largely guided Beethoven's layout of a sonata. It is clear, however, that he kept trying to find a way to give this looser form an importance equal to the first movement. Although from the outset of his career the finales are successful in their own terms, the problem of giving them greater weight did not find an adequate solution for many years.

The variety of Beethoven's forms in the sonatas is astonishing. He seems to have tried on every occasion to find a unique structure with a dramatic scenario that resembled no previous work. On the purely formal level, the range is startling: for example, an opening section in the tonic may be laid out spaciously (as in op. 2 no. 3 and op. 111) or it can be compressed laconically into seven seconds (as in op. 109). No other composer of sonatas has come near to such a wide range of character, style and form.

Phrasing

Curved lines and dots: legato, staccato, and the shape of the phrase

It used to be thought that Beethoven's indications for phrasing were so erratic that little weight could be attached to them. This was asserted by editors as distinguished as Artur Schnabel and Donald Francis Tovey. We may be thankful that editors have now become more pedantic. However, there is still the belief, tenaciously held, that when Beethoven gave different phrasing for different occurrences of the same theme, the text should be normalized.

Normalization amounts to a claim that different phrase indications or slurs for successive appearances of the same theme, when they occur, are mistakes made by the composer or the engraver. It is true that composers make mistakes writing down their inspirations, and Beethoven was certainly no exception; he could be exceedingly careful, even fussy about some details, and at the same time astonishingly careless about others. It is also true that at later appearances of a theme, Beethoven, like many other composers, could be somewhat summary in his indications (composers often rely, perhaps unwisely, on the intelligence, memory or good sense of the performers). What is unfounded about much editorial practice today, however, is the assumption that there is only one correct or ideal way to phrase a theme. Different slurs may bring out different aspects and different characters of the music, and Beethoven is, in fact, more consistent in the way he employs them than is sometimes thought. Long phrase lines emphasize the unity of the melodic contour, short slurs indicate the accents within that contour: both may coexist happily with each other, and the composer may have chosen to set in relief now one and now the other.

ATTACK AND RELEASE

The difficulty we may have today with Beethoven's indications of phrasing is that the phrase marks – the slurs – did not have quite the same meaning for a musician in the late eighteenth century that they do now.

The basic rules for slurs in the eighteenth and early nineteenth century are very simple:

1) The first note under a slur has a slight emphasis (it may be considered the minimal form of accent).

2) The last note under a slur is not emphasized or accented, but played lightly. In fact, the last note is, for the most part although not always, to be played somewhat shorter than written.

Today, with string players, and often with conductors, the delusion persists that eighteenth-century slurs were indications of bowing, which is what they are used for now. Once when rehearsing the Concerto in E flat major K. 271 of Mozart, I asked if bars 7 to 11 in the violins could be phrased the way I would play them when they occurred later in the solo part. In these bars

the last note under the slurs should be shortened, giving the passage more elegance and less eloquence:

When the conductor objected that the slurs were bowing marks, I pointed out that the slurs were also in my part, and I could not bow, only phrase. Most of the time little harm arises from this sort of error, as bowing will often coincide with phrasing – but not always, and in any case the fundamental meaning of the eighteenth-century notation is obscured. (The beginning of a slur indicates a minimal accent, and changing the direction of the bow is the simplest way – generally the only way – to achieve this on a violin.) Phrasing at the keyboard, indeed, is often based on an analogy with string playing and even more with vocal music: a mimicry of singing is the foundation for the expressive phrasing of instrumental music for centuries, including our own. The slur may indicate where the string player raises the bow or where the singer breathes or sings several notes to one syllable, but it is traditionally above all a direction of rhythmic emphasis and the articulation of the motif.*

---

*There is an excellent discussion of Beethoven's phrasing marks in William S. Newman, *Beethoven on Beethoven*, New York, 1988, which takes up most of the important issues, and is marred only by the tacit assumption that there ought to be one correct phrasing at each place.

The way to execute slurs like the ones in the Mozart concerto is explicitly given in Daniel Gottlob Türk's *Klavierschule* of 1789, but to his account it should be added that the first note of the two-note sets is not only to be played longer than the second but also with a little more weight:[2]

At times some tones should be slurred and others detached. It is customary to signify this type of execution as shown in a. I have given the correct execution in b.

When Beethoven changes the phrase marks at successive appearances of a theme, he transforms the sense of the melody. We may find a good example in the main theme of the finale of the "Pathétique" Sonata op. 13. At the opening of bar 2, the C is a firmly sustained note which needs a certain *cantabile* emphasis. The slur, therefore, stops over the eighth note before the C:

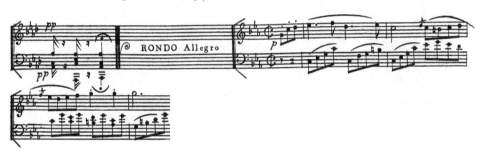

At the very end of the movement, however, Beethoven radically alters the accent of the theme: the note which came at the beginning of the second bar is no longer a half note but a quarter note followed by a rest, and it is now to be played lightly and released without accent, a moment of relaxed grace before the last phrase. Consequently the slur now extends to this final note, which must on no account by played longer than written (it may, indeed, be slightly shortened):

This alters the character not only of the motif but of the main theme as a whole, which is no longer accented on the second and fourth bars as before but on the first and third. Removing the emphasis on the second bar makes the motif hesitant, fragmentary, momentarily indecisive, and justifies the violence of the final cadence. It is true that, when Beethoven wrote very fast, it is sometimes difficult to tell when looking at his manuscripts exactly where his slurs are supposed to begin or end. When it was important, however, he could be very sensitive to the placement of the slur. For example, in the main theme of the scherzo of the Sonata in A flat major op. 26, the two notes C and D♮ in the second bar are clearly united under a slur and separated from the following note, and this establishes that the C is accented, the D♮ unaccented, and the E♭ in the next bar, held for four beats, accented. (The pattern is repeated four bars later with the F, G and A♭, but in Beethoven's manuscript, the slur is less precisely indicated, and the engraver has mistakenly interpreted it as a three-note slur.)

Scherzo
Allegro molto.

Eight bars later, however, when the motif occurs at the opening of the second part, the last of the three notes of the motif note is no longer held for four beats but quickly released after only one. In the autograph we can see how Beethoven started to write a two-note slur as before, but his pen suddenly changed direction, swooped down to avoid the second note and then moved back up to end on the next note, which no longer bears an accent:

The motif now tapers off gracefully instead of moving emphatically towards an accent and a continued development. The new phrasing indicates a fundamental transformation of character; the opening two bars are no longer an affirmation followed by a scherzando comment, but a question answered by an emphatic new motif.

Editors have not always realized the full significance of the slur as it was employed around 1800, and have often tried to normalize those changes of slurring by Beethoven that signify a change in the character of the theme, or project a different kind of emphasis. For example, even the editors of the so-called *Urtext* edition published by Henle in successive revisions of the text have reduced the variety of the slurs on the first page of the Sonata in C minor op. 10 no. 1. At the opening, the slurs of the dotted rhythm (bars 1–7) end on the quarter note:

This tells us that the first quarter note on the weak third beat is to be played lightly: it is the next quarter note on the down beat which receives the accent.

A few bars later, however, the accent of the motif has changed. The quarter note on the third beat is now dramatically accented with a syncopated effect, and the slur therefore ends now *before* the quarter note on the penultimate sixteenth note of the motif (bars 23–7).

This is the way it reads in the first edition (the manuscript no longer exists), but recent editors have extended the slur to the quarter note as before, perhaps thinking that it is evident that one cannot pause between the sixteenth and the following quarter notes. However, the end of the slur does not always imply a pause, but only the sense of an unaccented release. This betrays the ambiguity of the slur, which was used to indicate both a legato and the accent of the phrase. Normally in the eighteenth century this caused no trouble, as the two meanings generally coincided: one often began an individual motivic element of a phrase with an accented note, continued legato, and ended the motif with an unaccented release. The scores of Mozart are filled with short slurs which articulate the phrase in this sense, and so, largely, are the early scores of Beethoven.

Gradually Beethoven's slurs became much longer in his concern not to chop up the phrase into so many small elements. With the composers who followed him, Chopin in particular, the slurs become immensely long, enclosing dozens of bars and even several pages; execution and interpretation evolved towards a greater continuity. This did not necessarily mean more legato, but signified the need to think in terms of sustaining larger units.

The end of a slur can indicate a pause, the final note to be played shorter than written followed by a slight breath, but this is not always the case, as we can see from op. 10 no. 1, where no pause is possible or even thinkable when the slur ends on a sixteenth note. In Mozart's Sonata in B flat major K. 570, the opening theme is phrased as follows:

Later it appears with a more unified phrasing:

The first way emphasizes the rhythm of the bar. It can be executed with the slightest of pauses after the third beat, but that is less important than the graceful lilt given by the minimal accents imposed by the slurs. The last note, F, in the first version of the four-bar motif is a half note, and it is outside the slur; this signifies that it must have at least a certain fulness of sonority. The second phrasing, by contrast, sets in relief the unity of the motif, which now ends more gracefully, tapering off into a quarter note within the slur, and this directs a release without emphasis.

How different were the executions of the two notations of phrasing intended to be? It is clear that the end of each version, either a quarter note or a half note, was to provide a strong contrast with the other version, but whether the separation of each bar by a slur was to be markedly contrasted with the versions in which all four bars are united under one slur is dubious: neither the autograph nor the first edition, which may have incorporated changes made by the composer, is consistent in this regard. It is evident, however, that the first appearance of the theme, as an unaccompanied unison, needed to be more highly articulated than the later one that combines with a new motif in another voice.

In the exposition of the Sonata in C minor op. 111, Beethoven puts a slur over the first five notes of a seven-note motif:

Only the last two notes are marked staccato, so it is not necessary to break the legato before the sixth note. Today we would end the slur on the sixth note, but for Beethoven that would have implied that the sixth note was to be released without accent. Ending the slur on the fifth note, however, tells us that the sixth note is to be attacked with emphasis, and the sixth and seventh notes of the motif are therefore set off in this way, which dramatically transforms the character of the phrase.

The ambiguity of the slur (the end implying either a release of sound or simply an unaccented note) caused trouble for the composer only when he wished a full legato to extend into a final accented note. In the opening movement of the Sonata in A flat major op. 110, the two-note slurs in bars 28 to 31 indicate that the first note in a weak position is accented, and the second note is released and may even be followed by the slightest of pauses:

– but Beethoven indicates a *sforzando* on the last of the two-note elements. Leaving off the slur might have led here to detaching the first note. It is important to see that the *sforzando* reverses the accent of the two-note set implied by the slurs, but the reversal is a surprise. The motif of the ascending sixth is accented as strong/weak, strong/weak, strong/stronger (with the first strong accents in a weak position). In the eighteenth century this way of accenting notes in a weak position was one of the meanings of the term *rubato*. It does, indeed, demand a certain rhythmic freedom in order to be executed with sensitivity, and one should linger very slightly on the accented note, but not so much as to cause a real distortion of the larger rhythmic movement.

ACCENTS AND RUBATO

A similar and fruitful confusion exists in the eighteenth century between accenting a note and detaching it, and this ambiguity continued deep into the nineteenth century. In fact, playing a note slightly detached was a simple way of setting it into relief. This imitation of string technique was suitable to the weak volume of early keyboards, useful indeed for instruments like the harpsichord or the organ in which no dynamic accent was possible, and with the early pianos it permitted a great variety of emphasis from a simple detached note to a slight accent and eventually to a *sforzando*. See for example the beginning of the second part of the Adagio variation from Mozart's Sonata in A major K. 331:

The detached notes at the end of the phrase are not a staccato but an expressive portamento. The notes (G, A, B, C# and D) are not to be sharply detached but only given a little extra weight. Generally this effect is meant to be executed with an unobtrusive *rubato*, and the notation, in fact, directs a gradual slowing down of the rhythm.

The two ways of detaching the note, sharp staccato and weighted accent, were sometimes distinguished in the eighteenth century by writing the former as dots and the latter as vertical strokes. In the first movement of Beethoven's Sonata in A flat major, op. 110, the indications over every fourth note in the right hand are meant to indicate delicate accents, as staccato is obviously impossible and absurd:

Beethoven could be very firm with his publishers, insisting that his vertical strokes should be distinguished from his dots. However, a glance at almost any one of his manuscripts will show that it is often virtually impossible to tell one from the other: in his impatient handwriting the dots are often as large as strokes. The necessary distinction can only be made on a musical basis.

Writing staccato under a slur was a standard way of indicating an expressive emphasis that was to be performed *rubato* – in this case with a slight *ritenuto*. We can find examples in Mozart and Chopin, and playing the detached notes in absolutely strict tempo here would be intolerable:

Note that in the Etude by Chopin, all six detached notes in bar 57 are to be executed with the pedal held down. It is, therefore, not a detached sound that is intended here but a *ritenuto*.

This indication was employed by Beethoven, although the slowing down was perhaps less extreme than in the example from Chopin, and sometimes delicate, almost imperceptible, in fact, as in bar 2 of the theme of the second movement of the Sonata in E minor op. 90:

or in the third and tenth bars of the opening movement of the Sonata in A flat major op. 110:

The required slowing down, however, is clearly more emphatic in the Sonata in C minor op. 111, where it is forthrightly demanded:

SHORT ENDINGS

One aspect of Beethoven sometimes repugnant to modern performers is his occasional rounding out a phrase or even a movement with a very short note. In fact when it occurs elsewhere in eighteenth-century music, as it often does, we find it odd. The end of Johann Sebastian Bach's Fugue from the Toccata, Adagio and Fugue in C major BWV 564 can seem peculiar today:

The ending seems strange to us because it takes a second or so after the last chord to realize that the piece is really finished; modern performers prefer a more cleanly delineated end immediately perceptible to the listeners so that applause will be forthcoming at once. For this reason, it is rare that a modern pianist will resist the temptation to linger a little over the final note of the Sonata in D major op. 10 no. 3, although it should be evident that Beethoven intended the music not to be rounded off properly but to disappear as if vaporized:

Similarly, the last bar of the finale of the Sonata in A major op. 2 no. 2 may be freely executed with a delicate *ritardando*, but there is no reason to lengthen the final note:

These unemphatic endings, unwelcome to so many pianists today, are typical of
the period. Another example is the end of the scherzo in the "Moonlight" Sonata:

Playing the last chord here longer than written is a mistake in style frequently
made in concert: the final chord should be not only short but unaccented.
However – and this is what goes against the grain of modern performance –
when it is played properly as written, the average listener today may not realize
that it is final until a few seconds have gone by.

Similarly, the ending of even a single phrase with an unemphatic short note is
also not always acceptable to modern taste. In the transitional melody near the
opening of the exposition of the Sonata in D major op. 10 no. 3, few performers
will release the F# at the end of the phrase in bar 30 as quickly as Beethoven
directs:

It ought to be obvious that the composer wished for a very short note: it was certainly more of a bother for Beethoven to write a quarter note and two quarter
rests than to write a dotted half note, but the latter is what he generally receives
from most performers. The final F# is not included in the previous slur, and this
implies that it is allotted a certain weight without, however, being lengthened.*

---

* The indications of phrasing ask for a slight accent on the first beat of bars 1, 2 and 4 (i.e. bars
23, 24 and 26, and bars 27, 28 and 30) of each phrase, and another on the second half of bar
3 (bars 25 and 29), giving a lift to the upbeat of the fourth bar and increasing its weight. This
means that bars 2 and 4 are the strong bars. In the next phrase (bars 31–6), the weight shifts
to bar 1.

Two bars later (31–2), however, Beethoven writes a motif with a short unemphatic final quarter-note chord and three beats of rest in the left hand, but the dryness of that much empty space seems to be antipathetic to modern sensibility. This final chord (bar 32) is included as the last note under the slur, and this implies an immediate release with no accent. The expressive weight rests on the *sforzando* in the previous bar, and the release should be graceful, contrasting with the scherzando quality of the next two bars. Rendering the affective character of this passage requires strict and even literal attention to these indications of phrasing.

Unfortunately, traditional eighteenth-century notation of the length of notes was sloppy by modern standards. Beethoven seemed occasionally, as Mozart did, to try for a more accurate indication, but his attempts were intermittent. The basic convention that has become the stumbling block for performers and editors today was actually a simple one: any note or chord preceding a rest was generally played shorter than written. At the second phrase (bar 9) of the early Sonata in A major op. 2 no. 2, there is a good example of Beethoven's trying for a more precise indication and his inconsistent return to the old and (for us today) unsatisfactory convention. At the end of the phrase he writes an eighth note followed by an eighth rest and a quarter rest:

A dozen bars later he restates the phrase, altering the relation between right and left hands; this time he ends the motif less precisely with a quarter note and a quarter rest:

One might think that perhaps Beethoven was not just saving trouble by dispensing with the extra rest and that, since the phrase is minimally different, he now intended the note to be held longer, but one should turn to the recapitulation where the original phrase recurs unaltered, though the old imprecise notation reappears:

Here there is no change except for the less exact indication of the right hand's final note. Wherever this motif occurs, there is no musical reason to play the final note longer than an eighth note, but it is only on its first appearance that Beethoven so precisely writes it out as an eighth note with two rests, an eighth-note rest and a quarter-note rest: in fact, elsewhere (and this phrase returns in bars 165 and 176 of the development section) he always simply writes a note with a quarter-note rest, except in bars 169 and 180, where he is forced to write an eighth note with an eighth rest, as a new chord now appears on the second beat.

When Beethoven repeats a passage but changes the value of a note before a rest, there is a good rule of thumb for deciding whether he is indicating the rhythm precisely or merely returning to an old convention: if the new notation is less trouble to write, then he is probably using it as an abbreviation; if it is more trouble to write, then he intends a different value for the note in order to change the character of the motif.

It has been suggested that the convention of cutting short the notes before a rest accounts for the strange notation of the main theme of the Great Fugue for string quartet:

If Beethoven had written quarter notes with quarter rests here, all contemporary musicians would have played the equivalent of eighth notes followed by three eighth-note rests. The indication to hold the note by writing a horizontal line over it was not yet current. The two tied eighth notes, therefore, serve to tell the players to sustain the note until the rest. In this case, at the very least, Beethoven would have been given the duration of three sixteenth notes. (The only other solution would have been to write *tenuto* over each of the notes.)

For the same reason, the differences in notation of the following passages (bars 252 and 312) from the Sonata in A major op. 2 no. 2 do not, in fact, imply a difference in performance:

The eighth note A in bar 312 does not need to be sustained longer than the corresponding note in bar 252. The passage is an octave higher in 312, and Beethoven makes it less awkward by dividing it between the two hands. But he does not bother to write the last note in the left hand as a sixteenth and add two sixteenth rests. That would have been an unnecessary precision.

The eighteenth-century convention of giving a note before a rest only half its written value was particularly important for notes in the bass. Sir Charles Mackerras has pointed out that the famous extra-long cello and double bass notes in the first bars of Mozart's *Don Giovanni* did not appear when Mozart wrote down the opening bars for the catalogue of his works, and it is a surprising effect of sonority for him to have overlooked or forgotten. The bass instruments of the time, of course, were weaker than they are now, and perhaps the tradition of writing the bass notes longer than their real value arose in order to ensure their sounding effectively. In any case, today we oddly seem to prefer our bass notes to be sustained longer than their written value. In fact, many pianists often leave their left hand resting on the keyboard, holding on to the last note played before a rest as if it made it easier for the hand to find its way back when needed again. Starting with the generation of Chopin, composers of keyboard music preferred a general continuity of sound to the more highly articulated style of the previous decades, a style which Beethoven himself (according to Czerny) deplored as "too choppy" (*zu gehacktes*) when speaking of Mozart's way of playing the piano, and which he tried to attenuate over the years without, nevertheless, ever completely renouncing its system of articulation. His music and its phrasing did much to prepare the new era while still exploiting so much of the old style in which he had been reared. If we wish to grasp his conception of phrasing, we must learn to enjoy the more detached sound that he still used at times, and the consequent sense of air and transparency that he inherited from the style of his earliest years.

RESHAPING THE PHRASE

A motif almost exactly the same as the three-note left-hand motif in bars 31–2 of the first movement of op. 10 no. 3 quoted above (p. 24) (the motif is common enough in music of the period) can be found in the finale of the Sonata in C major op. 2 no. 3, starting in bar 9:

Like the example from op. 10 no. 3, the last chord of the motif is shorter than the first two. It must be lightly released at once. It may properly be played as less than the written quarter note but not more, or the contrast with the third playing of the motif, where the last chord is now written as a dotted half note, will not be effective. What is essential to the period is the immediate and unaccented release of a note preceding a rest: the grace of the style depended on it, and it is important in order to make the articulated contrast with accented endings, as in the last example. In this rising sequence, the motif should become more urgent and more forceful as it proceeds. (In the right hand the accents are clearly artic-

ulated by two slurs in each bar to bar 16, and then only one slur per bar afterwards: this decreases the emphases and increases the continuity; almost no break
in legato is possible at any point here and none is necessary.)

At the opening of the Sonata in E flat major op. 7, the same three-note motif
is found at bars 5 to 10 in the left hand, here inverted, once again played twice
with the last chord shorter than the first two, and then a third time with the last
chord now sustained. The first two playings (bars 5–6 and 7–8), all three notes
tied together by a slur, demand that the last chord be released lightly, and this
requires the motif to be executed with a graceful diminuendo: the third time
(bars 9–11), the last chord is sustained and a crescendo is actually directed, confirmed immediately by being followed by a *sforzando* that repeats the last chord
of the motif and transforms it into a dominant seventh:

After two bars lighter in texture (bars 11–12), the left-hand motif is transferred
to the right hand, and there is no slur (which implies here that each individual
chord is slightly more emphatic), the crescendo also returns, and the third chord
of the motif is now doubled in length with the *sforzando* on the next chord which
will resolve back to the tonic. This page magnifies a graceful two-bar motif with
a feminine ending into a more dramatic, masculine cadence of five bars (13–17).
Successfully realizing in performance the change in character depends on respect-
ing the indications of phrasing and on releasing the notes before a rest almost at
once without lingering over them and without trying to make a richer, more
homogeneous and more agreeable sonority.

When these bars return at the recapitulation, the right-hand version is now
extended, introducing the movement to the subdominant traditional in the eighteenth century immediately following the return to the main theme and the
tonic, and it is now unified by a three-bar slur and a longer crescendo to indicate
a greater intensity (bars 201–5). This three-bar slur is wrongly extended by most
editors to four bars, but leaving the last two notes outside the slur implies a separate emphasis that is musically effective. Note the change in the left-hand phrasing, with two slurs in place of one four-bar slur: this suggests an extra accent
which sets in relief the more dramatic reworking.

The subtlety of Beethoven's phrasing can be seen at its most remarkable in his treatment throughout the movement of the opening theme of the "Pastoral" Sonata op. 28 in D major:

In this nine-bar theme plus one bar of introduction, the phrasing tells us that there are delicate accents on the first beats of bars 3, 5 and 6, and that the last four bars are an individual unit, with the last note released softly and quickly in a feminine ending. In the immediate replaying (or counterstatement) of the theme an octave higher, the phrasing reveals that the first bar was not, after all, an introduction but an integral part of a ten-bar melody. The tenor part is now tactfully set in relief by an unusually long slur for the full ten bars, and this tells us that it is to be heard as a quiet counterpoint to the soprano.

The final four-bar slur in the right hand is the crucial one. On it depends the pastoral expression of the whole phrase: the first note under the slur, the A, receives the weight, and the next three bars move without a break into the quiet release of the last note, which vanishes into the two quarter-note rests. As the pitch rises, the dynamic level goes down and is rounded off lyrically into silence.

When the main theme returns at the subdominant at the opening of the development section, however, Beethoven begins to transform the phrasing:

At first the phrasing is the same (except that the tenor line commences with the second bar of the ten-bar theme). With the following counterstatement, however, the phrasing begins to change as radically new dynamics are introduced. The crescendo and offbeat *sforzando* in the third bar of the phrase and the *subito piano* in the fifth (bars 179 and 181) remove the unifying slur over the third and fourth bars. Above all, with the second indication of crescendo (bar 183), the phrase mark that held together the final four-bar motif disappears: the third bar alone has a slur. The first two bars of the concluding motif now have a separate individual weight, confirmed in bar 188 by a *sforzando* in the second bar after the forte in the first: the second bar is no longer less articulated than the first. Most important of all, the final note of the four-bar motif is not the last note under a slur, no longer, therefore, to be released gently. It now requires a slight attack. This not only adds rhythmic excitement but fits the new function of these bars: they are a preparation for the gradual fragmentation of the motif which results in the series of attacks beginning in bar 209, each bar marked by a separate slur and a *sforzando*, and finally with the motif shortened to two beats in the right hand (bar 219) with a syncopated accent. Dramatic violence replaces the original pastoral lyricism. The large-scale progressive structure of the development and its gradual build-up centres on the last two bars of the four-bar motif, and this necessitates the series of changes of phrasing and accent.*

The separate slurs for each bar continue (and in the left hand as well starting at bar 219) until 239. In this magnificently dynamic climax, which sustains a pedal point on the dominant of the relative minor for thirty-eight full bars with no remission, it is important to mark the underlying rhythm subtly, once there is nothing left but a simple repetition of the harmony of F sharp major for 18 bars. The slur is the minimal form of accent. (In passing, one should note that Beethoven introduces the sustaining pedal only in bar 252: this means that he wants bars 252–6 to have a special new sonority.)

One final example of Beethoven's rephrasing of an important theme may find a place here. The two versions are from the exposition (a) and recapitulation (b) of the second movement, Prestissimo, of the Sonata in E major, op. 109:

* For the exposition and recapitulation, we have the autograph manuscript, in which the phrasing is relatively consistent, if not completely so. Unfortunately, the development section is missing, as it was removed when Beethoven revised this section, and the new autograph page was not inserted.

b)

Beginning with the *subito piano* in bar 43, Beethoven uses a simple harmonic sequence that descends through the diatonic circle of fifths (V of F sharp to F sharp minor, V of E to E minor, V of D to D minor, V of C to C major), a common-place progression that many composers, including Bach and Mozart (and later Chopin and Schumann), have found useful for a moment of passionate expression. The sequence, once started, has an energetic force that impels it onwards, but its very conventionality draws the interest and the attention away from the harmony on to the melody, which, at this point of the Prestissimo, is beautifully expressive.

The phrasing chosen for the first version is remarkable: to understand its meaning one must, as usual, imagine the soprano line sung. In general, singers find it easy and most natural to make the highest note louder than the rest: singing a high note softly is an effect cultivated in that kind of *cantabile* singing called *spianato* on the operatic stage, and it is asked for here by Beethoven, who puts the high notes that twice leap up a sixth to F# and E as the last notes under the slurs. (There is a slight discrepancy here between the manuscript and the first edition: in bar 45, the manuscript starts the slur with the C♮, not the F#: the manuscript version is both more consistent with the rest of the phrase and more expressive). In the third part of the sequence (bar 48) the leap (on F♮) is an octave, and the high note is now in the middle of a long slur that extends for three bars. Playing the high notes without an accent demands from the pianist a special kind of playing, an almost imperceptible *rubato* on each one in order to make them sing out softly. The advantage in this passage is not only the grace of the arabesque line that is so outlined, but also the emphasis that is now given to the notes that are harmonically the most expressive. The slurs start with the D, C and B♭, each of them creating a dominant ninth chord with the harmony of the bass and a series of *appoggiaturas* of great poignance. In this way both the highest notes and the most dissonant notes of the melody are set in relief by Beethoven's choice of phrasing.

He makes a different choice, however, when the passage recurs in the recapitulation, rewriting it so that the highest notes of the first two parts of the sequence are transposed up with extraordinary effect from the leap of a sixth to the interval of a tenth, arriving at F natural and E flat. They are consequently no longer the last notes under the slurs, but singled out and separated from the other notes, and this notation implies that they are no longer a final release but are to be given a greater and more detached weight, an effect which is reinforced by the fact that they now double the bass line. The last part of the sequence returns to the leap of an octave with B♭: like the first two high notes, this one, too, is singled out, but here it is set apart by being placed at the beginning of a slur, which implies an initial attack. Each version of this passage has its idiosyncratic and characteristic style of expression. In executing this movement it is best not to play both passages alike, an intellectually lazy procedure, but to follow Beethoven's phrase directions for bringing out the contrast – unless one can think of something better (not an easy task).

LEGATO, NON LEGATO, STACCATO

In the same Prestissimo of op. 109, we find several passages in which bars with slurs and bars without slurs alternate:

The two-bar groups 9–10, 13–14, 17–18, 21–2, 33–4 and 37–8 have no slurs; 11–12, 15–16, 19–20, [23–4], and 35–6 all have slurs (and slurs begin again with 39–41); in addition, 19 and 23 are specifically directed "legato". (The

passage from bar 33 to 38 is repeated in the recapitulation, and an extra two-bar
slurred set is added there, and then the passage continues as before.) It should be
evident that, when *legato* is repeatedly signalled, something else probably ought
not to be legato, although I am ashamed to admit that I played this movement
for many years without coming to this obvious conclusion. For two bars at a
time, Beethoven alternates two kinds of touch, a legato and another touch which
is not specifically staccato, but which Beethoven would have called *non ligato*.
This is the term (and spelling) he uses in the fugue of the "Hammerklavier"
Sonata in B flat major op. 106, at bar 184, and he directs it for both hands:

In the nineteenth-century critical edition of Beethoven's works by Breitkopf &
Härtel, *non ligato* was here comically misprinted as *ben ligato*. (In general, the
nineteenth century did not fancy the *non legato* technique of the eighteenth century: throughout the piano concertos of the first critical edition of Mozart, then,
the editors added a completely inauthentic direction of legato over many dozens
of passages.)

According to Türk, who was fairly conservative, the non ligato touch was the
normal one for his time of 1789. He writes:[3]

> For tones which are to be played in *customary fashion* (that is neither staccato
> nor slurred) [my emphasis] the finger is lifted a little earlier from the key than
> is required by the duration of the note.

In the 1802 edition of his book he added:

> Bach [i.e. Philip Emanuel] says on page 112: "The notes which are neither
> staccato nor slurred nor to be sustained are held down as long as one half their
> value." But taken in general, this kind of playing does not seem to me to be

the very best. For (1) the character of a composition necessitates a variety of restrictions in this respect; (2) the distinction between the tone which is actually staccato and that which is to be played in the customary manner is practically abolished; and (3) the execution would probably become too short (choppy) if every note not slurred was held for only half of its value.

This probably represents the new emphasis after 1800 on a more sustained style of execution.

How serious at times this *non ligato* indication was still for Beethoven, however, may be seen by the contrast of the succeeding passage of op. 106 in which he writes out a super legato in the right hand in which the pianist is directed literally to blur the notes together:

In the Prestissimo of op. 109, the non legato touch makes the following legato much more expressive, and this is appropriate as the two legato bars each time outline a tritone or augmented fourth, the most dissonant and therefore the most expressive of all intervals in a tonal style. (Of course, at a prestissimo speed, the non legato touch cannot be distinguished from staccato.)

Beethoven himself did not, in principle, much care for the non legato style of playing, and was one of the composers and performers mainly responsible for a turn to a more sustained technique of performance. In 1817, Beethoven's nephew Karl was taking piano lessons from Carl Czerny, and Beethoven wrote to Czerny about the kind of touch at the piano he wanted his nephew to learn:

I should like him to use all his fingers now and then, and in such passages as

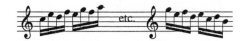

so that he may slip one finger over another. Admittedly such passages sound, so to speak, as if they were "played like pearls" (i.e. with only a few fingers) – but occasionally we like to have a different kind of jewelry.[4]

The "pearly" touch was the slightly detached, non-legato style, and Beethoven preferred a more up-to-date, sustained sonority.

Nevertheless, as we have seen, in spite of his opposition to the old-fashioned, detached sound, Beethoven often found it useful to return to it: he even directed a passage to be played only with two fingers (the fingering he deplored in the letter to Czerny) in order to achieve the *perlé* touch. This is to be found in the slow movement of the Sonata in G major op. 31 no. 1, and, ironically, it contains exactly the figuration that he wanted his nephew to learn to play with all five fingers, and not just two or three. Two editions of this sonata were published in 1803. Beethoven complained that the first, printed by Nägeli in Zürich, had many mistakes. The second (printed by Simrock in Bonn) cannot be said to be much of an improvement. I give the first sixteen bars of the slow movement from both. The notes and the phrasing in Nägeli are more satisfactory, but Simrock has the important indication of the fingering:

Simrock

Nägeli

Adagio

Grazioso

The *coloratura* writing of bar 10 and, of course, bar 12, needs to be played as directed with only two fingers in order to achieve that slightly detached quality and the *leggieramente* that the composer wants here. (In the descending scale at the end of each bar, three fingers may be employed, but four would result almost inevitably in a heavier legato unless one makes a great but unnecessary effort.) The whole movement is a delightful imitation, only partly humorous but mostly affectionate, of the traditional but already outdated style of operatic singing of long decorative passages.* (What follows the elaborate arabesques of bars 10 and 12 is almost all marked staccato; clearly it should not be a sharp staccato, but the detached *portamento* of Mozartean style.)

In this work, Beethoven employs an old-fashioned touch partly for parody, partly for character painting, but he never ceased to find it useful as a contrast to bring out the quality of the more singing legato on which he laid so much importance. The gradations from legato to non legato to staccato were easier to

---

* In illustration of the classical system of phrasing, we should note that at the end of bar 6 the slur stops before the beginning of bar 7, and the next slur ends on a thirty-second note that is certainly attached legato to the next note. In both these cases the following note is accented, and is therefore not included in the slur. For the rest of bar 7, however, in Nägeli the slur beginning with the G on the second beat continues until the F at the end of the decorative motif, as the F is unaccented, and must be released gently and immediately.

achieve on the old instruments since the sound was not as thick and the decay after striking a note was more rapid. It should be noted that there is more than one kind of legato, from a texture in which the notes are run together as Beethoven directed above (see page 36) to one in which each note is articulated although not separated. Beethoven's use of sonority was similar to his use of compositional procedures. He did not abandon any part of the tradition in which he had grown up: he enlarged and made it more various in unexpected ways. Even his last keyboard works have many passages in which the sound recalls the nuances and the transparence of Mozart and Haydn. In the same way, the last quartets have passages which hark back to the elegance of the string quartet writing of the 1780s.

MULTIPLE TEXTURES AND THE DRAMATIC SCENARIO

Except in the good-humoured irony of works like op. 31 no. 1, Beethoven does not use the old-fashioned, detached or non-legato technique of playing for its own sake for long stretches, but only in order to achieve a more interesting variety of textures. The detached sonority is generally followed at once by another kind of touch. The principal theme of the Sonata in C minor op. 111 (quoted on page 22) is first stated staccato and then with a still detached but heavier and more expressive sound. At the counterstatement, Beethoven goes still further:

It should be evident that the first playing of the motif is again staccato throughout, followed by a heavier and slower portamento, and then with a full legato for the first time, giving the motif the full range of touch. At each succeeding point the motif becomes more expressive. The hierarchy of touch is important.

The main theme of the finale of the Sonata in E flat major op. 27 no. 1 is phrased in a variety of ways so that the new function of the theme may be reinforced at each appearance. This can be seen at once in the first eight bars for the various motifs in both right and left hands:

In the first two bars, the sixteenth notes in the left hand are not legato; this detached sound in the bass is particularly difficult to achieve on many modern concert grands as the bass register today is often so thick that the sounds will not decay quickly enough; when playing this sonata it is necessary to choose an instrument that has a relatively clear and brilliant bass with a light sonority. The light, detached sound of the first two bars makes a wonderful contrast with the heavier legato and crescendo in the upward rush for both hands that follows. The pattern is repeated in the next four bars, but the dynamic is now *forte* throughout (the unaccented short ending before a rest in bar 8 demands a *diminuendo* from the preceding *sforzando*).

The phrasing of the initial right-hand motif is altered in bar 5 to fit the new and louder dynamic, as the slur in the opening bar is not repeated. At the opening, the right-hand texture is in opposition to the detached sixteenths in the left hand, and the motif begins with a delicate lilt that comes from a legato attack and release of the two notes in bar one: when they return in the *forte* of bar 5, however, they are no longer legato, the slur has been removed and the second note is no longer a weaker member.

The main theme is given a new function sixteen bars later, and the two notes become powerfully accented, detached but not staccato, while the rest of the theme has now been altered by a staccato touch, which is echoed at once softly with a *scherzando* effect:

The motif returns in the development for fugal purposes. It is now staccato in both dynamics of forte and piano:

In bars 121 to 129 (foreshadowed from 108 on) we come upon the two-note motif in diminution, initially staccato and forte, followed by a *subito piano* which changes the touch into an unvaried legato that goes over three bars. Each appearance of the theme receives a new style of performance that brings out its new character.

The final transformation of the two-note motif is found at the very end in the coda, marked Presto:

In the initial playing of the two-note motif in bar 1, the second note was gently released, but here in the coda the two notes construct a rising sequence, and in bars 268 and 272 it is the second note that receives the accent, with a *sforzando* that gives a grotesque and forceful response to the syncopated bass.*

The significance of the two-note motif is reinterpreted at each of these points, and every time it calls for a new form of execution: 1) legato and piano with an unaccented release, 2) detached and forte with the two notes equal, 3) both notes heavily accented, 4) both sharp staccato, 5) staccato and legato mixed with sudden changes of dynamics, and finally 6) legato with a continuous crescendo and the second note made stronger than the first with a syncopated *sforzando*. It should be clear that in this progression, the motif gains steadily in power and force. The changes in phrasing and touch are integral to the scenario, the conception of dramatic development. We can find precedents for Beethoven's procedures, particularly in the work of

---

*The opening of the coda divides up the new four-bar theme first into two-bar groups, and then repeats the phrase unifying all four bars under a slur. Since the autograph manuscript is lost, we cannot be sure that this was Beethoven's intention or the engraver's.

Haydn,* but the transformations of a musical idea by touch, dynamics and phrasing had never been seen before Beethoven on such a scale or with such concentrated intensity. Nor was it ever seen again. This is one of the many reasons the sonatas remain so fascinating to play.

* See the remarks of James Webster in "The Significance of Haydn's Quartet Autographs for Performance Practice", in *The String Quartets of Haydn, Mozart and Beethoven*, ed. Christoph Wolff, Cambridge, Mass., above all pp. 76–8 and 80–2.

Tempo

It is not illegal to play a piece of music at the wrong tempo: we risk neither a jail sentence nor even a fine. A certain school of aesthetics considers it immoral to contravene the composer's intentions, but sometimes it may even be a good idea. We have all heard performances at clearly inauthentic and even absurd tempos which turn out to be revealing, instructive, moving or brilliantly effective. The wrong tempo might be still more effective than the right one. This leads some musicians to conclude that there is no correct tempo, and this may be true for certain styles of music in some periods. Nevertheless, Beethoven evidently thought there was a right tempo for each of his works, although it is not entirely clear that he himself always knew or had correctly decided on what that tempo should be. Composers often write wrong notes (there are quite a few in Beethoven's manuscripts, although not as many as in those of Debussy or Schoenberg, who hold the record for slips of the pen), and may just as well write down the wrong tempo or misjudge a metronome indication. Nevertheless, even if we decide to play at an inauthentic or incorrect tempo (for reasons of effectiveness, or perhaps just to be original), it is a good idea to know what the right tempo might be, and how to go about defining it.

It is a fundamental mistake to think that a tempo with which we are comfortable today is bound to be correct. Instruments have changed, concert halls are different, habits of listening have altered. Sensibilities have changed as well. It is true that the majority of tempos at which we now perform Beethoven raise few problems. However, when we study the way Beethoven employed tempo indications, there will be some surprises. We have a bad habit of dismissing a tempo which goes against the grain, which makes us ill at ease – claiming that Beethoven must have been in error, or that the copyist or engraver was at fault. If, like all composers, Beethoven did on rare occasions make mistakes, we would always need some evidence to be able to claim this – an instinctive reaction is not enough. Ironing out those aspects of Beethoven which catch us off guard may be convenient, but it risks obscuring some of his extraordinary individuality. We must always be prepared to find ourselves at times initially out of sympathy, and very occasionally we shall be forced to find new ways of performing even familiar pieces which will accommodate the composer's originality and his idiosyncrasy.

Of course, in the end we have to choose a tempo that we find both viable and comfortable, or with which we have finally found a way to be comfortable. What is important, however, is to avoid the initial rejection of a tempo which seems alien or awkward, and to be able, when necessary, to reject an interpretation which presents itself with a specious facility.

"*TEMPI ORDINARII*" AND THE METRONOME

On 18 December 1826, Beethoven wrote to the publishing firm of Bernhard Schott & Sons in Mainz:

> The metronome markings will be sent to you very soon. Do wait for them. In our century such indications are certainly necessary. Moreover I have received letters from Berlin informing me that the first performance of the symphony [no. 9] was received with enthusiastic applause, which I ascribe largely to the metronome markings. We can scarcely have *tempi ordinari* any longer, since one must fall into line with the ideas of unfettered genius.[5]

This letter hints at some of the problems of tempo indications in Beethoven. *Tempi ordinari* are "standard tempi", and what is meant are the simple and conventional indications like Allegro, Allegretto, Andante, and so forth. *The New Grove* (under *tempo ordinario*), quoting this letter, misinterprets the plural *tempi ordinari* as if it were a singular, and claims that Beethoven is describing "the ordinary, noncommittal tempo that required no tempo designation". But the standard tempos of the late eighteenth century are not the same as *the* standard tempo or *tempo ordinario* of the age of Handel, which is based loosely on the pulse.* The plural *tempi ordinari* of the second half of the eighteenth century are multiple, conventional and more tightly defined.

What Beethoven is saying in the letter is that the standard eighteenth-century tempos are no longer acceptable "in our century"; in other words, nineteenth-century genius demands less conventional tempos, more subtle gradations. It may seem paradoxical to us that this greater freedom was to be achieved by metronomic indications. It was, however, by the metronome that slight, nuanced deviations from the standard speeds could be indicated. Beethoven was, of course, aware of the dangerous constraint imposed by the metronome. On the manuscript of his song "Nord oder Süd" he wrote:

---

*The most cogent account of the meaning of the term in the first half of the eighteenth century is Robert L. Marshall, "Bach's *tempo ordinario*: A Plaine and Easie Introduction to the System", in *Critica Musica: Essays in Honor of Paul Brainard*, ed. John Knowles, New York, 1996, pp. 249–78.

100 according to Mälzel, but this must be considered applicable only to the first bars, for sentiment also has its tempo and cannot be completely expressed by this number [i.e. 100].

This, however, is a question of how Beethoven's metronome marks are to be interpreted, to which we must return.

Equally crucial is Beethoven's implication that the standard tempos were previously acceptable. If "in our century" we can no longer tolerate the standard tempos, that means that they were once workable and valid. This raises the problem as to what exactly these *tempi ordinari* once signified, a subject that had already exercised Beethoven some years before. In 1817, he wrote, in a letter often quoted, to a Viennese musician, Ignaz Franz, Edler von Mosel:[7]

> I am heartily delighted that you agree with me about our tempo indications which date back to the barbarous ages of music. For, to take one example, what can be more absurd than "Allegro", which always means "merry", and how very far removed we often are from this conception of time, so much so that the piece itself says *the very opposite of the indication*. . . . But the words describing the character of the composition are a different matter. We cannot give these up. Indeed, the tempo is more like the body, *but these refer to the spirit of the composition*. As far as I am concerned I have long thought of giving up the nonsensical designations Allegro, Andante, Adagio, Presto; Mälzel's metronome gives the best opportunity to do this. I give you *my word* that I shall *never use them again* in my new compositions.

Of course, as we know, Beethoven did not keep his word and never abandoned the old standard terms "Allegro, Andante, Adagio, Presto". He continued to retain Italian terminology in general except for brief attempts around 1815 to substitute German expressions.

What is clear, however, is the distress caused by confused or ambiguous significance: did these standard terms indicate different characters or specific speeds? It is evident that for a late eighteenth-century musician "Allegro" no longer meant "merry". The term was used, as it is today, basically as a neutral indication solely of tempo, although it gradually developed a secondary association to mean a movement of a certain weight and magnitude. Similarly, Adagio did not simply mean slow, but generally implied a work of earnest and meditative character (in the mid-eighteenth century, it often signified as well a movement that required ornamentation, improvised or written-out). These confusions arose from the fact that certain tempos began to be regularly associated with certain characters and forms of sentiment – or tropes, to use today's more fashionable term.

Nevertheless, we cannot dismiss Beethoven's clear implication that *tempi ordinari* as indications of speed were once understood by musicians – and this means generally accepted and effective – and Beethoven's own practice even at the end of his life was rooted in the traditions he had learned when young, however much he may have inflected and altered these practices. This means that at the beginning of Beethoven's career standard terms like Allegro, Allegretto and Andante were taken as more or less precise determinations of speed – as, we might say, proto-metronome marks before the metronome was invented. A study of the music from 1780 to 1800 will in fact reveal relatively coherent uses of some of the terms, although we shall, of course, inevitably come across anomalies.

One important proviso must be added, however: the understanding of the *tempi ordinari* was not international or even national, but municipal. Just as each city in the eighteenth century might have a different idea of pitch, so each musical culture understood the indications of tempo as a part of its local idiom. When Mozart went to Italy, he wrote to his father that the Italians wrote *Presto* in their scores but they only played *Allegro*: evidently, a Viennese Presto was faster than an Italian one. Late eighteenth-century Vienna was a small city by modern standards, and the number of professional and even of enthusiastic amateur musicians was relatively modest and cohesive, a social sub-group in which everyone must have known everybody else. Not only are Mozart's and Haydn's tempo indications more consistent than is sometimes thought, but Beethoven's use of the standard terms also remains to a large extent in line with those of his predecessors. For example, the notorious 138 to the half note of the Allegro of op. 106 is in fact a perfectly normal Mozart Allegro; the stumbling block comes above all from the fact that Beethoven is both more difficult to play and more complex to hear than Mozart. He was not often concerned, however, with the comfort of either performer or listener.

On the other hand, determining today exactly what the standard terms meant for a period that had neither metronome nor recordings is a very delicate matter (the metronome came into general use around 1813, although there were primitive devices before). Metronome marks, like those of Hummel and Czerny for Mozart symphonies, given more than twenty to thirty years later than the composition cannot always be trusted, although they may certainly represent some of the earlier practice; changes in performing style, however, can alter radically in a single generation, sons rebelling against fathers. There have been attempts by distinguished scholars to fix the meanings of the tempo marks of the last decades of the eighteenth century, of which the most famous are the still influential studies of Rudolf Kolisch.[8] What is valuable in Kolisch's work is the consideration of works of similar affective character and rhythmic texture. His final recommendations for tempo, however, derive much more from the performance tradition that developed in central Europe in the late nineteenth century and early twentieth than from any reconsideration of contemporary witnesses to practice during Beethoven's lifetime. For example, his suggestion of 30 to the half note for the opening movement of the Quartet in C sharp minor op. 131 has more to do with the reputation for the sublime acquired by this work than by Beethoven's mark of *Adagio ma non troppo e molto espressivo*: not even an unqualified *Adagio* without the *ma non troppo* could have been performed that slowly while Beethoven was still alive. Kolisch's work is an invaluable guide to the reception history of Beethoven's music as represented by the character of the execution. This value can be underestimated. For many works, we might well claim that the most significant virtues of Beethoven's music may be better captured by the performance tradition worked out by decades of experience with the music than by a simple attempt to recover the practice of Beethoven's contemporaries. In short, it may be a good idea to play the opening movement of op. 131 at a tempo unthinkable in the 1820s, but we should be aware that our performance is a fundamental revision of Beethoven's intentions, to which the words "ma non troppo" are an unequivocal testimony.

In general, the methodology of most of these researches, even some of the most scholarly attempts to recover "authenticity", is still unfortunately guided, at least to some extent, by the method we use to determine the tempo of a nineteenth- or twentieth-century work. The normal and apparently reasonable way is to consider first the musical text and only afterwards the tempo indication – Andante, for example – and then try and fix upon a pace that will make the music sound Andante in an effective way. But if Andante is already to some extent a preset, standard tempo, equivalent for the contemporaries of the young Beethoven at least roughly to a metronome indication, the modern procedure stands things on their head. In other words, if Andante had something like a standard meaning for a composer during Beethoven's early years, then the speed had already been decided: it was a given part of the equation. One did not search for a tempo which would make the piece sound like an andante: the andante *was* the tempo. What had to be done instead was to find a way of playing the music *at that given tempo* which would be effective. What made the process more complex is that to some extent Andante could shift its meaning, depending on the form or type of the piece in question, but these types were also, to a large extent, conventional.

Although a nineteenth-century tempo mark is generally more an indication of character than a precise indication of the needed velocity, the contrary is more often true of the tempo indications of the previous period. In spite of the confusion of character with tempo that had already begun to exist in the eighteenth century, it is clear that Beethoven felt that the indications of Allegro, Adagio, and so forth were basically conventional determinants of standard speeds, although they had affective associations. They did, however, lack for him the subtle gradations necessary for his new music, so that the metronome would be useful for communicating finer nuances even if it, too, was, in the end, too coarse a measure to allow for the necessary suppleness of tempo demanded by sentiment. We have, therefore, to begin by assuming a relative consistency of meaning for tempo indications from 1770 to 1800, and it is astonishing to what an extent such an assumption will prove to be valid if the application is not unreasonably rigid. It is significant that Beethoven in his letter to the publisher Schott affirms that the use of the metronome is to set tempos which are not conventional, not standard, but individual in order to allow genius to create idiosyncratic move-

ments outside of the *tempi ordinari*. The standard tempos were largely understood by consensus within the small homogeneous musical society of Vienna.
Such a community would not have needed a mechanical instrument like the
metronome to come to an agreement on such important matters that were
accepted collectively. It was to some extent the desire for unconventional tempos
that stimulated the use of the metronome.

Of course, besides setting unconventional tempos, the metronome was useful
to convey to foreigners – barbarians like the English and the Russians – what the
correct standard movement should be. Haydn could appear personally in
London to teach the English how to perform his symphonies, but Mozart (after
the tours of his childhood and early youth) and Beethoven did not travel (except
for Mozart's famous stay in Prague). It was in the first decade of the nineteenth
century that the reputations of Mozart and Beethoven were gradually established
outside of Austria and its immediate neighbours, and were imposed above all in
Paris and London, where they were acknowledged by 1810 as the supreme
modern composers of instrumental music. Mälzel's invention of the metronome
followed hard upon this development, and it was enthusiastically promoted by
Beethoven. The metronome was a useful engine in the Viennese campaign to col-
onize European musical life.

AN EXAMPLE: THE CLASSICAL ALLEGRETTO

Beethoven often (but not always) sought for tempos which did not conform to
the standard, "ordinary" tempos of Viennese musical culture – which fell
between the cracks, so to speak – and for this reason we must begin by trying to
grasp how these *tempi ordinarii* worked: this is the tradition of performance, the
context from which his music derived its meaning.* Perhaps the easiest of these

---

* In *The Tempo Indications of Mozart* (New Haven, 1988), Jean-Pierre Marty has usefully com-
piled the indications of Mozart, and some of his arrangements into categories are persuasive.
What is not convincing is the wildly different interpretations of, e.g., Andante, and other standard tempo marks. A danger signal is already raised on page x of the preface, discussing the slow
movement of the Concerto in C major K. 503, where Marty concludes that "the sixty-fourth
notes of bar 98 are almost impossible at more than [quarter note] = 44". The Andante should
apply to the quarter note, and the sixty-fourth notes are properly very fast indeed. Marty's 44
is indistinguishable from Largo, and it is dubious that an indication like Andante could range
from 44 to 96, as he believes. Most of Marty's judgements are based on modern recordings,
rather than on the metronome indications given by Hummel and Czerny: it is true that these
were given long years after Mozart's death, so they should not be accepted uncritically and
already contain some clearly skewed interpretations, but they give a better idea than the habit
that has gradually developed over two centuries of simply choosing the most comfortable tempo
in each case. We cannot ignore the later tradition, of course, but it did, in some cases, produce
some extraordinary misconceptions, which scholars are trying today to correct little by little.

tempo indications to investigate is the Allegretto in duple time, as it exhibits more homogeneity than the Allegro, which had more differing types. We may look, above all, at a conventional genre, the Allegretto finale, although it will overlap with the Allegretto slow movement: there are also two kinds of form within this genre, the rondo and the variation set, but the tempo remains fairly consistent when applied to both forms.

In the case of the Allegretto finale, we are lucky to have a work which allows us to fix a speed with considerable precision, as it presents a number of different rhythms arranged successively in a controlled accelerando, and only one tempo will allow us to realize this progression comfortably. This is the finale of Mozart's Concerto in G major K. 453, which is a set of variations in common time *alla breve*. The scheme goes as follows:

1) Theme in quarter notes
2) First variation in eighth notes
3) Second variation with triplet eighth notes
4) Third variation with sixteenth notes

//

3)

Since a nineteenth-century Allegretto implies a faster tempo than an eighteenth, many pianists begin this movement somewhat too fast and are forced to slow down as the variations proceed. But if Mozart goes from quarters to eighths and then to triplet eighths and finally to sixteenths, it should be evident that he intends an increase in motion by discrete steps within a unified frame. (There are variation sets in which tempo changes must be introduced, as in Beethoven's "Diabelli", but many sets require a steady beat, and Mozart's notation of a controlled accelerando here obviously demands a unified tempo.)

The fastest tempo at which the third variation can be executed by both oboist and pianist without sounding like a scramble is 76 to the half note. This is a fairly moderate tempo for the theme to begin with, but by the third variation the sixteenth notes will be played at 152 to the quarter, which gives sufficient brilliance. Starting with a quicker tempo and slowing down the variations, as we hear at

some performances, destroys one of Mozart's most remarkable effects: a simul-
taneous increase of rhythmic excitement and lyricism. The opening of each
phrase of the third variation demands a cantabile more intense than anything in
the movement before, but the ends of each section enter into a virtuosity more
brilliant than the passage-work of the second variation. Not to keep a fairly strict
tempo from the second to the third variation would be to thwart one of Mozart's
most successful inspirations.

It is important to note that the movement ends with a *Presto* coda in opera
buffa overture style, in which the main theme is now played twice as fast.
Increases of tempo in this period are often related in the proportion of one to
two, so the tempo of the *Presto* is now 76 to the whole note (double the 76 to
the half note of the *Allegretto*), and the entire movement is therefore conceived in
one tempo:

It is rare to be able to fix a tempo of the past with any certainty; in the case of
Mozart's Concerto in G major, we are only able to do so because the logic of
Mozart's scheme requires that the theme and the first three variations be played
at the same tempo to make sense, and only 76 will accommodate that beautifully
planned succession.

When, in 1815, Beethoven gave metronome marks to his symphonies, the only simple, unqualified *Allegretto* is the second movement in 2/4 of the Seventh Symphony. It is marked 76 to the quarter note, which is exactly the same tempo as Mozart's 76 to the half note *C alla breve* (there ought to be a difference between a 2/4 and 4/4 *alla breve*, and perhaps there is one both in theory and sometimes psychologically, but in practice, as we shall see, they usually merge):

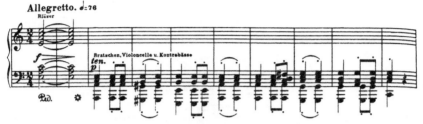

In the Eighth Symphony, on the other hand, the second movement is *Allegretto vivace,* and it is consequently marked slightly faster by Beethoven, ♪ = 88. It is in duple time 2/4, but the notation makes the eighth notes equivalent to the quarter notes of the seventh symphony (and, of course, to the half notes of Mozart's *alla breve* finale of K. 453).

It is clear that the meaning of Allegretto is not always altered by the character and function of the movement, or even by an *alla breve* notation. Beethoven's slow movement of the Seventh Symphony and Mozart's finale are in the same tempo, although the affective type of each work and its place in the larger structure of concerto and symphony are radically different. It should be emphasized again, however, that, for Beethoven as for Mozart, Allegretto is a much slower tempo than it was to become later in the nineteenth century. In the third quarter of the eighteenth century, Allegretto had the affective meaning, as Leopold Mozart wrote, of a work that was *"artig, tändelnd und scherzhaft"*[9] (charming, playful and humorous), but it lost much of that significance, as we can see from the slow movement of Beethoven's Symphony no. 7 and many examples from Mozart. Like "Allegro", it had shed most of its affective meaning by 1790 and become basically an indication of pacing. Later in the nineteenth century it took back some of the meaning of a light-hearted Allegro, but several decades were needed for this development (the "Dona nobis pacem" of Beethoven's *Missa Solemnis,* for example, is an *Allegretto vivace,* and it is by no means charming, playful or humorous). It also became not only lighter but considerably faster: for Brahms, the Allegretto finale of the Second Piano Concerto is marked 104 to the quarter note, which is 30 per cent faster than an Allegretto of the previous era, for which the median was about 76. The only other symphonic movement directed by Beethoven to be marked simply *Allegretto* without further qualification is the finale of the Sixth Symphony, but that is in 6/8 time, and the metronome marking is 60 to the dotted quarter, which is very tranquil – slower, indeed, than most conductors are willing to take it.

To understand Beethoven's Allegretto, we must first situate it in the tradition in which he grew up, and appreciate its partial consistency. Allegretto was often used by Mozart for certain types of movement, the most important of which is the finale. Since Beethoven continued to produce finales of this type, although less often than Mozart, a brief survey of Mozart's practice is necessary here. There are many examples, and it becomes evident that a pace of roughly 76 to the basic beat (either in 2/4 or in a 4/4 *alla breve*) may be accepted as a *tempo ordinario*. I do not mean that every Allegretto of Mozart is to be fixed at a precise 76, but that it is a median which provides a standard that can be inflected by the performer. The *alla breve* rondo finale of perhaps the most often played Sonata for violin and piano, that in B flat major K. 454, falls into this category:

and the relatively slow 76 to the half note is imposed by the final page where the conventional brilliance will come out as 152 to the quarter:

The variation set finale of the Sonata for violin and piano in E flat major, written a year later in 1785, is notated in 2/4.

THEMA

The tempo of around 76 to the quarter is forced on us in the same way as it was with the finale of the G major concerto and the violin sonata in B flat major. Variation 5 introduces triplet sixteenths (a), and then thirty-second notes (b):

The final variation, Allegro in 6/8, will sound almost double tempo if it is played at about 66 to the dotted half note, which is effective and not too difficult. The *Allegretto* opening tempo of the finale of the Sonata for violin and piano K. 306 demands a similar pace:

and the *grazioso* of the "Rondeau" finale of the Sonata for violin and piano in F major K. 376 marked *Allegretto grazioso* may imply a notch or so less on the metronome. The finale of the great Sonata for violin and piano in G major K. 379 is a set of variations notated in 2/4, in which the theme is marked *Andantino cantabile*, but it returns at the end as an *Allegretto*:

THEMA

and the thirty-second notes of the coda once again require a pace of about 76 to the quarter. Changing from Andantino to Allegretto here means that the return is not intended to provide a marked contrast, merely a more invigorating execution.

Although for us today Allegretto is close to Allegro, an Allegro somewhat moderate and light in character, for the composers of 1780 to 1820, Allegretto was very much closer to Andante. Two works of Mozart make this evident. The great third-act sextet in *The Marriage of Figaro*, originally *Allegretto* in the manuscript, was changed to *Andante* (I give bars 1 to 24, as we shall consider later the motif divided between bassoon and oboe – and Marcellina and Bartolo – set to the words "beloved son" in bars 17 to 24):

In a reverse decision, the Rondo for piano in F major K. 494, originally *Andante,* was published as the finale of the Sonata for piano in F major K. 533, and the tempo was changed to *Allegretto*:

The slightly faster tempo was perhaps stimulated by the revision of the piece, which added greater brilliance with a written-out cadenza and some contrapuntal virtuosity, as well as giving a new importance to the lower register. These two examples serve to show that a composer may not always be sure of the tempo, and we may conjecture that different conditions of performance – a small work to be played at home and the finale of a sonata to be performed in slightly more impressive circumstances – will legitimately affect even the composer's idea of the tempo. In any case, we can see that in the 1780s Andante and Allegretto were not far apart.*

This is demonstrated even more clearly by the revision of the tempo indication for the Kyrie in 2/4 of Beethoven's Mass in C major. Originally a relatively simple *Andante con moto* in manuscript, it was changed and published as *Andante con moto quasi allegretto moderato ma non troppo vivace,* the marking of a composer almost paranoid with the certainty that the performers will get it wrong (as they mostly do). What has happened is that Beethoven had already begun to exercise what he thought was the prerogative of genius that he was to claim later,

---

* Mozart also changed the *Allegro* of the Minuet from the String Quartet in C major K. 465 to *Allegretto,* but most editors seem to feel that the *Allegro* of the manuscript is more suitable. Minuet tempi, however, are an independent problem, a special case because of the tradition of the dance.

and demand a tempo that fell between two of the standard tempos (or *tempi ordinari*), in this case between Andante and Allegretto. The Mass in C major predates the metronome. A standard Andante would have been around 63 to 66, the standard Allegretto about 76 to 80. What Beethoven evidently wanted was roughly 69, but he could not yet ask for it. We can see he felt that a standard tempo was comprehensible to average musicians, but that they would be on shaky ground once they stepped outside it. No wonder, then, that Beethoven greeted the metronome with such enthusiasm, tempered with a distaste for the rigidity that it imposed.

There are also Allegretto finales in Mozart's Sonatas for piano in C major K. 330 and in B flat major K. 333. The latter presents itself as a mimic concerto rondo with contrasts of solo and tutti, and it needs the standard tempo to work:

This last movement falls into the same category as several important concerto finales of the allegretto type: it has not only what sounds like awkward piano reductions of tutti sections (the awkwardness helps to convince us that we are dealing with an attempt to render orchestral writing) but also an elaborate cadenza.

The variation finale of the Concerto in C minor K. 491 has no tempo indication in the manuscript but is traditionally labelled *Allegretto*, and with good reason, as 76 to the half note remains more or less the inevitable speed for its weight and brilliance. The fact that the *Allegretto* tempo mark was added not by the composer but by the editors is evidence of the way this tempo was considered standard: any speed much more or less than 76 to the half note is rarely attempted with this movement. Like the G major Concerto K. 453, the notation in K. 491 increases from quarter notes (a) to eighth notes (b) to sixteenths (c):

This completely conforms to the allegretto variation type of finale that we have found before.

These numerous allegretto finales pose an odd dilemma for modern taste. Only when Mozart increases the speed within the notation do we find the brilliance that we feel necessary for a last movement. Sir Charles Mackerras pointed out to me that a study of the metronome marks given to the Mozart symphonies around 1820 shows that the first three movements were generally faster than today but that the finale was often performed a little more slowly. I think the explanation for this lies in the traditional behaviour of the audience at that time: every movement was applauded, and the slow movement sometimes encored. Conductors therefore did not yet find it necessary to whip up enthusiasm with the finale, which could retain its less brilliant character.

Nevertheless, the late eighteenth century (and Beethoven well into his last years) did not always consider a brilliant finale indispensable. There are the numerous and modest minuet finales of the Haydn piano sonatas and piano trios. A brilliant and imposing finale was not yet the norm that it was to become (and for which Beethoven, in op. 111, like Tchaikovsky and Mahler later, would substitute an impressive and meditative slow movement). We can still find lyrical and amiable finales in the last decades of the eighteenth century, above all in *Hausmusik* and chamber music, but even occasionally in symphonies and concertos. This tradition had already weakened by the generation after Beethoven, and I think that is why his pupil Czerny, who only studied very briefly with him, was so often to give metronome marks for Beethoven's finales that are too rapid, while his suggestions for the earlier movements are mostly circumspect: the demands of the public for closing brilliance and virtuosity had begun to corrupt even the private tradition.

The *Allegretto* finale of Mozart's Concerto in C major K. 503 shows how far the concept of performance had changed by the twentieth century. The tempo of 76 to the quarter seems today too amiable, even flaccid, to most pianists:

although the tempo works ideally for the rondo's central lyrical section in the subdominant F major:

It is only in the final pages that Mozart begins to add the sparkling virtuosity that we now consider absolutely necessary for a concerto, and here any tempo above 76 to the quarter (or 152 to the eighth note, as Mozart increases the pace to thirty-second notes) will begin to sound impossibly rushed:

I have seen it suggested, in desperation, that this coda should be played freely like a cadenza, but playing the easy parts at a fast tempo and slowing down for the difficult passages is an unworthy policy, and there is no need for that if the proper allegretto *tempo ordinario* is accepted from the beginning. This, however, is a matter for the individual temperament of the pianist, and whether he or she believes it is possible to make the more moderate tempo interesting enough to hold the attention of the public.

Some of the allegretto finales in duple time of other large works by Mozart require a similar decision: the Quintet for piano and winds in E flat K. 452, the Quartet for piano and strings in E flat K. 493, the Trio for piano and strings in G major K. 496, the Trio for piano and strings in B flat major K. 502, the Trio for piano, clarinet and viola in E flat major K. 498, and the finale (as well as the opening movement) of the String Quartet in D major K. 575. The final *Allegretto con variazioni* in *alla breve* of the Quintet for clarinet and strings in A major K. 581 is another example, and the standard tempo is imposed once again by the progressive rhythmic structure: theme in quarter notes, variation 1 dominated by eighth notes, variation 2 by triplet eighths, and variation 4 with an almost unrelenting sixteenth-note motion; and then, after an *Adagio*, a coda marked *Allegro*. In spite of the great individuality of each of these works, they all fall into a well-defined category, and this explains the similarity of tempo, making this relatively easy to determine. I have no reason to think that 76 or thereabouts does not adequately fit the basic beat of all of these works.

One finale in duple time from the Trio in E major for piano and strings K. 542 resembles all these listed here, but it is not in 2/4 or *alla breve* but in four, and it is marked *Allegro*:

Nevertheless, the rhythm is basically *alla breve*, it has a concerto texture with the entrance of the *tutti* in bar 10, and it develops the sixteenth-note brilliance that characterizes so many of the other allegrettos. Like these, it can be played at about 76 to the half note – or, if one wants to keep the Allegro common time designation, at 152 to the quarter note. For some reason, Mozart seems to have thought of this movement in four, although the *alla breve* phrasing is as clear in the opening theme as it is in any of the other examples. Probably Mozart wanted a slightly more moderate tempo than an *alla breve* allegretto, and perhaps we ought to think of this movement as an Allegro at 138 to 144 to the quarter note. (An Allegro in common time might be said to equal an Allegretto moderato in *alla breve*.) Another finale of exactly the same type is that of the Quartet for piano and strings in G minor K. 478, but it is marked only *Rondeau*, and is traditionally labelled *Allegro*: it needs a faster tempo, perhaps an *alla breve* 96.

Before leaving the Mozart tradition, one more work needs to be considered to illustrate the causes for modern misinterpretation: the finale of the Sonata for piano in D major K. 576. The *Allegretto* is almost always played at a much faster tempo than 76 to the quarter:

In this movement Mozart does not increase the inner divisions all the way to the brilliance of thirty-second notes; triplet sixteenths are as far as he will go. It is true that at the standard allegretto tempo this will sound very sedate. However, on 12 July 1789, Mozart wrote to Michael Puchberg,[10] "I am composing six easy sonatas for Princess Frederike" (K. 576 was written in July 1789). No concert virtuosity was intended here. It has been doubted by some musicians that K. 576 could be one of these easy sonatas (it was, in any case, the only one finished, although K. 570 in B flat major written the same year is very easy to play). The *Adagio* is ostentatiously easy, as if Mozart was demonstrating his ability to create the sublime for the inexperienced fingers. Bars 26–30 show how little he could demand from the performer, and how much he could achieve with absolute simplicity:

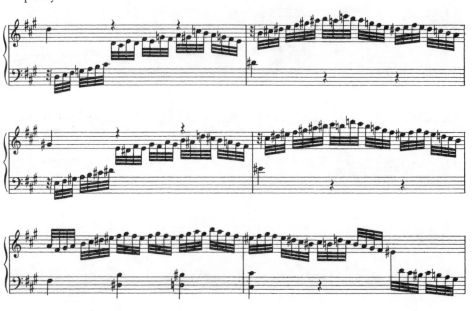

Precisely because of its simplicity this passage is harder to play than it looks.

The first movement, however, is one of the most difficult ever written by Mozart (I have heard the finest pianists, including Gieseking and Solomon, come momentarily to grief in public with it). But the reason for this is Mozart's almost self-indulgent contrapuntal ambitions: he could not resist showing off his compositional virtuosity, and plays the main theme with every possible stretto in two-part counterpoint:

1) At a distane of six beats

2) at a distance of three beats

3) at a distance of one beat

The last is extraordinarily difficult, but Mozart, like Bach with his Two-part Inventions, was evidently under the delusion that two-part counterpoint was easy for amateurs and beginners, which seems plausible since they have to play only one note at a time in each hand. In fact, the only places in the first movement of K. 576 that are at all hard to play are exactly the passages of two-part counterpoint. K. 576 is not a concert piece and is not intended to be effective for an audience. Furthermore, the motif in bars 16 to 20 of the example from the finale quoted above is identical with the expressive line starting at bar 17 of the sextet from *The Marriage of Figaro* (see page 61 above). I do not think that Mozart would have conceived a melody that outlined the dissonance of a tritone to be performed at a tempo too fast to allow it to sound expressive, and that would make it ugly by his standards. The *Allegretto* indication of this work is consequently not an exception in Mozart's relatively consistent use of the designation.* This forces pianists to make a choice: they can perform the last movement of K. 576 in public at the proper tempo and forgo public admiration for their technique; they can play it at a brilliant, rapid tempo and miss the expressive quality inherent in the music; or they can play another sonata instead.†

It is revealing that so many of Mozart's allegretto movements are the finales of concertos (including K. 414 in A major) or of works of chamber music that closely imitate concerto texture with a mimicry of the alternation of solo and tutti sections, like K. 333, 452, 456, 493, 496, 502, and 542, all mentioned above. In this way, a certain tempo became gradually associated with a specific genre or type of work, and helped to define it. Even the finale of the D major Sonata K. 576 employs the concerto texture, as bar 17 in the example quoted above clearly appears like the arrival of a ritornello or tutti section. Allegretto was

*An exception may be the Allegretto *Rondo alla turca* of the Sonata in A major K. 331, for which a faster tempo is probably required. This is, however, a character piece (or "characteristic" piece in the old sense of that word), and a different tradition may be in force. First-movement Allegrettos are very rare, but Mozart uses the direction in common time or *alla breve* in some of his later quartets (K. 499 and 575 in D major – the final movement of the latter is also *Allegretto* as is the minuet); his last quartet in F major K. 590 begins *Allegro moderato*. Whether anything very different from a basic beat of 76 was intended for a first-movement *Allegretto* is not clear: perhaps in these ultimate works Mozart was turning towards a more easygoing or more intimate style. At any rate, the last three quartets were written for the King of Prussia, who would probably not have welcomed any grave technical difficulties, and would have preferred moderate tempi.
† In *Eighteenth-Century Keyboard Music*, ed. Robert L. Marshall, New York, 1994, p. 338, Robert Levin writes: "There is scarcely a more dashing, more flamboyant movement by Mozart for solo piano than K. 576's finale.... The storm ensuing from the substitution of D minor for D major is spellbinding, all the more so in that the fiery temperament of the passage is achieved almost exclusively in two-part counterpoint." It would seem that even the most distinguished and brilliant proponents of "authentic" performance practice sometimes take our traditional twentieth-century practice without critical examination.

a useful tempo for an easygoing last movement which could develop a certain brilliance in the final pages.*

Except for minuets, Haydn did not care for Allegretto finales (he preferred Presto even for the German dance, the *Teutscher,* and most of his allegretto movements are in triple time (generally the minuets) or in 6/8). A rarity is the *Allegretto* finale of the Quartet in D major op. 33 no. 6, and the slow tempo would make this grand exception to Haydn's very fast finales irresistibly witty. Among the later string quartets, op. 76 no. 6 opens with an *Allegretto* variation set in 2/4 which is most often performed faster than 76 to the quarter: it turns into a double fugue marked *Allegro,* and the opening section would benefit immensely from a tempo less than 88 in order to make a more striking contrast with the following *Allegro.* The Quartet in F minor op. 55 no. 2 opens with a 2/4 *Andante più tosto Allegretto* (suggesting once again the kinship of Allegretto and Andante at that time) for which the standard tempo of 76 would be perfectly satisfactory. In the later symphonies of Haydn, the great *Allegretto* slow movement march *alla breve* from the "Military" Symphony in C major no. 100 with all the "Turkish" effects cannot be played far from 76 to the half note:

* Both of Guglielmo's arias in *Così fan tutte* are marked *Allegretto,* and are generally performed fairly briskly, often like an Allegro con brio: perhaps in opera the old affective meaning of Allegretto as light-hearted came into play. But it is also possible that some of Mozart's tempos in the operas would surprise us today. For example, I have always thought it odd that Papageno's entrance aria, "Ein Vogelfänger bin ich ja", in *Die Zauberflöte* should be marked *Andante,* as it is traditionally sung at a much livelier pace; but Alan Tyson, with whom I discussed this, informed me that there was some evidence that the original Papageno, Schikaneder (who was also the librettist and the impresario), sang the first stanza from behind the scenes, entering only with the second stanza. In this case, a very deliberate tempo would have been reasonable so that the public could catch the words.

and the slow movement *Romance*, also in *Allegretto* cut time, from one of the "Paris" Symphonies (no. 85) is similar. The Symphony in C major no. 82 has an *Allegretto* slow movement in 2/4, which has a rhythmic structure like the *Andante più tosto Allegretto* of the Quartet op. 55 no. 2. Although in purely instrumental works Haydn is not as fond as Mozart of the Allegretto in duple time, there is no reason to think that his use of it deviates in any significant way from that of his younger colleague.

There are a number of amiable pieces in *The Seasons* designated Allegretto: the first one, Simon's aria in 2/4 time, "Schon eilet froh der Akkersmann" [Already the farmer hurries joyfully], is the most significant. Since the farmer is hurrying, we should not assume a slow tempo, but starting at bar 17 Haydn incorporates an extensive reminiscence more than twenty-four bars long of his most popular work, the slow movement of the "Surprise" Symphony. Since this was originally *Andante*, I cannot conceive that the tempo of Simon's aria – while certainly faster – would have been radically different, and this shows that for Haydn, as for Mozart and Beethoven, Allegretto was closer to Andante than to Allegro.

I have focused on the Allegretto in duple time because it provides the easiest demonstration of the relative consistency of at least one standard tempo, and fixing it approximately. The procedure can serve as a model for determining the sense of other indications. Movements in triple time demand a consideration of whether the basic beat is one to a bar or three. "Allegro", the most common designation of all with many varying types, is also a more complex term for similar reasons: the opening movement of Beethoven's Sonata op. 2 no. 2, for example, is in 2/4, but there are evidently four strong beats to the bar, while the opening movement of op. 106 is in an *alla breve* 4/4 with only two strong beats. Things can be even more ambiguous: the *Allegro moderato* of Beethoven's Fourth Piano Concerto, for example, begins as if it were in *alla breve*, quickly moves to 4/4 and finishes towards the end of the exposition with eight strong beats per bar. The *Allegro* finale of his Third Piano Concerto in C minor in 2/4 is a tempo exactly the same as the 6/8 of the *Presto* coda, and they actually have to be metronomically equivalent – that is, the dotted quarter of the Presto must equal the half note of the Allegro.

We can be sure that there was a certain consistency or consensus about the *tempi ordinari* of Allegro and Adagio from 1780 to 1810, but it would need more research to fix their contours. (The *Allegro* 3/4 opening movement of Beethoven's Sonata in D major op. 28, for example, may be reasonably expected to be in the region of the suggested metronome mark that the composer gave the opening 3/4 Allegro of the "Eroica" Symphony.) What I wish to establish, nevertheless, is the nature and existence of the standard tempos asserted by Beethoven, and his effort to free himself from their tyranny – which means, however, that we must still take account of their existence for any understanding of how a more individual tempo was determined.

I have principally considered Mozart, with a glance at Haydn, not only because it was their practice which would have had the greatest importance for Beethoven, but also because they represent the closest parallels with Beethoven's work. The early Dussek sonatas, for example, do not contain an Allegretto in duple time, and Clementi wrote few Allegretto finales in 4/4 or 2/4 (one of them is in the easy sonata op. 38 no. 2 in B flat major, evidently intended only for amateurs). For his last movements he preferred Presto with astonishing consistency. Both Schubert and Beethoven, however, continued and extended the Mozartean (or Viennese) tradition of the Allegretto finale in duple time in which a relatively slow tempo attains by subdivision a certain virtuosity, and they both continued to work within the framework of the standard tempos.

BEETHOVEN'S ATTEMPTS TO FIX THE TEMPO

Beethoven's use of even the standard indications of tempo is less consistent than Mozart's. In any case, uninflected standard indications – simple Andantes or Allegros and so forth – are relatively infrequent in his works compared to the practice of other composers: he tended to privilege more complex directions, like *Allegro vivace e con brio, Andante molto moto*. Perhaps this makes the change from *Allegro assai* to the unconditional *Allegro* for the "Hammerklavier" Sonata op. 106 all the more significant: this movement was finally determined to be in a standard tempo, and 138 is more or less an acceptable standard Allegro for a good deal of the classical Viennese tradition.* Indeed, the opening Allegro of this sonata is in many ways much less eccentric than the first movements of the three that preceded it, opp. 81a, 90 and 101.

From the beginning, Beethoven produced occasional examples of the finale in a relatively easygoing tempo so characteristic of Mozart, along with Presto finales that recall Clementi and Haydn. The finale in common time of the Sonata in A major op. 2 no. 2 is not marked *Allegretto*, but *Grazioso* (and headed *Rondo*), and it needs a tempo of about 69 to the half note or 138 to the quarter (Czerny originally suggested 144 and then lowered it to 132). The Sonata in E flat major op. 7 has a finale in 2/4, *Poco Allegretto e grazioso*, that needs to be even slower. With op. 22, however, we reach the true type of the Mozart Allegretto finale, with a controlled increase of motion from sixteenth notes to thirty-seconds; the Mozartean model is enlarged by Beethoven through more dramatic inner contrasts and also a more expansive lyricism:

Czerny gave 69 to the quarter as a tempo in his *School of Practical Composition*, but suggested 76 in the edition published by Simrock: the more standard 76 seems to me preferable, but only if it is interpreted with the necessary suppleness and freedom. In any case the general character of the pacing is not in question.

---

* There is some discussion whether *Allegro assai* is faster or slower than Allegro, and therefore whether Beethoven was marking the tempo up or down. I would think that *Allegro assai* is faster, and *Assai allegro* may be slower. There does not seem to be a way of deciding this point.

With the works of Beethoven's middle period, tempo indications become more problematic. With the exception of op. 106, he gave no metronome marks for the piano sonatas, or for other works with piano, like the concertos, the sonatas with violin or cello, or the trios. We have only the metronome marks he published for the nine symphonies and for the string quartets through op. 95 to use as a guide for the way he construed terms like Allegro, Adagio, and so forth. These marks have been subject to a lot of controversy over the years. We need to start with a number of observations:

1) Some of Beethoven's metronome marks were given as long as fifteen or twenty years after the works were composed. A composer's memory of his intentions does not always remain very fresh.*

2) It is not only a metronome mark that might be mistaken. Composers may decide that terms like Andante and Allegro need to be changed, as we have seen above (pages 58 and 64) with both Beethoven and Mozart. The metronome marks given by Beethoven years after composition are not, I believe, elucidations of the meaning of tempo marks like Allegretto ma non troppo, but fresh interpretations of the musical text. They are therefore dubious as a general guide to the meaning of the terms, unless we are convinced that he had not changed his mind about the work and its character.

3) Composers are not infallible judges of the best form of interpretation of their own works. Like anyone else they need the experience of performance to refine their ideas of execution. When the composition is exceedingly original, even revolutionary, the composer may not yet have evolved a style of performance suited to the new conceptions. Beethoven did revolutionize the style of playing the piano very early in his career, but it is not clear that the radical originality of his piano music starting with op. 31 was accompanied by any immediate change in performance. I do not think the way of executing the early works can be successfully applied to those that followed.

4) Beethoven was not always sure of the tempo of his music. His change of the first movement of Symphony no. 9 from 112 to the quarter to 88 is an indication of how uncertain his decision might be. (Chopin, too, vacillated on occasion, giving the metronome marks of both 120 and 160 to the Etude in A minor op. 25 no. 4. Many other similar instances can be adduced.)

5) Beethoven's metronome marks have not come down to us without a few mistakes. The misprint of the trio (*Presto*) of the scherzo of Symphony no. 9 as 116 to the half note instead of the whole note was perceived very early. The most impossible indication in the symphonies is that of the finale in 2/4

---

*When I consulted Stravinsky about what I thought might be misprints in his *Sérénade en la*, he lamented to a friend, "Some young American pianist is asking me about my early pieces. What am I to do? I don't remember them very well." He took a long time to answer any of my queries, and I am by no means certain that I received the right answer in every case.

of the Symphony no. 4 in B flat major, in which the *Allegro ma non troppo*
is given as 80 to the half note. As long ago as 1872, Gustav Nottebohm
remarked "a mistake may be assumed". This makes for an absurd presto at
160 to the quarter, the bassoon passages are literally unplayable, and the
tempo is clearly not "ma non troppo". It is most likely that 80 is a simple
misprint for 60.

6) When Beethoven gave the metronome marks, he could no longer hear himself perform at the keyboard. This made his task of finding the pace for all of
the earlier works much more problematical.

7) Beethoven's remarks about the necessity of escaping from *tempi ordinari*
were written late in life. When he wrote down the metronome markings in
1817, he may already have been trying, not to give the measure of his earlier
indications, but to find subtler and more nuanced tempos than he would have
conceived a decade or more earlier.

Nevertheless, even with all these negative factors taken into account, it is unlikely
that Beethoven was often mistaken about the pacing of his works, and extremely
unlikely most of the time that the indications he finally fixed upon deviated by
more than a notch on the metronome from a viable and sensible tempo for each
work in question. To understand the tempos of the piano sonatas, therefore, we
need to take into consideration both the tradition of the tempo indications in
Vienna during Beethoven's lifetime (above all the early years, when his conceptions were formed) and the metronomic interpretation he gave of those marks for
the quartets and symphonies, an interpretation occasionally but not always idiosyncratic. I think that his conception of tempo was like that of structure: he most
often began with the standard forms of his earliest years to develop subtler, more
original ideas, but he never ceased to look back and refer to procedures he had
learned many years before.

BEETHOVEN AND THE CLASSICAL ALLEGRETTO

Controversy over some of the tempos in middle-period Beethoven begins early.
The *Allegretto* finale of the Sonata in G major op. 31 no. 1 provoked disagree-
ment soon after Beethoven's death. In *On the Proper Performance of All
Beethoven's Works for the Piano*, Czerny wrote about this movement:

> As the *Allegretto* is in *alla breve* measure, the whole must be played a remark-
> ably quick *Allegro molto*. The beautiful, expressive, and extremely melodious
> theme, must be played as *cantabile* as possible. . . .

On the face of it, there is an evident absurdity in claiming that an Allegretto is to
be played Allegro molto. In any case, Schindler protested:[11]

Did Beethoven really have such a limited, schoolmaster-like notion of the *alla breve* measure that he would establish it, or any time signature, as the first law in interpreting a piece of music, rather than the particular character of the music itself? He himself played this rondo, and would have played it, "at a comfortable pace". The whole movement has much the character of a quiet narrative.

It seems to me that Schindler is right about the character of the music (although his claim to have heard the composer play it may be doubted, as he had a tendency to lie about such matters with complete effrontery).

The finale of op. 31 no. 1 is an *Allegretto* in cut time of the type of the Mozartean Allegretto rondo finale:

I see no reason that this movement should not be played as a standard Mozart Allegretto, around 76 as the basic beat. Donald Francis Tovey wrote about this piece:[12]

> Resist the temptation to take this movement too fast. Allegrettos are gentle creatures. And this one has a very gentle theme.... It is inadvisable to work these [difficult] passages up to a faster tempo than you will need – viz., a comfortable amble, not far over the border of *alla breve*, and, for example, no faster than the Rondo of Op. 13 [Allegro].

The finale of the "Pathétique" (op. 13) is an *Allegro* in cut time. There is something illogical in recommending that the tempo for an allegretto should not be faster than an allegro. It is evident that for Tovey, as for Czerny, allegretto is not strictly a tempo mark but an expressive indication, meaning a light-hearted allegro, which is what it became during the nineteenth century. As we saw above, however, this will never do, given Beethoven's use of the term for the slow movement of the Seventh Symphony, and his employment of it in the tempo marks of the Kyrie of the Mass in C major and the "Dona nobis pacem" of the *Missa Solemnis*.

We might add that when Schubert used the finale of op. 31 no. 1 as a model for the finale of the great posthumous Sonata in A major,* he also chose Allegretto as an indication, but marked the time signature as common time, not *alla breve*. It obviously goes not far from the Mozartean tempo of around 76 to the half note, however, if slightly slower and more emphatic:

*This was demonstrated by Edward T. Cone and myself independently some thirty years ago. Two other finales marked Allegretto were composed towards the end of Schubert's life: the Sonata in G major, and the String Quintet in C major. This turning back to a Mozartean type is testimony to the continuing life of that tradition. I think this implies that both movements are generally performed too quickly, particularly the finale of the quintet. The *Più presto* towards the end of the quintet is not a *Poco più presto* as it is ordinarily interpreted, and demands a decided dramatic contrast impossible when the opening tempo is too fast.

Another *Allegretto* finale by Beethoven is very close in character and style to this work of Schubert, and extends the Mozart tradition in a way very similar to Schubert. This is the last movement of the Sonata in A major for violin and piano op. 30 no. 1. It is a variation finale, and uses the Mozart examples as models:

It is evident that the standard Viennese tempo of around 76 to the half note is appropriate, and it would be difficult to imagine anything much faster or slower.

Nevertheless, Beethoven's own view of Allegretto was somewhat more ambiguous and more complex than Mozart's. The 2/4 *Allegretto* of Symphony no. 7 may have been marked the standard Mozartean 76 to the quarter by Beethoven, but he marked the 2/4 *Allegretto* finale (a set of variations) of the String Quartet in E flat major op. 74 100 to the quarter. This still makes the opening of this finale proceed at a relatively slow pace, and Beethoven needed to add successive accelerations to accomplish a brilliant end:

100 to the quarter in this piece, nevertheless, comes out as a very moderate tempo. In spite of Czerny, there is no evidence that Beethoven ever indicated Allegretto for a fast or brilliant tempo.

The evidence of Beethoven's own metronome marks for a simple Allegretto in duple time with no further qualification goes, therefore, from 76 to 100. To this we must add his fixing the *Allegretto vivace* of Symphony no. 8 at a basic 88 (to the eighth note), and the *Allegretto ma non troppo* of the slow movement of the Quartet in F minor op. 95 at 66 to the quarter:

None of these markings produces a really fast tempo; even the one for the finale of the E flat major Quartet gives a pace that sounds closer to an Andante than to an Allegro. In addition, no one, as far as I know, has ever thought that any of these markings was too slow, and many conductors prefer a heavier and more portentous tempo for the second movement of the Seventh Symphony.

Further evidence of Beethoven's feeling for Allegretto as a relatively slow tempo is the second movement of the Trio in E flat major op. 70 no. 2, marked simply *Allegretto*. This is a "slow" movement with a humorous scherzo-like character. It would be difficult to conceive it in a tempo faster than 76 to the quarter, and it might, indeed, benefit from 69 to 72. (Czerny proposed ♪ = 116 for this, or 58 to the quarter note, which suggests more an Andante than an Allegretto.) In any case, the meaning of the Allegretto designation is the same as in the Seventh Symphony, even if the emotional tone of the piece is so radically different:

The tempo mark here is consistent not only with the other examples of it in Beethoven but with the ones in Mozart as well.

To avoid complication, I have not so far closely considered the markings for Allegretto in triple metre or in 6/8, but most of those, like the finale of the "Pastoral" Symphony, are moderate: the 6/8 *Andante con moto quasi Allegretto* of the String Quartet in C major op. 59 no. 3 is 56 to the dotted quarter (slower than it is generally performed), and so is the 3/8 scherzo of the Quartet in F major op. 59 no. 1. In fact, at 56 to the dotted quarter, the quarter note would be 84, which is fairly close to the standard 76 metre of Allegretto either in 2/4 or *alla breve*. In any case, in duple metre Beethoven's suggested markings give us a range for the basic beat in binary rhythm going from 66 for *Allegretto ma non troppo* to 100, a wide margin – wide enough, in any case, to suggest that these limits should not be infringed.

MISUNDERSTANDINGS, EARLY AND LATE

Most interpretations of the *Allegretto* finale of the Sonata in F major op. 54 present us with a genuine anomaly. It is a perpetual motion in 2/4 with a coda marked *Più Allegro*:

Czerny suggested a metronome mark of 144 to the quarter, which would be a tempo slightly faster than an ordinary Allegro (faster, oddly enough, than Czerny's own mark for the *Allegro ma non troppo* finale of the "Appassionata", which is 132); later, in his Simrock edition, he reduced this to 108. Paul Badura-Skoda (in a note to his edition of Czerny's *On the proper Performance of All Beethoven's Works for the Piano*) believes that Czerny mixed up the marks of the two movements: in the book the indications are 108 and 144, in the edition they are 120 and 108. If this is the case, Czerny had reduced the 144 of the book only to 120.

Most performances, including Artur Schnabel's and Maurizio Pollini's, range from 126 to 144. The most extreme marking comes in the Haslinger edition of 1830: 76 to the half note (or 152 to the quarter). This suggests that the editor of this first "complete" edition may have referred to the standard Allegretto measure of 76 and, like most contemporary musicians, assumed that the perpetual motion implied an exceedingly swift rendition: one wonders at what tempo the *Più Allegro* of the last page of this movement could be negotiated in this case.

There are very few works in the history of music that are commonly played at a demonstrably wrong tempo, but this is one of them: the cause in each of these rare cases is always a misunderstanding of the nature of the piece in question. Examples include Chopin's Etude in E flat minor op. 10 no. 6, which is marked by the composer as 69 to the dotted quarter but played invariably at half that speed or less (the basic beat of this *Andante* is the dotted quarter, and Chopin conceived the bar as two slow beats, while most pianists interpret the work in a slow six to the bar):

Another of these misinterpretations is the minuet of Mozart's Symphony in G minor K. 550. Sir Charles Mackerras and others have pointed out that the practice of Mozart's time would interpret an Allegretto minuet at about 80 to the dotted half, and this is now widely accepted, although we still hear some performances at the stodgier tempo that used to be the rule (a heavy three quick beats per bar instead of one relatively light beat). A model tempo in Beethoven for a minuet Allegro – to be distinguished from the slow minuets like those in Beethoven's Sonata for piano in E flat major op. 31 no. 3, or in the Symphony no. 8 in F major – can be found with the third movement of the Sonata in D major op. 10 no. 3, or, indeed, the scherzo of the Symphony no. 5 in C minor (writing on the conversation pad he carried around when his deafness increased, Beethoven's friends called this a minuet, and it is, indeed, in fast minuet tempo). The slow movement of Brahms's Concerto no. 2 in B flat major is still another work almost never performed at the faster tempo intended by the composer.

All of these misinterpretations have reasonable explanations. The slow movement of Brahms is misconceived as a slow six which makes it sound, in fact, as if it were in a very slow three, while Brahms paradoxically wanted it to sound not in three, but in a slow two in hemiola (the basic beat is given by the pizzicato double bass, not by the solo cello), and this requires a faster tempo:

The scherzo element of the Mozart minuet in the G minor Symphony went unrecognized, and the movement was performed with an understandable but misplaced seriousness in order to fit with the extraordinary character of the outer movements. The chromatic complexity of the Chopin E flat minor Etude still makes the intended tempo shocking to most pianists, who think of the work as an expressive Nocturne, the better to savour the radical and expressive harmony of the inner voices.

The misunderstanding of the final movement of op. 54 has a double root. First, the change in meaning of Allegretto by the late 1820s to indicate a faster tempo, something like a modest Allegro of not too heavy or serious an expressive type. Second, the belief that a perpetual motion must necessarily be a fast piece. This last unfounded idea has also had an unfortunate effect on performances of Schumann's Toccata for piano op. 7, which, in spite of Clara Schumann's suggestion of 96 to the quarter for the composer's *Allegro*, is generally the occasion for a test of velocity – above all, ever since one pianist succeeded in the *tour de force* of recording it on a 10-inch 78 rpm disc. There is some small, if insufficient, excuse for this, since the Schumann Toccata has the character of an étude, but there is none for the misinterpretation of op. 54. Czerny, however, seems to have thought of the finale of op. 54 literally as a finger exercise (he writes that it "may serve as an excellent study for every good pianist"), and the fast tempo he suggests turns the movement, in fact, into what sounds like an educational piece by Czerny.

Beethoven, however, makes no attempt at achieving any effective brilliance before the final page. He even opens with a double indication of *dolce* in bars 1 and 3 (see the example above, page 87), and at a rapid tempo it is impossible to give this its full effect, combined as it is with the offbeat *sforzandi*. This indication is basic to an understanding of the character of the movement. Furthermore, the contrast within a *dolce* sonority between a *sforzando* on the second sixteenth (in bar 3) and one on the third (in bar 5) should not be an awkward dynamic opposition, but an exquisite detail. In this piece, Beethoven draws out from the simplest, most ordinary motifs the lyrical possibilities implied by the double indication of *dolce* in the first bars. The whole movement is one of his most triumphantly subtle and poetic works.

The misjudgement of character was responsible for the early disgrace of this sonata. One of the finest and most sympathetic early critics of Beethoven, Wilhelm von Lenz, famous for imposing the now popular division of Beethoven's music into three periods, detested op. 54, and was clearly puzzled by it: [13]

This sonata of two pieces which are two fragments (tempo di minuetto; allegretto) is only bizarre. First there is a minuet which is not a minuet, and of which the motif, if it is a motif, makes a noise for a moment in the lowest basses before losing itself in a forest of octaves, piled one on top of each other and which excludes any melodic idea. The allegretto is no less uninteresting. This must have fallen from the pen of the master when he was in God knows what kind of a mood; when he wasn't even thinking, when he had to content a publisher in the shortest possible space of time. This sonata shows the first traces of the third manner of Beethoven. The allegretto could pass for a kind of toccata, or rondo; the first piece, even if it is called a minuet, presents none of the parts, nor the reprises, nor the style of a minuet. This shapeless production has the faults of his third manner without having the beauties.

Perhaps Lenz disliked the minuet even more than the finale – at least he had more to say about it, but he clearly found the *Allegretto* boring, and I think his failure to comment on it even more telling than his critical assault on the minuet.

Since Beethoven's metronome indications for Allegretto go from 76 to 100, and all of the movements throughout his life that he called Allegretto, but to which he had no opportunity to give a metronome mark, fit easily into this range, most of them decidedly towards the bottom or slowest part of it, it is more than improbable that he would have used Allegretto in this one piece for a speed of 132 to 144. The rapid tempo commonly encountered in performance turns it into a routine composition, and prevents us from appreciating either its subtlety or its experimental character. Written between the "Waldstein" and the "Appassionata", like them it is an attempt to compose a finale at once simpler, less complex than the opening movement and at the same time with greater weight. It also represents a first essay at insisting on a reprise of the entire long second half, an experiment that he was to try again immediately after in the finale of the "Appassionata". The latter is also a *perpetuum mobile, Allegro ma non troppo*: Czerny gives 144 or 132 for this, which has become traditional, but which does not distinguish it from a simple Allegro, and amounts to affirming that Beethoven made a mistake in adding "ma non troppo".

The finale of the "Waldstein", in turn, is *Allegretto moderato*. Tovey is amusingly stern about this piece in his edition:

Allegretto indicates a moderate tempo, and *moderato* intensifies the warning; very necessarily, for this movement is often played in public too fast. Players who are bored by its breadth and wish to speed up its climaxes should leave Beethoven alone.

There is good cause for renouncing a slavish or pedantic following of metronomic indications, but that is no excuse for not taking Beethoven's tempo directions seriously. Allegro ma non troppo should not be as fast as Allegro; Allegretto should be slower still and even, from 1770 to 1820 as we have seen, not too far from Andante. Taking the last movements of the "Waldstein", op.

54 and the "Appassionata" with brilliant virtuoso tempi makes them more commonplace and vulgarizes them, confounding the tempo with an ordinary Allegro pacing, while it makes the contrast with the faster coda in all three sonatas less effective. In op. 54, above all, a fast tempo voids the finale of a large part of its significance, trivializes its character. It is only sensible to maintain the hierarchy of Allegretto, Allegro ma non troppo (or Allegro moderato), and Allegro in Beethoven's sonatas in order to preserve the distinctive meaning of different types of movement.

If we combine the authority of Beethoven's occasionally idiosyncratic metronome marks with the weight of the Mozart and Haydn tradition, we can approach an indication of Allegretto in Beethoven with an initial assumption, to be corrected by the performer's sensibility when necessary, of a basic beat of 76, with Allegretto vivace as 88 (using the scherzo of the Eighth Symphony as a model). For the opening movement, *Allegretto*, of the String Quartet in F major op. 135, 76 to the quarter is absolutely convincing:

This tempo preserves all the wit, emphasizing humour in place of brilliance, and yet is still lively enough, given Beethoven's thirty-second notes. The scherzo of the Sonata in E flat major op. 31 no. 3 is *Allegretto vivace* in 2/4: Czerny first suggested 80 to the quarter note and then sensibly raised that to 88. Faster than 88, even if one could play the following passage with the exact rhythms, one could not perceive the thirty-second notes as staccato:

The quicker tempo most often chosen in recital nowadays is merely the result of the prejudice that all scherzos have to be fast.* At a very slightly slower tempo, this movement sounds more original and much more humorous.

There is one further Allegretto finale in duple time in the Beethoven piano sonatas, but it is not labelled Allegretto as Beethoven, in a brief chauvinistic phase at the time he composed it, was insistent on having only German tempo and expression marks. This is the second and final movement of op. 90:

The tempo is *Nicht zu geschwind und sehr singbar vorgetragen.* Czerny translates this as Moderato, but Allegretto molto cantabile would be more adequate. Both tempo and character are reminiscent of the finale of op. 22. (Czerny suggests 88 to the quarter; somewhere between 76 and 84 would seem to me more judi-

---

*Badura-Skoda (in the notes to his edition of Czerny's account of Beethoven's piano music (see above)) insists that Czerny's tempo is too modest, and prefers 96. At this tempo the staccato touch on the thirty-second notes would disappear even on an older keyboard instrument.

cious.) The steady persistence of the Mozartean tradition in Beethoven's thought
is significant.

Another finale written around the same time reveals a similar reliance on the
Mozartean model of Beethoven's earliest years, the last movement of the Sonata
for violin and piano op. 96, a variation set, *Poco Allegretto*:

Once again, most performers, desiring a brilliant finale more in accord with
modern taste, take a relatively quick tempo, but the more standard Mozartean
pace of around 76 (perhaps 80 or 84 at most) would allow the precise articulation of the second beat of the first bar demanded by Beethoven (it is rare that
performers pay any attention to this and at a fast tempo it would sound ridicu-
lously fussy). Indeed, the indication *Poco Allegretto* suggests an even more deliberate pace. It would also make possible a graceful execution of the succeeding
variations:

Above all, the slower tempo would endow the transformation into the final Allegro with a contrasting brilliance:

The form and the character of this movement are so close to the Mozartean variation finale that the traditional Allegretto of Mozart would be more suitable than a realization of the theme with the sense of Allegretto found only later in the nineteenth century. Tempo, form and stylistic tradition are bound together in so many instances that we need to have forceful reasons for disassociating them, and the example of Mozart was still very much alive for Beethoven in those difficult years before he embarked on op. 106.

Nevertheless, these were to be the last Allegretto finales in Mozartean style that Beethoven would compose, although he still continued to employ Allegretto as a modest, easygoing tempo, with the beautiful opening 6/8 *Allegretto ma non troppo* of the Sonata in A major op. 101. Perhaps this derives from lyrical opening movements in 6/8 rhythm by Mozart, like the Trio in E flat major for clarinet, viola and piano K. 498 (it is interesting that in both movements the reprise of the exposition is omitted).

THE INTERPLAY OF TRADITION AND INNOVATION

It should be clear from this discussion that although we can only rarely attain any absolute certainty in deciding what Beethoven required for fixing on a tempo, we can determine a satisfactory range for the meaning of Beethoven's terms and avoid some absurdities. Beethoven himself was inconsistent, after all, perhaps because he was experimenting with tempo as much as he was innovating with other aspects of musical form. Nevertheless, we can set limits to the range of meaning of the standard terms as he conceived them. We should be conscious, however, that these limits were almost certainly narrower for Beethoven's contemporaries than for us today, particularly in his earliest years: the *tempi ordinarii* were intelligible conventions in his world that are now hard to grasp after two centuries. How conventional a tempo mark could be for Beethoven even relatively late in life, how independent of the character of the music, is shown by the fact that the slow movement of the Seventh Symphony and the opening movement of the Quartet op. 135 are both clearly at more or less the same metronomic speed and have the same *Allegretto* tempo mark. We need to continue to explore the more complex conventions of the Allegro, and to build on the research already accomplished by Rudolf Kolisch, Neil Zaslaw* and others; Adagio and Andante are probably more uniform than Allegro, although Adagio by tradition certainly demanded a great freedom of execution. Above all, we cannot isolate Beethoven's tempos from the Viennese tradition in force when he arrived in Vienna, in spite of his evident and even radical dissatisfaction with the conventional aspects of that tradition. In this respect, the composers that Beethoven studied before he was twenty-five are more useful for comprehending his cast of mind and even his later development than his coeval contemporaries. It would appear that he was relatively indifferent to the work of more recent composers once his own style and individuality had been set – except for opera, where he studied with envy the successful productions of French composers and Cherubini, while still relying essentially on the example of Mozart, and except, in a much less significant way, for the composition of his Violin Concerto, where he borrowed figuration from the up-to-date French works. He grandly transformed the Viennese tradition, but in this process he remained relatively isolated. He was untouched by any influence from Spohr or Rossini, for example (although Rossini was immensely popular in Vienna and left more than a trace of his style in the work of Schubert).

In the end, when studying what evidence we have for the tradition and for the way Beethoven attempted to inflect it, we must be prepared at times, as I remarked above, to find tempos that may feel uncomfortably fast and others that will seem awkwardly slow – that is, until we find a style of playing that makes sense out of them. We need, in short, to work up sympathy for ways of playing – and hearing, too – which feel alien to us. It is evident that Beethoven liked some tempos that we find incredibly fast. Even if we reduce his metronome mark for the final fugue of the Quartet in C major op. 59 no. 3 by a notch or two, it will still be faster than most quartets like to play, and fast enough to make it difficult for an audience to hear. The metronomic indication for the fugal finale of the "Hammerklavier" Sonata shows us that Beethoven liked his concluding fugues to be difficult to play and to listen to. (The final fugue, *Allegro* 3/4, of the Sonata in D major for cello and piano, op. 102 no. 2 for this reason must have been conceived in a tempo close to the one indicated by Beethoven for the 3/4 *Allegro* of the opening movement of the "Eroica" Symphony, which has a similar rhythmic shape and drive, although more complex.) On the other hand, the finale of the "Pastoral" Symphony and the scherzo of the Sonata in E flat major op. 31 no. 3 are both to be taken more slowly than our habits have led us to

*Neal Zaslaw, "Mozart's Tempo Conventions", in *Report of the Eleventh Congress Copenhagen 1972 (International Musicological Society)*, Copenhagen, pp. 720–33. This is the most judicious of all treatments; its only shortcoming, a minor one, is that it does not give greater weight to the evidence from Mozart's contemporaries and from the musical milieu closest to his world than to earlier writers on tempo.

believe, and I think the same thing is true of the final *Allegro ma non troppo* of the "Appassionata". The last movement of the "Emperor" Concerto, as well, is misrepresented in most editions: the tempo should not be *Allegro* but the more deliberate *Allegro non tanto*, and the dance movement sometimes requires six emphatic beats per bar and not simply a more graceful two:

The *Allegro moderato* finale of the "Archduke" Trio also demands a slower tempo than most performers will choose today. (To take only the category of the finale, Beethoven evidently preferred tempos that are either faster or slower than we are likely to hear in today's concert halls.) It is almost impossible in most of these cases to prescribe an exact metronome indication with any certainty that one has discovered Beethoven's intentions, particularly as he was not always sure what these were, and in his work we cannot expect anything like the relative consistency of indications that we find in Mozart, largely because Beethoven has less of the consistency of certain types of forms that we find in Mozart. Nevertheless, Beethoven's indications of tempo are to be taken seriously, and, in the works we have considered here, we should preserve the progression from *Poco Allegretto* through *Allegretto ma non troppo, Allegretto moderato, Allegretto, Allegretto vivace, Allegro non tanto, Allegro moderato, Allegro ma non troppo, Allegro, Allegro assai,* up to *Allegro con brio*. To play an *Allegro ma non troppo* at the speed of an *Allegro molto* seems to me to show a lack of respect for the text comparable to changing the harmonies or rewriting the melodies.

RHYTHMIC FREEDOM AND RUBATO

Many of our difficulties with what may at first seem odd about Beethoven's tempos will disappear when we remember the freedom with which he expected the initial pace to be interpreted as the piece proceeded (see page 45 above). A passage from the *Prestissimo* of the Sonata in E major op. 109 will show his directions for that freedom:

Un poco espressivo is followed four bars later by *a tempo*. This direction is some-times interpreted to mean a *ritardando*, but this is incorrect; it should be a *ritenuto*: the *espressivo* is immediate and not progressive. This is confirmed by the opening movement of the Sonata in C minor op. 111, in which every *espressivo* is accompanied by *Poco Ritenente*. There are several occurrences. In bars 29–36 below, the first *poco ritenente* implies a *poco espressivo*; the following *espressivo* and *poco ritenente* together demand more intense expression and greater freedom:

Ritardando is generally spread out by Beethoven separating the syllables, so that the word covers the whole space of the slowing-down. In bars 94–100, we can see the extensive spelling-out of *ritardando*. The *espressivo poco ritenente* of bar 99, however, practically applies to only one chord, the dominant ninth of the sub-dominant F minor with the D flat in the melody. (In spite of the notation, the *a tempo* of bar 100 should start with the upbeat of the previous bar.) We are jus-tified in generalizing (at least about the late work with certainty but also, I think, about the earlier) that *espressivo* in Beethoven always implied a slight slackening of the basic tempo. It should not, however, sound simply like a new and differ-ent tempo, but like a deformation or remoulding of the initial tempo; that is what gives the expressive character as far as the pacing is concerned.

Unfortunately, most of the time musicians vary between paying no attention to Beethoven's metronome marks or else executing them with relentless rigidity from beginning to end of the movement. This happens largely with performances of the symphonies, for every one of which we have the metronomic indications of the composer. Having announced with a certain fanfare an "authentic" per-formance of the cycle of Beethoven symphonies to be performed according to the original metronome marks, a conductor will then feel obliged to justify the pub-licity by hewing to these indications with dogged fidelity and to suppress within himself any instinct for freedom – with predictably disastrous results.

A certain suppleness that acknowledges the importance of slight variations of tempo for expressive effect will, in fact, make sense out of the majority of Beethoven's metronome marks. The slow movement of op. 106 is an example: it has seemed too fast to many sensitive musicians. But the opening page is specified by Beethoven to be played both *mezza voce* and with the soft pedal throughout, and this implies that he wished to avoid any kind of extrovert eloquence at this place: the emotion must be at once intense and repressed. A page later, however, the soft pedal is lifted and the music opens out with the section marked *con grande espressione*: following the model we have seen in opp. 109 and 111, this means a slight slackening of the tempo and a greater liberty of rhythmic inflection – *tempo rubato*, in short, if this is interpreted with a sense of the period. As a basic tempo, the ♪ = 92 given by Beethoven works for a great part of the movement and, indeed, sets off the freedom of the more openly expressive passages with more conviction.

TEMPO RELATIONS

One guide to Beethoven's tempo marks is proportion. There are a number of cases in which a tempo change within a movement displays certain elements in both the old and the new tempos which must be kept rhythmically invariant in order for the change to make sense. One case, generally misunderstood, is the transition from the *Maestoso* introduction of the Sonata in C minor op. 111 to the following *Allegro con brio ed appassionato*:

It ought to be self-evident that when Beethoven commences a trill in thirty-second notes in the *Maestoso* and continues it in sixteenths in the *Allegro*, he does not intend a break in rhythm but expects a continuous trill to bridge over into the new section. This means that the *Allegro* is pretty much exactly twice as fast as the *Maestoso*. Unfortunately, most pianists interpret the *Maestoso* to mean an Adagio, although there is no warrant for that beyond the hazy belief that all introductions are Adagio, and performances generally begin with a tempo four times as slow as the following *Allegro*. I used to do this myself because that is the way I had always heard it, but at least I gradually accelerated the trill into the faster speed so that a semblance of uniformity was achieved. I now believe the very slow tempo to be wrong, but a gradual acceleration is not as foolish as a sudden doubling of the speed without warning in the middle of a trill. Correctly viewed, the *Maestoso* should be much faster than it is usually performed, which would make most pianists nervous (above all because the opening skip, properly played with only one hand, is dangerous and tricky). The *Maestoso*, of course, may be interpreted with a certain freedom, and the relation to the *Allegro* need not be rigidly metronomic, but either the introduction must end at more or less half the speed of the *Allegro* or the trill must be gradually accelerated. The mathematical exactness is not important, but the proportional relation of the introduction and main section must be convincing to the ear. (The rhythm demands this relationship. The trill is a four-bar group: one bar of Maestoso (that is, two bars of Allegro) and two bars of Allegro. The trill is the opening of the Allegro within the Maestoso. Playing the trill too slowly ruins the phrase rhythm.) The technique is the same as the relation of the introduction of Schubert's Symphony in C major to the *Allegro* that follows:

146 **Allegro, ma non troppo.**

The time signature of Schubert's *Andante* introduction (wrongly printed in most scores as common time) is cut time (*alla breve*), and the rhythm at the end shows clearly that the eighth note of the introduction is equal to the quarter of the *Allegro*. The new tempo already begins hidden in the last bars of the old.

Relationships of this kind were important to Beethoven, who gave, for example, the same metronome mark to the 3/4 Scherzo of the Ninth Symphony and to its 4/4 trio marked *Presto*, in this case directing an acceleration into the faster tempo:

This keeps the basic beat the same, while changing the rhythm from 3 to 4 beats per bar. Beethoven made an almost identical demand in the finale of the Quartet in F minor op. 95, where he marked the *Allegretto agitato* in 6/8 as 92 to the dotted quarter note, and the coda in *Allegro* [*alla breve*] as 92 to the whole note. With eighth notes in the *Allegro* to sixteenth notes in the *Allegretto agitato*, this is the same tempo but with eight notes in the place of six.

These specific metronome marks of Beethoven foreshadow the change from *Allegretto* to *Poco più presto* indicated by Brahms in the coda of the finale of the Piano Concerto no. 2 in B flat major: the *Allegretto* (the faster nineteenth-century sense of this term) is marked 104 in 2/4 with sixteenth notes; the *Poco più presto* is 138 in triplet eighth notes. Multiplying 104 by 4 gives 416, which, divided by 3, gives 135.33 – close enough to 138 (the nearest notch on the metronome) to show that Brahms intended the sixteenths of the *Allegretto* to become the triplets of the coda. Indeed, Brahms even begins to divide the sixteenth notes in the last bars of the *Allegretto* into groups of three so that the new tempo starts within the old one:

This is more irrational in effect than the classical system that Beethoven inherited and that he continued to practise, and we should not try to introduce such sophisticated rhythmic effects before they became stylistically justified. Beethoven's changes of tempo generally keep the basic beat uniform and alter the subdivisions within the bar: Brahms keeps the subdivisions uniform and alters the beat of the bar, which has a more radical, syncopated effect.

In any case, one ought to make a distinction in Beethoven between indications like *Poco più allegro* and *Più allegro*. They seem to me to be radically different: the former can be fairly subtle, but the latter should make a dramatic contrast, generally as far as doubling the tempo, although this need not be interpreted dogmatically with a strictly mathematical measurement: it is the impression on the listener's ear, not on the metronome, that counts. (The possibility of doubling a later tempo is frequently undermined by the habit of taking the initial tempo so fast that the succeeding quicker tempo is only possible technically within a notch or two more on the metronome.) Nevertheless, some sense of a common beat freely rendered between two contrasting tempos makes a more convincing musical effect in works of that period than a more arbitrary juxtaposition (in the *Prestissimo* coda to the *Allegretto moderato* finale of the "Waldstein" sonata, the relation is not double but more or less quadruple – even on Beethoven's instruments the coda needed to be that fast in order to play the glissando octaves with ease).

A small note of caution: the indication of tempo applies to the basic beat, not to the subdivisions of the beat that Beethoven may introduce, sometimes at the very beginning of the piece. The "*Adagio*" of the slow movement of the "Hammerklavier" Sonata applies to the eighth notes of the opening, not to the thirty-seconds that are introduced into the main theme at the recapitulation. This is largely understood, but pianists sometimes take too slow a tempo with the *Adagio* in 9/8 of the Sonata in G major op. 31 no. 1, perhaps because they notice the faster rhythms introduced in bars 7 and 10 (see the quotation on page 38). The basic rhythm here is not the eighth note but the dotted quarter, and it is the dotted quarter which is meant to sound Adagio. The imitation of Italian opera *coloratura* is gracefully rapid. The decision as to the basic beat is essential: in the *Adagio* of the Sonata for cello and piano op. 102 no. 1, the basic beat is the eighth note. This means that the arabesque in sixty-fourth notes is fairly fast:

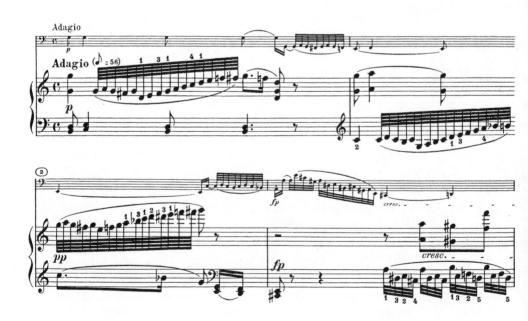

The tempo of the *Largo* in the Trio for piano and strings in D major op. 70 no. 1, the so-called "Ghost" trio, may be the most often misjudged in Beethoven literature, as performers see a number of passages in sixty-fourths coming up:

a)

Here the basic beat is the eighth note, not the sixteenth, so the tempo should be about double the excruciatingly slow pace usually heard in concert, and the sixty-fourths ought to be fast enough to appear frighteningly spectral, not just sinister.

TEMPO: INSTRUMENTS, ACOUSTICS AND SOCIAL CONDITIONS

We tend to play Beethoven's Adagios today more slowly than they were played during his lifetime. The reasons for this are multiple. One important reason is that classical music has become a more pretentious part of culture (although it was already beginning to develop in that direction in the late eighteenth century), and playing a Beethoven Adagio very slowly is a way of making the public aware that they are undergoing a deeply spiritual experience. This is important now that an audience for a Beethoven sonata might be fifty or one hundred times larger than the twenty or thirty people who would have had the opportunity to listen to it in early nineteenth-century Vienna. An unnaturally slow tempo in the wrong hands might lose the attention of the audience: with the right artist, however, it can magnify and intensify the act of listening. At too slow a tempo, of course, some salient aspects of the piece may be diminished or even lost, but there is also a gain if the public listens with greater interest – and consequently greater understanding – and feels spiritually rewarded at the end for its effort.

The slower tempo for an Adagio is encouraged as well by the modern piano, which not only makes it possible but even tempting. This is not the place to argue at length the merits of old and new keyboards, except to recall that the pianos of Beethoven's time are not effective in the concert halls seating two or three thousand people demanded by many concert promoters, so that it is unlikely that the modern piano will ever be permanently replaced by examples or replicas of the older one. The faster decay of sound on the old pianos was partly an advantage, and made for a greater clarity and essential lightness of texture, but it can also be a disadvantage in Beethoven, failing to sustain lines effectively even at a more moderate tempo that does not drag. Every note on any piano of any era begins to die away the moment it is struck. The achievement of a legato effect on the piano is therefore partly dependent on the imagination and good will of the listener, who disregards and discounts the rapid decay as irrelevant to the musical conception. Sometimes Beethoven's music makes too great a demand on the listener's imagination even with the modern piano, giving long, lyrical lines in the upper regions that only a violin could sustain effectively, and in other places the old instruments entail an even greater constraint; there are moments that clearly cry out for a constancy and unity of line that no piano can succeed in realizing. In the acoustics of a small room seating twenty to a hundred bodies, this constraint may be acceptable, but not in the cavernous space of the modern hall. For this reason, it generally makes the most sense to approximate the original tempo and resist the temptation to drag the Adagio in a soulful manner.

Not only the sound of the instrument and the acoustics of the hall influence tempo: the social nature of the concert also has its effect. An informal talk to ten or twenty people becomes, with an audience of hundreds and more, an oration, which must proceed at a different speed as well as in a different tone of voice. I do not think that a pianist consciously changes interpretation because of the size of the audience, but it must have an influence which is more than superficial, and rightly so. In any case, most pianists start working out their interpretation as if they are going to play for many hundreds. The public concert, not the private performance, is the norm for our musical experience today.

The thicker sound and stiffer action of the modern piano also induce slower speeds in the quick movements, but the older and faster tempos can be mastered today with a little care, particularly by preventing the murkier bass of the new instruments from swamping the treble. Many artists, however, have made a career based largely on playing either faster or slower (or both) than anyone else.

Even if one has a good reason for choosing a pacing that Beethoven had not imagined, or would not have countenanced, it is still wise to try and ascertain what might be lost by this deviation from a more authorial tempo. The loss can often be made up or at least compensated by phrasing and touch. In the end, the demands of modern musical life can benefit, not by the arbitrary and blind imposition of our own taste or, alternatively, from the pedantry of imagining that we have found the One Authentic Way, but from a knowledge and acceptance of the different options open to a performer in Beethoven's lifetime, an understanding of both the freedom and the constraints that existed when the music was written.

Pedal, trills, extending the keyboard

BEETHOVEN'S USE OF THE PEDAL

The unacknowledged problem with the pedal in Beethoven's piano music is not how to use it, but where not to use it. It must certainly be true that Beethoven employed the pedal much more than he indicated in his scores, as Czerny claimed, but that does not mean that he used it as Chopin or Schumann did, or as pianists do today. A glance at either the manuscript or the first edition of the finale of the "Moonlight" Sonata is instructive. At that time the pedal was not simply and discreetly indicated by *P* or *Ped.* below the bass, and where to lift it was not directed only by a star or an asterisk, like *. The pedal was called for by writing out in full the words "Without dampers" ("*Senza sordino*"), and lifting it by "With dampers" ("*Con sordino*"). The notation consequently looks much more commanding and serious than the one in use today. The finale begins:

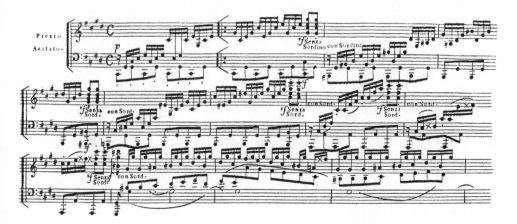

The pedal comes in for one beat at the end of the second bar, *Senza Sordino*, but Beethoven immediately directs the next seven beats without pedal, *Con Sordino* and continues to write out that injunction every two bars after one beat of pedal.

It is clear not only that all those arpeggios are to be played without pedal, but also that they are non legato. Slurs are first introduced only in bar 7: this is to be interpreted as the first appearance in the movement of a legato touch. The initial light detached sonority is much harder to achieve on a modern concert grand than on the instruments of Beethoven's time. There are three kinds of sonority employed here in this opening page: detached without pedal, legato without pedal, and *subito forte* with pedal. The unremitting use of pedal common today abolishes these distinctions.

How important the opposition of pedal and no pedal was for Beethoven can be confirmed at the most dramatic climax of the finale:

The manuscript indicates the first set of arpeggios, bars 163–4, without pedal (*con sordino*), and the second (the indication mistakenly omitted by the engraver) with pedal (bars 165–6), which makes the second set doubly effective. Some editors think this is a slip of Beethoven's pen; I see no reason to suppose this. Starting with the following bar, Beethoven again expressly directs no pedal, and this runs against the grain for most of us who play the piano today.

In short, the pedalled sound is still a special effect for Beethoven as it was for Haydn, and he used it above all for contrast. The first movement of the "Moonlight" Sonata is perhaps the only exception in his work, a unique essay in tone colour: here he wanted the entire piece to be played with pedal, to be played, in fact, delicately and pianissimo without ever changing the pedal, that is, without lowering the dampers on to the strings. Even on his piano this made for a slight blurring, a wonderful atmospheric sonority which can, in fact, be reproduced on the modern piano, but only by exercising great care, with half changes and delayed changes of pedal.

Much more typical of his idea of how the pedal was to be employed are the sole indications of pedal in the main part of the scherzo from the "Hammerklavier" op. 106:

This brief appearance of a pedalled sound comes back fifteen bars later when this
section is repeated with the registers changed:

The main motif, repeated so often, is coloured suddenly with the pedal for one solitary moment, and then the dry sound returns. This is an exquisite and sensitive detail, which sets off a single appearance of the motif, ruined if the pedal is much in evidence before it enters. (One might envisage only an absolutely minimal touch of pedal to aid the legato that Beethoven demands in bars 35–8.)

For the generation after Beethoven, the basic Romantic use of the pedal was very different: it was no longer the classical opposition of dry and wet sonority, but above all the sustaining of the bass so that its upper harmonics could vibrate with the other voices and produce a richer tone colour as the open strings were permitted to react in sympathy. Beethoven, indeed, already makes use of this function on occasion, particularly the sustaining of the bass, but he almost always contrasts it at some point with a drier, unpedalled sonority that makes the richer texture doubly effective. The scherzo of the Sonata in A major op. 101 suddenly offsets the quirky dryness of its humorous tone with a lyrical pedal point on D flat lasting four bars, and the more complex sonority of the slight blurring is welcome both for its expressive quality and its relief from the drier march texture:

And the finale of the same work interrupts the good-humoured exposition for a unique effect of pedal, cutting short a rare lyrical passage marked *dolce* with a pianissimo horn call that seems to come from far away (the blurring of the pedal aids the effect of distance) only to be interrupted in turn by a boisterous and exceedingly brief new theme:

The primary concern of the pianist here should be to preserve the extraordinary variety of tone colour and not iron out all the changes in an effort to make a more beautiful sound.

It is clear that pedal must often be added to Beethoven's indications as long as the principle of contrast is preserved. In order to realize this, it should be remembered that the contrast requires that the pedalled sound be very much in evidence when it is needed, and that the habitually discreet employment of the pedal taught to the more docile pianists at conservatoires is out of place. When the pedal is used in Beethoven, it should be perceived to be used. We might say that it should be remarked. Often we use too little pedal in places where it is obviously required. It is curious that the three sonatas of op. 31 contain no indications of pedal except for the first movement of the second sonata, which contains some very heavy directions indeed. For example, the end of the development section of the Sonata in G major op. 31 no. 1 is absurd without pedal:

Everyone uses pedal here, of course, but most pianists change pedal every four bars or so, and almost no one uses a lot of pedal in bars 189 to 192. In my opinion, Beethoven's treatment of dominant minor ninth chords with pedal elsewhere should inspire us to hold the pedal unwaveringly down and not change at all starting at bar 170 (perhaps, indeed, at bar 162) until the recapitulation opens in bar 193, after which no pedal at all should be used for several phrases (the opening theme of this movement needs to be heard almost completely without pedal for most of its course). Above all, bars 189–93 should swim in pedal, and any sense of decorum here should be renounced. This movement should not be played to please Proust's grandmother.

The model for this effect of a climactic minor ninth chord with pedal may be found in both the "Waldstein" and the "Appassionata" Sonatas, where Beethoven expressly directs a great deal of pedal to bring out this dramatic and dissonant harmony. The famous blurring of the D♭ and C in the middle of the coda of the "Appassionata" is well-known, but the long pedal at the end of the development of the finale of the "Waldstein" is equally instructive:

The dominant pedal lasts seventeen and a half bars. The minor ninth A♭ is introduced in the eleventh bar, to the shock of many musicians, who would like very much to change pedal here, at the very point when the foot should remain steady. This is the moment when the dynamic sinks to pianissimo, and the effect of sustaining the pedal is magnificent when the sonority is sufficiently delicate. What is rarely observed, however, is Beethoven's directions to remove the pedal for the last half of bar 312, and to play the last beat dryly. This allows the return of the pedal in bar 313 to set the beginning of the return of the main theme into high relief.*

The similar directions to remove the pedal at certain points of the opening pages of this movement are equally important:

---

*For further considerations on Beethoven's pedal, see my *The Romantic Generation*, Cambridge, Mass., 1995, pp. 13–27.

The instruction to take away the pedal for most of bar 8 is an exquisite and illu-minating detail if carried out: the soft dry sonority has extraordinary delicacy. The pedal has three purposes in this page: 1) it sustains the bass for a pastoral, drone effect; 2) it helps the pianist to make it clear that the bass note is always an integral part of the melody that goes from bass to soprano without a break, and the line must be heard as a unity; 3) it adds a delicate atmospheric blurring that reinforces the pastoral mood (this can be achieved on the modern piano by play-ing the right hand as softly as possible, and if the notes are only touched so that they just speak, they will actually sound much louder than we might think). The atmospheric haze will appear with its full quality only if bars 23 to 30 are played absolutely without any pedal whatsoever. Any attempt to eke out the legato with the pedal here would be self-indulgent laziness on the pianist's part.

A paradox of the way phrasing is notated at the time is the fact that the first note of the melody in bar 1, an eighth note followed by a rest, and the first note in bar 8, similarly an eighth note followed by a rest, imply diametrically opposed types of execution. Starting the phrase with an eighth note and a rest means that it is attacked with an accent: ending the phrase at the end of a slur with an eighth note and a rest means that it is to be released without an accent. This is the irri-tating ambiguity of notation at the time. It arose from the desire to articulate clearly the opening of the phrase, and to contrast the initiation of a motif or a phrase with the rounding-off of each element. In neither case here is the duration of the note in any way indicated by the notation, since in both the pedal is to be held through the succeeding rest.

How serious Beethoven was about exactly how long to hold down the pedal through the rests each time in this movement may be seen from bar 101. Beethoven originally wrote an initial eighth note followed by an eighth-note rest and a quarter-note rest: he scratched out the quarter rest and substituted two eighth rests, and put the release of pedal under what was now the third of the three eighth rests in the bar. He wished to specify that the pedal was to be held down throughout all the rests until the very end of the bar. Bars 105 and 113 are subsequently notated in the same way. Later in the movement, he directs the pedal to be held through full bars of silence sustaining the chords in the preceding bars, and accordingly writes two quarter-note rests instead of a half-note rest in order to make it clear that the pedal is only to be raised at the end of the bar.

It is no use hiding the problem that Beethoven's pedal indications, particularly his clear intention to have certain passages dry, are not always welcome to the modern performer. It is not only that today's instruments damp somewhat more efficiently than Beethoven's and make for a slightly drier and less pleasant sonority when no pedal is used. In the large concert halls now more or less standard throughout the world, the unpedalled sound does not carry well. The modern public, furthermore, have become accustomed to the richer vibration of the sonority with pedal, just as they have become used to the continuous vibrato of the modern violinist and find the absence of a vibrato oddly disturbing. Nevertheless, without demanding a dogmatic purity, the variety of tone colour that Beethoven desired can be preserved for modern audiences if the pedal is not simply applied mechanically and thoughtlessly wherever it does not disturb the harmony.

TRILLS

In the eighteenth century, trills generally began with the upper note, although there are certain exceptions. Chopin still held to the old-fashioned tradition, but the fashion was changing. Hummel is popularly supposed to be responsible for establishing the fashion for starting the execution on the principal or lower note. Beethoven's place in this development is unclear.

The inconvenient truth is that Beethoven himself was not always sure how to play his own trills. Towards the end of the finale of the "Waldstein" Sonata, the trills are very important, and on the back page of the manuscript, he made a stab at writing out the execution of one of the trills, the one starting in bar 485:

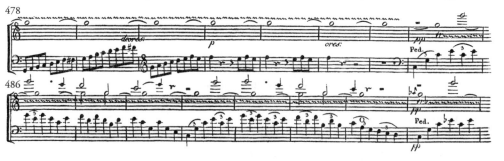

Beethoven first began writing the trill starting with the lower note, G, on all of the main beats, then crossed it out and rewrote it starting with the A. If one plays the trills with four beats, i.e. with eight notes per bar, Beethoven made the wrong choice. He also wrote out an easier version with only three beats of the trill per bar, but I cannot imagine anyone capable of playing the "Waldstein" wanting to use the simple form. In bar 487, the melody note G on the second half of the bar would be obscured by being played with the A above it. We would not hear the melody but only the dissonance of a major second.

Beethoven's indecision arises from an uncertainty about the function of a trill. Originally the trill is expressive, a simple but lengthy extension of the most expressive ornament in Western music, the *appoggiatura*. Basically the trill extends and repeats the *appoggiatura*, and the most traditional way of playing the trill in baroque music brings out that character by beginning slowly, speeding up, and sometimes ending with a snap. It is the upper dissonant note that receives the initial weight, which is at the end of the trill finally resolved into the lower note.

A second function of the trill which develops a little bit later is motivated not by expression but by sonority: the trill exists merely to sustain and extend a note on the keyboard. Simply repeating a single note rapidly on a keyboard instrument always has an effect of brilliant or picturesque virtuosity, and it was used by Domenico Scarlatti to imitate the guitar on a harpsichord or early piano; it is hard to play a rapidly repeated note very softly. A trill is a much softer effect on the piano, rather like a *tremolo* on a bowed instrument. It helped to sustain long notes which, on old keyboards, would otherwise die away very rapidly; and it also added a little excitement to the sound. At this place in the "Waldstein" finale, the trill is essentially fulfilling the second function, which is why the composer began by writing it out beginning with the lower note, but he evidently thought it could also be made to sound expressive, so he revised his writing in favour of the more dissonant effect. If one wishes for the more expressive sound, then one must alter or adjust it in bar 487 so that the melody is not ruined. The basic function of the trill in this passage, however, is the sustaining of the principal note as a kind of upper pedal throughout the section.

The decision how to play the trills in Beethoven should not be an attempt to reproduce ancient or even authorial performance practice, but ought to be the result of considering what the function of each trill is, a function that might change as it recurs even in a single movement. In the final fugue of the "Hammerklavier", the main theme is the leap of a tenth starting on the dominant, with a trill on the second note, the leading tone, resolved into the tonic. How should this trill be executed? If one wishes to emphasize the interval of the tenth, it would be sensible to begin it on the lower note. If one prefers to give it an expressive quality, making it dissonant to the surrounding harmony, the advantage would be to start it on the upper note. How did Beethoven think it should be played? At one place he writes it out, in the final stretto when the theme is played in the original position and inverted simultaneously:

The inverted version in the right hand specifies that the trill begins on the upper note. The left hand plays the original version, where the trill is directed but its execution is not written out. Beginning the left-hand trill on the upper note like the right hand, however, would lead to the revolting sonority of a double trill with a perfect fifth and an augmented fourth: in spite of all of Beethoven's revolutionary courage and his willingness on occasion to write something ugly for dramatic effect, he cannot have wished for anything that crude, and, in fact, writes out the trill in the right hand to prevent any such parallelism. This might suggest that he generally expected the trill in the original version to start on the lower note, but in my opinion there is no reason to assume that he wanted the rendition to be uniform throughout the movement. In any case, whatever the composer's intention, since we have seen that he himself was not always sure of the correct decision, the pianist is at liberty to decide each time what may be considered the most musical solution. No amount of research can ever do away with that fundamental responsibility. All that research can accomplish is to make the pianist aware of the range of possible choices.

THE LIMITS OF BEETHOVEN'S KEYBOARD

During Beethoven's lifetime the piano keyboard was extended in both treble and bass. At the beginning the limits went from a low F to a high F. Early in the nineteenth century, the range was extended upwards, and by 1815 an octave had been added above, and the bass was enlarged by a fourth below to the C.

Beethoven welcomed the extensions, and he certainly chafed against the barriers. In work after work, the music pushes to the limits of the keyboard and implies notes beyond the available ones. In the Sonata in D major op. 10 no. 3, for example:

The powerful rush of octaves almost makes us hear the high F# at the end even when it is not played. Beethoven said that he wanted to rewrite his earlier works to include the new range that became available, and, in fact, he revised an early version of the Third Piano Concerto in order to make use of the high notes that piano manufacturers had introduced. Should we, today, follow suit and rewrite?

No simple, global answer can be given. In the passage from op. 10 no. 3 quoted above, not to play the F# on a modern instrument does not make sense, except to a few connoisseurs in the audience who know that the early pianos stopped at F. On an early instrument, indeed, the absence of the F# has a kind of dramatic power, as if Beethoven were literally pushing against the physical limits imposed by the material object he was playing. (The advantage of playing the older instruments, in fact, is not that they are more suitable, but that they are so evidently inadequate and consequently reveal the composer's ambitions more clearly, his refusal to allow the physical limitations of instrument or musician to dictate his inspirations.)

However, when the conception of a movement or a passage is evidently shaped by the available range, and Beethoven exploits the limitation, we ought to refrain from any revision. The return (b) of a passage of the exposition (a) of the finale in the recapitulation of the Sonata in D minor op. 31 no. 2 is so effective that no one has ever thought of changing it although it is obviously imposed by the limited keyboard. The two passages are:

a)

b)

The rewriting by Beethoven was forced upon him by the fact that he did not yet have the high G implied by the transposition of the passage from A minor to D minor, but the repetition of the upper D makes the passage more dramatic, and it fits better with the motivic treatment of the finale as a whole.

We should not think that Beethoven was the first composer to push at the physical boundaries of the instrumental means available to him and to be inspired by them to more expressive forms. In Bach's Partita no. 4 in D major, a lovely arabesque in A minor (a) returns in B minor (b):

a)

In this partita, evidently written somewhat earlier than the others, Bach did not yet have the high D on his harpsichord, which stopped at the C. As Beethoven did later in op. 31 no. 2, he reworked the phrase repeating the upper note many times, and the arabesque gains in pathetic effect.

The reason that no straightforward global answer can be given for the problem in Beethoven is that in so many cases the advantages of extending the range or of sticking to the original are fairly equally balanced. My own preference in these cases would be to stay with the original. The following passage from the finale of the Sonata in F major op. 54 will demonstrate the possibility of choice:

It is evident that Beethoven was forced to stop writing octaves in the bass (indicated by an 8 under the note in bars 37–40) because he had nothing below the F. It would not be unreasonable to continue adding the octaves. Nevertheless, the return of the octave doubling in bar 44 gives the end of the sequence added power, and makes the upbeat to the following section more interesting. One might also maintain that keeping the F as the lowest note in the movement as a whole makes the tonic F major more cogent at its later appearances.

Similarly, in the fugue of the "Hammerklavier", the octaves of the augmentation of the main theme cannot descend to the tonic B♭ in bars 114 and 115:

It may seem perverse not to allow the bass octaves to descend to their natural goal of B♭. The climax, however, is actually reached in bar 116 with the low C that starts an insistent presence of the harmony of the dominant ninth on C that lasts for ten beats. This climax is considerably more effective if it remains the lowest note in the bass and is only spoiled by playing the lower B♭ just before it. Before altering a passage in Beethoven, the character of each instance must be considered, and the different circumstances weighed. (We shall return to the problem with the low Es in both op. 90 and op. 109.) The question remains a small part of the larger consideration of the realization of the sonatas, and no dogmatic answer seems to me ultimately satisfactory.

PART II
The Sonatas

The Eighteenth-Century Sonatas

THREE SONATAS, OPUS 2
COMPOSED IN 1795

The three piano sonatas op. 2 assert the young composer's individuality and his range. Beethoven does not reserve the work in the minor mode for the last, as he did with the three piano trios op. 1, but opens with it. Each work is strikingly different in character and form. Pathos is succeeded by sociability and brilliance. Formal patterns typical of Mozart are followed by techniques learned from Haydn. The sonority incorporates textures from concerto, symphony and chamber music.

The Sonata in F minor op. 2 no. 1 is a homage to Mozart, transported into a new and more violent affective world. The opening theme of the first movement forces us to remember the main theme of the finale of Mozart's G minor Symphony. For this sonata, Beethoven recalled a theme he had written many years ago for a piano quartet when he was a child even before Mozart had composed his G minor Symphony, but he made this theme sound more like Mozart's finale when he used it in the sonata. The second theme in the traditional relative major, A flat, is derived directly from the first theme, but in a way that is triply surprising: it is a free inversion of the first theme, it does not start with the harmony of a root position tonic but on a more intense dominant pedal, and it is coloured strikingly throughout by the chromaticism of the minor mode. This gives an unprecedented excitement to the new version of the theme, and it emphasizes the role of the pathetic minor mode in the movement. In addition, it replaces the light staccato of the first theme with a more intense legato. The closing theme, unavoidably in the accepted relative major, is also coloured by the accidentals of the minor mode. Beethoven clearly tries to reduce the space of the major mode in this work: when the second and the concluding themes return in the recapitulation, they are now not merely coloured by the minor mode but firmly in the tonic minor. It is surprising how little has to be changed later to anchor the themes in the minor, and even more surprising how little difference it makes to the character of the themes on their return, as the pathetic charge was initially so great.

There is a wrong note in all editions of the development section:

The pairs of bars 73–4, 75–6 and 77–8 are in a parallel sequence, and for that reason the first note in the right hand in bar 75 should be a B♮, not a D♭. The difference is almost imperceptible but the change to D♭ in the sequence makes no sense. I do not know if the engraver made the mistake or Beethoven himself in a moment of inattention; the autograph manuscript has disappeared.

The F major Adagio (all the movements of this sonata are in F) is in the style of an aria with traditional operatic ornaments. In bar 16, it closes firmly on the tonic to start up again in the relative minor (with a phrase reminiscent of the slow movement of a Mozart concerto) as if to continue in ternary form, but it quickly moves to a traditional exposition closing section on the dominant, and it turns out to be in cavatina form (a sonata exposition and recapitulation without a development, as in the outer section of a *da capo* aria). In the recapitulation the return of the section in the dominant follows a full close on the tonic, avoiding a tightly knit structure.

The minuet and the trio are both in the orthodox three-phrase pattern. In the trio, bars 59 to 65 are an interpolation in the pattern, suspending it for seven bars. With only the slightest revision one could skip from bar 57 or 58 directly into bar 64 or even into bar 66. Beethoven employs here a well-known eighteenth-century technique for enlarging a melody discussed by Koch.* The trio is also interesting in that the return of the first phrase as the third phrase is more regular than its initial appearance: it seems as if the final appearance is the original form and the first appearance the rewriting.

The Prestissimo finale is a work of youthful violence with its many indications of fortissimo and its brilliant arpeggios. None of the movements in the minor (the first, the minuet and the finale) allow an ending in the major. This insistence on the minor mode is unusual for its time, and, in fact, there is a higher proportion of works in the minor among Beethoven's sonatas than in those of his

* See my *The Classical Style*, p. 87, and the reference to Koch's *Versuch*.

predecessors or his contemporaries. Might one call this a prefiguration of the later importance of the minor mode?: all of Chopin's works in sonata form are in the minor mode, and all of the piano sonatas of Schumann and Liszt as well.

The Sonata in A major op. 2 no. 2 follows a tripartite model derived from Haydn for the exposition of its opening movement, in contrast to the binary Mozartean exposition of the first sonata. The main theme is complex in two parts, bars 1–8 and 9–20. The first eight bars oppose two separate brusque motifs; the second phrase flows more smoothly. After an abbreviated counter-statement, a new brilliant motif starts (bar 32), derived largely from the rising scale of the second phrase of the main theme (bars 9–10) played three times as fast, but entirely new in character, almost like a cadential tutti ritornello, going from forte to fortissimo. The standard technique of modulating to the domi-nant is employed by setting up a pedal on the dominant of the dominant (B major) and a few hints of the dominant of the dominant of the dominant to strengthen the process (F sharp major, V of V of V). All this is orthodox, but not the subsequent move to the minor mode with a *parlando* duet between right and left hands and an expressive slowing down:

This initiates a new theme with a bass that rises, first diatonically and then chro-matically, through a ninth from E to F#. We cannot overestimate the revol-utionary character of this passage, and a good deal of nineteenth- and twentieth-century music springs from the exciting innovation of this mounting bass and the final dissonant *fortissimo* violence.

Beethoven wanted the broken octave arpeggios in bars 84 to 90 to be played in one hand. Most pianists take Czerny's advice and play them with two hands. The sound is very different. The two-handed realization of such a passage had already been used by Domenico Scarlatti, so Beethoven was probably aware of it, and he could have thought it up for himself, but he specifically prescribed the fin-gering for one hand. The difficulty of playing the passage with one hand reveals itself audibly in performance even on one of Beethoven's pianos with its narrower keys. The effect of the performer's having to struggle even slightly with the pass-age gives it psychologically greater force with the public.

In spite of the arrival of a dominant cadence at bar 58, all of bars 32 to 104 form a unity, framed by the brilliant new figure at bar 32, which returns at the end of this section like a ritornello and precedes a brief closing theme. The expressive theme with its rising bass that follows the cadence at bar 58 is so clearly attached affectively to the previous passage, and seems to continue to develop its characteristic expression so closely, that a Mozartean division at bar 58 would be hard to maintain in performance: the large-scale rhythmic structure of the whole section is closely allied to the sweep of a Haydn exposition in many of his symphonies, although the emotional violence and excitement of Beethoven is novel. The brevity of the closing theme (derived from the rising scale of bars 9 and 10 of the main theme transfigured by a legato touch) is Haydnesque as well: Mozart generally needed two or three conventional flourishes to end an exposition.

We might outline the exposition as follows:
A Bars 1–20 principal theme
        21–32 counterstatement
B Bars 32–46 Ritornello at the tonic, movement to V
        46–58 Establishment of the minor mode
        58–83 Section in dominant minor with rising bass
        84–91 Virtuosity in dominant major
        92–103 Ritornello at the dominant
C Bars 103–16 Cadential theme

The development section descends from the ending of the exposition on E to C major, then to A flat major, and then to F minor. This is the first example of Beethoven's beloved descent in thirds that reappeared throughout his life. At the end of this process, changing the mode from F minor to major leads naturally to D minor, and this prepares the standard move back to the tonic A major through A minor. On the way, Beethoven takes the opportunity to write some virtuoso broken tenths in order to realize a triple stretto of the motif originally heard in bar 9. The pianistic techniques used in this sonata are among the most original of the period, as are the resulting sonorities.

The sonority of the Largo appassionato is even more striking: a hymn tune marked *tenuto* accompanied by what sounds like a *pizzicato* bass.* This movement is in ternary form with long outer sections of 19 bars each, and a shorter 11-bar central section that abandons the hymn-like texture for a more speaking texture, a duet between soprano and tenor. At the return to the first section, many pianists do not realize that the use of white and black notes in the same

---

* The staccato bass will sound even more like a *pizzicato* if it is very rapidly arpeggiated, or played slightly before the tenor part. This is a technique for making bass notes sound like *pizzicato* invented by Haydn in his late E major Piano trio.

chord was a traditional way of indicating an arpeggio, this one to be played not rapidly but slowly and expressively (and the arpeggio should be extended to the right hand as well):

The most extraordinary aspect of this movement is the immense coda of 31 bars, which takes up more than a quarter of the whole. At bar 50, a new motif that sounds like what should be a final cadential four-bar codetta starts, and is repeated with expressive ornaments. In place of the expected final chord, the hymn, heard only softly until now, suddenly crashes in with six bars of *fortissimo* and octave doubling: there is no question that this is a sonority as loud as Beethoven's instrument could support. Then, after a brief and much softer transition, the hymn is replayed in the major with greater transparence in a higher octave (and we are probably intended to continue the pianissimo of the previous transition), along with a new and delicate ostinato in the alto. A new closing theme brings the movement to an end. There are precedents for such a grand expansion of a coda with new and complex developments of the main theme in Haydn, but none in Mozart.

The Scherzo is in three-phrase minuet form. The first phrase ends on the tonic, so the second part naturally begins with the dominant. There is an exquisite interpolation that expands the expressive cadence in G sharp minor:

Without the interpolation, we can skip directly from the end of bar 18 to 25 (and bars 25 to 32 are also clearly a transitional extension of the second phrase of the three-phrase structure), but we would miss the moment of greatest lyrical expansion, which depends on the arrested motion. The last four bars of the scherzo are a coda to the third phrase.

The Rondo (Grazioso) is an amiable finale of the kind that we have seen so often in Mozart, and needs to be slightly slower than the traditional Allegretto. It is marked in common time, not *alla breve*, but the rhythm is often an *alla breve* type. The downward swoops of intervals of thirteenths and fourteenths in the main theme are an imitation of violin technique. Marked with a two-note slur for an eighth note and a sixteenth with a sixteenth rest, they must sound legato although the hands of few pianists can realize that literally. Even without the use of the pedal, however, the phrasing and accentuation can give the illusion of a legato, particularly if the following sixteenth-note rest is not only observed but tactfully exploited. The lyrical grace of the theme depends on this detail. The most inspired stroke is perhaps the transformation in bar 100 of the opening two-beat arpeggio into a long four-beat scale that goes from the bottom all the way to the top of Beethoven's keyboard. Nineteenth-century critics like Lenz felt that the central episode in A minor made an unnecessarily brutal contrast with the outer sections, but what is most remarkable is the relaxed spaciousness of this finale.

The third sonata of op. 2, in C major, stakes a claim to the grand public style: this work is intended to impress listener and performer. It begins quietly and perhaps strangely with the texture of chamber music. The opening phrase, famously awkward to play, resembles the beginning of a string quartet (although more complex, it sounds somewhat like the first bars of op. 18 no. 1) even more than it does a quiet string opening of a symphony or a concerto. Like op. 2 nos 1 and 2, the initial two-bar motif is repeated at once with many of its elements transposed up a second, a pattern that will continue to recur later in Beethoven's works. The second part of the theme is replayed (bar 9) as if with the melody transferred to the cello. The intimate opening is belied immediately in bar 13 with a public *fortissimo* section of 14 bars, which has some piano concerto figuration but is more symphonic in character. A half cadence in grand style on the dominant is succeeded by three beats of silence.

After the silence, the sudden turn to the dominant minor is arresting, and an expressive theme of 12 bars is closed with some traditional concerto solo figuration directed to a half cadence on the dominant of the dominant and a new theme marked *dolce* in G major. (The five-bar-long slur starting at 51 shows the effort Beethoven was making to replace the heavily articulated style of the time with a more cantabile legato.) The tutti section first heard in bar 10 returns (bar 61), acting as a ritornello. Full cadences, *forte* and *fortissimo*, on the dominant G take place three times (bars 77, 85 and 90), with two *pianissimo* full cadences (bars 79 and 81) as well; there is a profusion of closing themes. The invention is lavish.

The development, starting with one of the closing themes, moves to E flat major, with 12 bars of arpeggios of a kind considered indispensable at that time for the traditional development (or second solo) of concertos. The concerto style of this movement becomes more and more apparent as it proceeds, finally resulting in a full-scale cadenza, and the closing bars of both the exposition and the movement as a whole sound like a piano transcription of a massive orchestral tutti.

The recapitulation opens with the first eight bars of the exposition, but then the traditional injection of subdominant harmony at this point inspires some expressive two-part counterpoint (bars 117–25), followed by an abbreviated version of the ritornello. The subdominant leaning of the new passage justifies the replacement of the following dominant minor section of the exposition by the tonic minor (subdominant harmony makes a turn to the dominant improbable and unconvincing and persuades us that the tonic is imminent).

The slow movement in E major treats a simple form, *A B A B A*, with great ingenuity in one of Beethoven's most dramatic creations. The originality lies more in the dynamics and texture than in the harmonic pattern. The ten bars of the opening theme, which has an operatic cast, have a pause in every bar, as if the singer stopped for breath after each brief motif: every silence, as in an opera, has an emotional power. The *B* section is in the tonic minor, and is in cavatina form (exposition and recapitulation with no intervening development); the exposition has two sections of a unified flowing texture in E minor and G major: the first theme of this new section is only three bars long, played first in E minor and then at once in G major; a new theme based on a motif of written-out *appoggiature* continues in G. The exposition is all played quietly, but the recapitulation begins with a shock, an immediate *fortissimo*; the return of the opening theme of the *B* section takes on something of the character of a harmonic development, as the three-bar theme appears successively in the tonic minor, the subdominant minor and the dominant minor (E minor, A minor and B minor). The return of the second theme with the *appoggiature* has an inspired transformation: repeated in E minor, it is now consistently over a dominant pedal, which radically alters its function. While the recapitulation of the first theme of the *B* section works partially as a development, the pedal under the return of the second theme transforms it into an elaborate dominant preparation for the reappearance of the *A* section.

The ten bars of *A* are simply repeated without alteration until the end, where the greatest shock of the movement is produced. Instead of the soft resolution on to the tonic, the harmony drops to the flat submediant, C major, and the opening two bars of the principal theme are played *fortissimo*. This matter is dropped at once for the reappearance of the *B* section: the first theme modulates from C major back to the tonic E, and then the second theme, no longer on a dominant pedal, is played in the tonic major. The contradictory tensions of the middle section are now completely reconciled, as all dissonant harmonic structure is resolved into the tonic major. The opening theme returns once again with added ornaments. In a short coda of operatic recitative, Mozart's expressive effect of having the soprano descend with a leap from the highest to the lowest register is reconstituted as only the piano could do it; the vocal line descends from the soprano to the bass, but as if it were sung by one voice:

The scherzo, in three-phrase form as usual (bars 1–16, 17–28 and 40–55), interpolates a relentless suspension on the dominant for eleven bars at the end of the second phrase, and a nine-bar coda from 56 to the end. The rhythm is insistent and exhilarating. The trio, also in three-phrase form, makes a powerful melody out of sweeping arpeggios. There is a coda after the return of the scherzo, which follows a dramatic orchestral effect of unison octaves with two eight-bar ostinato pedals, first on the dominant and then the tonic. The scheme is simple but remarkably individual in sound.

The finale, Allegro assai, returns to the concerto style of the first movement. It follows the standard model of a sonata rondo with the Mozartean effect of a new and independent theme in the subdominant to complete the development section (Mozart's form is often *ABAdevCBA*, and Beethoven enlarges this with another appearance of the main theme, *ABAdevCABA*). The development ends in the conventional relative minor (bar 101). The subdominant theme that follows is like a chorale, and impressed Brahms sufficiently to produce an imitation of it in the finale of his F minor Sonata op. 5. One of Beethoven's flashier technical accomplishments as a pianist was a triple trill. He employed it in his concerto cadenzas, and he produces a cadenza with one at the end of this movement. He evidently wrote this sonata, and the others of the opus, to show off his performance style to the greatest advantage.

SONATA IN E FLAT MAJOR, OPUS 7
COMPOSED BY 1797

This is one of the longest and most difficult of the thirty-two sonatas. It is considerably longer than the "Appassionata" or than any of the last three sonatas. The technical difficulties of the first movement (where Beethoven demands a very fast *Allegro molto e con brio*) include long skips, legato octaves, very fast broken

octaves, scales that must be almost as rapid as a *glissando* (bars 97–8), and a written-out *tremolo* (bars 111–27) in which different voices must be emphasized.

In this sonata, perhaps for the first time, Beethoven radically alters the accent
of a theme at its final appearance. At the opening, the main theme is accented
on the first note of the motif of a descending third, and on the odd-numbered
bars:

The opening motif is not slurred, but a slur is implied, and in a later page all the
notes of the opening chord are tied into the second chord except for the soprano,
which has an effect equivalent to a two-note slur. The accents are consistently on
bars 1, 3, 5, 7, and 9;* the first offbeat accent is in the second half of bar 10. Bar
13 is only accented on the second beat, and bar 16 throws the emphasis squarely
on an even-numbered bar, to which bar 17 acts at least partially as a release before
reestablishing the original pattern.

The end of the movement reverses the accent of the motif:

The accompaniment in the left hand now throws the accent of the motif on to
the second note (perhaps that is why Beethoven did not bind the two notes with
a slur, but any accent on the second note of the motif at the opening of this
movement would be unmusical and would, in addition, spoil Beethoven's effect

---

* See remarks on the phrasing of this passage on p. 29.

of reversal of accent at the end). In the final bars, the accent-creating pattern in the left hand occurs every two bars, but then the motif is speeded up in diminution in the right hand, and the left hand also speeds up its accenting pattern to every bar.

Note that there is a final empty bar over which the fermata is placed, instead of a fermata over the final rest in the previous bar. That is because Beethoven is clearly thinking in terms of a two-bar pattern with downbeat accents on the odd-numbered bars. The motif now begins on even-numbered upbeat bars starting on bar 352, and this shifts its accent. The last chord is on 361, a downbeat, and the final empty bar merely completes the pattern. (The end of the first movement of op. 2 no. 2 has a similar empty bar, but it is not gratuitous there as Beethoven asks for a repeat of the second half of the movement. No repeat is called for at the end of op. 7.)

In the *tremolo* figuration at bar 111, the main melodic line is at first in the lower voice changing to the soprano in bar 116, and to the middle voice in the latter half of 119, where it remains. This requires very tricky tone control (the voicing is altered at the end of the passage in the recapitulation and goes to the lowest voice at the end of 303 and to the middle voice in the second half of 305). These voices should not be set excessively in relief but only delicately emphasized, as Beethoven is clearly striving for a unified texture, but that does not make the control of tone any easier.

The introduction of subdominant harmony after the beginning of the recapitulation is not this time the occasion for any lyrical sentiment but a grand sonority of *forte* (bar 305), repeated *fortissimo* with an insistent *sforzando* on every beat. It is an event that stands out (see the example on page 30).

The *Largo, con gran espressione*, combining the opposing and almost contradictory technique of a hymn with an operatic accompanied recitative, demands an intensely expressive performance. It is in the submediant C major: as in op. 2 no. 3, Beethoven was following Haydn in his use of mediant relations for the key of the slow movements. The rhythmic structure of the outer part of an *A B A* form is exceptionally varied, and the dynamics go quickly from *pianissimo* to *fortissimo*, the texture from legato to sharp staccato without warning. The central section, a chorale which goes to the flat submediant A flat major, was sufficiently impressive to inspire Schubert to imitate it in the central section of the slow movement of his Sonata in B flat major. The melody, *sempre tenuto*, is strikingly contrasted with a staccato accompaniment. After the return of the *A* section, newly ornamented, a coda briefly brings back the chorale, transferred to the left hand, followed by several new motifs. The last bars of the movement have an amazing sonority: a legato bass descending chromatically in heavy octaves, pianissimo, under the opening melody interrupted by rests as before, a sudden *fortissimo* at the penultimate moment of greatest intensity, released astonishingly into two short, detached chords, *pianissimo*. Nothing like this had ever been heard before:

The three phrases of the minuet form are bars 1 to 24 (expanded by rests and a suspension on V of V between bars 12 and 18), bars 25 to 42, and bars 43 to 86, with a coda from 87 to the end at bar 95. The first phrase plays the opening of the main theme twice: for the second playing, the third phrase substitutes the tonic minor, and then adds a long lyrical development from bar 55 to 70, beginning and ending pianissimo: this section is one of Beethoven's loveliest inspirations.

The trio of the minuet is an atmospheric exercise in tone colour, with the melody hidden in an arpeggiated motion of triplets, pianissimo with sudden accents of *ffp*. These accents appear to cover only the first note of the bar, and therefore only the lower voice, but at least some of the time I think they would be better applied to the whole of the initial triplet. (Liszt had not yet invented his notation for an accent that covered more than one note, which he unfortunately abandoned later in life; if three notes must be accented together, it is misleading to write three separate accents. If Beethoven, as I think, wanted the whole broken chord set in relief, he had no adequate notation to indicate that.)

The last movement is an amiable finale, *Poco Allegretto e grazioso*, in a style that extends the numerous Allegretto rondo finales of Mozart, adding both a more marked cantabile style and an arrestingly brilliant middle section. The twelfth bar of the main theme comes to a halt on a dominant B flat in simple unison octaves *sforzando* with a fermata. At the first return of the theme, Beethoven follows the B♭ octaves, now a *subito* piano after a crescendo, with unadorned B♮ octaves *sforzando*, an ostentatiously laconic way of establishing the C minor of the middle section (Beethoven actually asks for a crescendo on the sustained B♭). The fermata over the B♭ is heard again when the main theme reappears for a third playing. The last playing of the theme, however, now heavily ornamented, holds a surprise. It is as if Beethoven had been planning to exploit the climax of the theme, keeping back the greatest effect for the end:

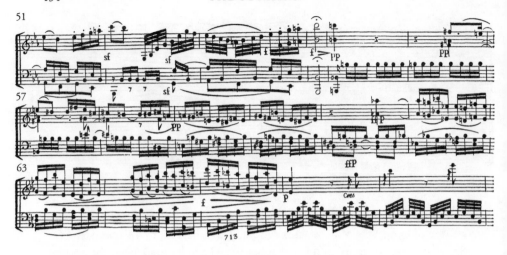

the pianissimo dynamic is essential for the sense of mystery that the strange harmony of the flat supertonic brings. Beethoven stops the motion at this point, makes the listener wait for resolution. It comes fortissimo in bar 161. Here it would be nonsensical to interpret the *ffp* in the left hand as applying only to the third under which it is written; the following B♮ must be included in the grand accent. It is the resolution of the B♮ into the B♭ (which must be *piano*) that carries the meaning of the passage, and the *fortissimo* must remain constant into the entrance of the right hand. This passage is one of the first examples of Beethoven's ability to make an initial and striking detail on the first page reveal its full significance only much later in the work (many of us will think, of course, of the C# in the seventh bar of the "Eroica" Symphony, and how much is made of it when it returns).

THREE SONATAS, OPUS 10
COMPOSED BY 1798

Beethoven in C minor has come to symbolize his artistic character. In every case, it reveals Beethoven as Hero. C minor does not show Beethoven at his most subtle, but it does give him to us in his most extrovert form, where he seems to be most impatient of any compromise. In opening his set of op. 10, he chose to present himself to the public at once in that aspect. He reserved the most pretentious sonata of the three, the one in D major, for the end. As with op. 2, he begins with the passionate heroic, continues in a wittier vein, and closes expansively with the grand style.

The C minor Sonata is the most compressed and laconic of the three, like op. 2 no. 1. It is evident that in this movement, Beethoven worked consciously with an alternation of strong and weak bars (like the first movement of op. 7, the opening *Allegro molto e con brio* ends with a fermata over a silent bar, as it is the penultimate bar which has the strong accent, and the silent bar completes the unit), but he was exceptionally subtle in this work with the use of periodic rhythm.

It is with the presentation of the main theme that we can see Beethoven's play with bar accent. The phrases start at first with a strong downbeat on odd-numbered bars, but the counterstatement begins on bar 22. Where does the change to accenting the even-numbered bars take place?

Tovey believes that it starts at bar 9, and is confirmed by 17 onwards.[1] This underestimates Beethoven's supple handling of the rhythm. Bars 10 and 12 begin to add extra weight to the weak bars, which results in an expressive syncopation that any pianist will wish to bring out, but the *rinforzando* and the arpeggio reaffirm the supremacy of bar 13. Both 14 and 15 recall the expressive accents of bars 10 and 12, but the end of the phrase on bar 16 is a weak release, and restores the original unit grouping. (Note the phrasing of the left hand, which demands an unaccented release at bar 16.) From bars 9 to 14, Beethoven steadily adds intensity to the weak, even-numbered bars, which increases the excitement until bar 16 relapses into the subordinate place, but I believe that it is more effective if the pianist continues to privilege the accents in bars 9, 11 and 13: it keeps the expressive urgency constant without relaxation. What follows is a rhythmic paradox, but it will not be the last of its kind in Beethoven. Bars 17, 19 and 21 are strong measures, but the first beat is always blank; bars 18 and 20 supply feminine endings, and to play them with a strong accent must be rejected as stylistically unacceptable: the phrasing demands that what accent there is should be looked for on the third beat of the previous bar. It is only with the first chord of bar 22 that the pattern is reversed: it is a bar that dovetails two phrases, the end of one and the beginning of the next. Both 21 and 22 are strong bars in immediate succession, and this gives a jolt to the phrase rhythm.

Leaving the strong first beats of the strong bars empty is a dramatic syncopation, very effective if it is exploited by the pianist: it extends the tension through the silence. A more spectacular use of the technique will be found much later in Beethoven's work. At the end of the scherzo of the Sonata in A flat major op. 110, all the chords are on weak bars and all the strong bars are silent. In the finale of the latter work, the transition to the second fugue presents all the chords on weak beats, and all the strong beats void. In op. 10 no. 1, the pianist must try and feel the accent as falling on the rests, and this will guide the interpretation of the four bars of pianissimo.

The movement opposes short, articulated fragments with long lines, the latter particularly in the bass. The most lyrical theme in this mostly angular work is a new theme in the subdominant minor that is introduced in the development and takes up most of it. This has its consequences in the recapitulation, where the main theme of the second group, originally in E flat major, returns, not in C major, but in F major, a relationship possibly unique in a sonata structure of the time. A change of mode to F minor prepares a replaying of the theme in the tonic minor: as in op. 2 no. 1, Beethoven avoids the tonic major. He was disinclined to work with the traditional classical ending in the major of a work in the minor mode, and must have been uneasy with the comfortable reconciliation that was implied by the tradition. He would only accept it, in works like the Fifth and Ninth Symphonies and the Sonata op. 111, when he could construct a spectacular justification.

The *Adagio molto* of op. 10 no. 1 is almost the last slow movement to make use of the ornamentation that was traditional for an Adagio. In this respect, it resembles the work of Beethoven's contemporary, Hummel, a master of such graces. Beethoven originally composed another such slow movement for the "Waldstein", but removed it (it became the separately published "Andante favori"), replacing it with the inspired short movement in arioso style now in place. Later slow movements of Beethoven were characterized either by much greater sobriety, as in op. 13 and op. 57, or by the invention of original ornamentation that differed considerably from the earlier conventions, as in the return of the main theme in the slow movement of op. 106. The slow movement of op. 10 no. 1 is in cavatina form: the exposition is separated from the recapitulation only by a very short, brusque arpeggiated dominant seventh chord, *fortissimo*. There is an eleven-bar coda, a long bass line that imitates the sound of a cello.

The finale is as angular and violent as the first movement and even more compressed. No modulation is needed in the exposition to set up the traditional move to the relative major; a half cadence with a fermata on the dominant of C minor and a jump into E flat is all that Beethoven will allow. In the recapitulation, a substitution of C major for the original E flat at this place does not, of course, require any justification, and it soon switches back to the minor. The development section is only eleven bars long, but ends with exceptional ferocity. Perhaps the most interesting point of the form is the beginning of the coda, with the theme originally in E flat now at the Neapolitan D♭, with six bars marked both *ritardando* and *calando*: it is clear that Beethoven wanted an intense effort from the performer here to achieve a grandly expressive effect. The quiet ending is in the major, but, except for the tonic chord, all the other harmonies are inflected by the accidentals of the minor mode.

The Sonata in F major op. 10 no. 2 is in the comic mode, and it proclaims its witty eccentricity at once on the first page of the *Allegro* with the move to the dominant, which begins already with bar 13. It establishes a firm half cadence on the dominant of A minor (V of iii), and then starts a new theme in C major with no further preliminaries. A minor is the relative minor (or vi) of C major, and going back to the tonic at the end of a development section by leaping from V of vi into I was already banal when Beethoven composed this sonata, but no one had ever tried the trick in an exposition before.* The sonata may seem modest, but the opening theme is complex: four scherzando bars made up of two tiny motifs are followed by a longer, more lyrical and legato cantabile of eight bars.

The end of the exposition is a simple I V I in unison octaves, played fortissimo. Beethoven takes this extremely bare version of a conventional cadence and develops it for the first ten bars of the development, an early example of his fondness for stripping the language of triadic tonality down to its most fundamental elements presented nakedly, and then using them as the basic material of his work.

The banal convention of going from the relative minor back to the tonic at the close of a development returns here as an extremely elaborate joke. Beethoven ends in D minor with a half cadence on V of vi (an A major chord) dying away pianissimo, followed by a long pause. Instead of going back to the tonic and starting the recapitulation, he stays in D, changes the mode to major, and, simply and innocently, begins his recapitulation softly in the wrong key. He keeps this up for twelve bars. Then six bars of pianissimo return to the tonic F major, a transition accomplished by the repetition of a fragment of the theme, a technique Beethoven had learned from Haydn.

There is no slow movement: the *Allegretto* is a minuet. Both the first phrase, repeated, and the second phrase of the three-phrase structure are completely regular 8 bars in length. The third phrase, however, is expanded to 14 bars by interpolating a two-bar elaboration of two-part counterpoint after bar 4, and then repeating the last four bars. There is an eight-bar coda, which arrives after the piece is clearly finished. The richly sonorous trio, beginning *pianissimo*, is also in three phrases, but the lengths are 16, 8 and 16, which unites phrases 2 and 3 and brings the effect closer to a binary form. The returns of phrase 1 and then of phrases 2 and 3 are rewritten with disconcerting syncopated accents on the second, or weakest, beat of 3/4 time. The *da capo* of the minuet, with the repeats

* See my *Sonata Forms*, New York and London, 1980, pp. 235–56, for a discussion of this passage.

written out, is reformulated as a *rubato* – that is, the right hand is always half a
beat late (although the first phrase is first played straight once as it was originally
heard). There is a full bar of silence at the end, as the last phrase ends on the
strong bar of a strong/weak unit.

The final *Presto*, with elements of fugal style, derives immediately from many
Haydn finales, particularly from the string quartets with contrapuntal display,
but by its long sections of delicate staccato in an inflexibly unchanging fast uniform rhythm, it is also the ancestor of the Mendelssohn scherzo.

Of the three sonatas of op. 10, the third is on the largest scale, the only one with
four movements. Most of the first movement derives directly from its first four
notes: rarely has so much been made of so little. For the capacity to draw inspiration from the smallest motif, Beethoven has no rivals in music history with the
possible exception of Bach, and it was from the *Well-Tempered Clavier* that
Beethoven learned music as a young boy.

The importance of the first phrase is established by ending it with a fermata:
this is a good way to make an opening proclaim that it is providing the basic
material to which we must pay attention for the rest of the movement:

The first four notes of the opening phrase are picked up by the second phrase and
played, now legato instead of staccato, three times (four times in the left hand).
The third phrase freely repeats the second with a texture of broken sixths. The
fourth phrase takes up the first phrase again and leads it further and higher, so
high in fact that the last note, F#, was just outside the range of Beethoven's piano
which stopped at an F natural. The previous phrase led the left hand down to one
note below the range of Beethoven's piano, which reached only to the low F. It
would be a foolish act of Puritan self-denial not to play these two notes on a
modern piano, as they are so obviously implied by the music – in fact, to the
point that one thinks one hears them even when they are not played, except that
one misses some of the climactic sonority.

The first four notes are the basis of every other theme in the movement except one. Most interesting is the way they appear in the first theme of the dominant group:

Here the first four notes are not transposed, but nevertheless in a different key, no longer in D but in A major. This keeps the original pitch, but changes the significance. Throughout the exposition, this simple motif is played relentlessly – about fifty times, in fact, and that does not count the inverted appearances.

The only unrelated theme is in B minor, starts immediately after the fermata on an F#, and initiates the move to the dominant.* In the first movement of every one of the piano sonatas in the major mode so far, the move to the dominant is accomplished in a different manner: in op. 2 no. 2, by going directly to V of V; in op. 2 no. 3, by a sudden move from a half cadence on the dominant to the dominant minor; in op. 7, through the subdominant leading to the dominant minor; in op. 10 no. 2, through V of iii. Beethoven does not often repeat his procedures, and he had a greater repertoire than his colleagues. The road taken by op. 10 no. 3 is impressively simple, even graceful. The B minor leads naturally to a cadence in F sharp minor, the relative minor of the dominant, A major. Beethoven reserves the subdominant G major for the coda: with its effect of reducing tension he can create a soft sense of mystery, heightened by a pianissimo move from G major to G minor. The four-note motif, with inverted variants derived from it, dominates the coda. In this work the motivic relationships are far from subtle: they cannot be missed even by the musically illiterate. It would seem as if Beethoven wanted everyone to perceive some of the secrets that make up the art of composition.

The extraordinary pathos of the *Largo e mesto* presents a temptation to play too slowly, and pianists today often choose a tempo that would be unjustifiable with the weaker sustaining power of Beethoven's keyboards. The opening of the development section is, I think, influenced by the similar place in the slow movement of Mozart's Sonata in A minor K. 310; otherwise the stylistic sources for this

---

* For this theme, see pp. 24–5.

piece are both operatic and symphonic. The thirty-second-note offbeat figuration in the development comes directly from string playing. They turn into pathetic gasps that clearly represent sobs. The sonority, particularly in the lower register, is richer here than in any other previous composition of Beethoven, and the atmosphere of tragedy, brought to a grand climax in the symphonic coda, would remain unsurpassed, if not unequalled, in his career.

The menuetto is a lyrical triumph, opening piano *dolce*. The three phrases are 16, 8 and 19 bars respectively; there is an 11-bar coda. The first phrase ends on the tonic. The second phrase is a mini-development section, a simple sequence of rising fourths worked out contrapuntally, starting from a conventional V of vi: F# B E A, so ending simply on the dominant. The return of the first phrase as the third phrase is subject to a magnificent transformation: every element of the original is intensified. The melody starts again accompanied by a trill above it, and springs to greater and more passionate heights. The dynamics, originally piano throughout, become dramatic, including an unexpected *fortissimo*; on the return to the level of *piano*, a four-bar crescendo is interrupted by a *subito piano* that restores the unpretentious lyricism of the opening bars. The trio makes a rough contrast. It is based on a two-note motif played staccato the first time and repeated legato. With motifs as simple as the ones Beethoven used for his basic material, these transformations of significance by touch and phrasing were indispensable to his sense of composition.

The Rondo finale incorporates effects that go from irony to burlesque. The first phrase opens with a short motto, like a repeated question; the long pauses were certainly intended to be comic. The two bars that follow provide an expressive answer – too expressive, in fact, with its fermata and a tiny cadenza that is, indeed, expressive but hopelessly conventional; it should not be glossed over, but played with sentimental conviction in order to bring out the humour. The motto is played again three times in a rising sequence leading to an even more conventional cadence with a surprise resolution. After another long pause, the curious motto returns *fortissimo*, and the conventional cadence once more closes the section.

A new theme at the dominant is also comic in its simplicity, being at first nothing but a chromatic scale:

A raging central section leads to a *fortissimo* passage in unison octaves, the original theme returns in B flat major, continued briefly with one bar of pathos, and another long pause. A slower and much longer passage in unison octaves rises from the bass with a mysterious chromatic shape. When the main theme returns for the last time, the pauses are filled with freely inverted comic echoes (bars

84–5). This inversion, which becomes a stepwise descent of a fifth, leads to an original pianistic invention in bar 91; the extremely brief descending motif is played rapidly in both hands out of phase and *fortissimo*. Mysteriously rich sonorities (bars 102–5) lead to twelve soft repetitions of the motto with a tonic pedal over which rising and falling scales and arpeggios finally die away (see example on page 23). Few movements have synthesized so many different textures and so many different moods. In some ways this is the most complex finale that Beethoven had written until then. The only thing that prevents it from having a weight equal to the first movement is the continuous appearance of a quirky, even grotesque, humour, which lightens the atmosphere.

SONATA IN C MINOR, OPUS 13
GRANDE SONATE PATHÉTIQUE
COMPOSED BY 1799

In 1855, Lenz wrote about this work:[2]

We should not like to have to speak about this work after the suffering it has gone through for fifty years in boarding schools and other institutions where one learns to play the piano. Is the name of Beethoven heard there by chance? The mistress of the establishment takes out, not without difficulty, from under volumes richly bound in morocco leather, a dog-eared paper which has not had even the honours of burial in leather.... Don't listen to the charming child, her hair in spiral curls, serve you up the "pathétique" with barley sugar. Poor little innocent creature who has just gone through Cramer's finger exercises, if she dares to put a timid foot into a Czerny rondo ... the *pathétique*, the feared score, becomes inevitable.... It is worse when an adult plays the sonata for you, above all very compromising for her, as she could only come to that by an extreme devotion for you? How can men really like that? she says. If the pianist is a renowned lady, one of those with a sovereign disdain for some wretched quarter notes, even for some simple eighth notes, there is no salvation.... The martyrdom ended, open the score to amuse yourself and find "Carefully revised, corrected and with fingering by Czerny" (Cranz edition): that's the clap of thunder! Czerny correcting Beethoven when all he did was correct the proofs of a thirtieth edition. Let us not go into the details of the pathetic sonata, with fingering by Czerny, metronomised by Moscheles and which will not escape chloroform. Let us hasten to say that it is simply magnificent, that the crowds of crickets who have devastated the adagio until the present day were not able to destroy its calm grandeur.

I have quoted this at some length, as it gives an illuminating image of

Beethoven's role in European culture only three decades after his death, and a male chauvinist account of his importance for the female amateur and professional. Above all, it demonstrates the reception history of Beethoven's first successful effort at the sublime. It was already evident by 1855 that the popularity of the "Pathétique" was a threat to its appreciation.

It has been argued that the repeat of the exposition of the first movement should include the *Grave* introduction, and Rudolf Serkin used to perform it so. We cannot settle the matter by consulting the manuscript, which has been lost. In the first edition, the opening of the *Allegro di molto e con brio* certainly is preceded by a bar line with dots, and this normally directs a repeat: oddly enough we do not find the standard two dots, but four. Is that significant? It makes musical sense to begin the repeat at either the beginning of the *Allegro* or at the *Grave* – at least it does not make musical nonsense to begin at the later point as it does with the Sonata in B flat minor of Chopin. If we judge by the resemblance of the form to the Sonata in C minor op. 111, starting the repeat from the *Allegro* would be the more likely choice.

The first edition is unusual in that there is a genuine attempt to make what Beethoven considered the important distinction between his strokes (or wedges) and dots, the first indicating detached accents with a certain weight, the second staccato. It is unfortunately only too clear that the engravers were unable to do that with any consistency. There are wedges in bars 11–14 and 19–22, but there is one wedge in bar 121 and dots in 122–4, although the motif is similar in all these places. Except in bars 159–60, the wedges disappear after the exposition and are all replaced by dots, as if the engraver was discouraged by the distinction. The only place where I think one can have the kind of complete confidence in the engraver's version which would make much of a difference in interpretation is in bars 65–88:

I am not sure whether the dots in 71–2 are intended to be different from the similar bars that follow with wedges at 79–80, but the dots in 82 and in 86 plausibly offer a tone colour and weight that can reasonably be contrasted with the wedges in 83–4 and 87–8, which need a more emphatic and expressive sonority, as do the wedges on the last two beats of both 95 and 96. Bars 93 to 99 have only wedges,* but the similar place in the recapitulation has only dots (bars 257–64). Whatever the notation, no one can reasonably think these last are anything but heavy accents, and a sharp staccato would be physically impossible – that is, inaudible as such if one tried to carry it out. The evidence is interesting, however, as it must reflect inaccurately the composer's concern for varying the touch.

The high seriousness of the work is shown at once. The minor mode dominates. The exposition goes to E flat, but Beethoven goes further than he did in op. 2 no. 1, where he only added the chromatic colouring of the minor mode to the major, but settles for 30 bars firmly in E flat minor before turning to the major. As in op. 2 no. 1, the recapitulation of the second group can remain in the minor throughout. Bringing the *Grave* introduction back at the end was surely borrowed from Mozart's Viola quintet in D major, but returning to it at the opening of the development is novel. Even more radical at this place, however, is the harmony: having moved rapidly from the E flat cadence at the end of the exposition to the dominant minor, Beethoven goes from G minor in four succinct bars to E minor, an enharmonic relation that must have been very disquieting when it first appeared.

The phrasing of the famous *Adagio*, marked *Cantabile* at the outset, is exquisite and rarely carried out:

The phrasing is repeated almost exactly at each return of the theme, so there is good reason to think it reproduces Beethoven's intention correctly. It calls for a

---

*Tovey (*A Companion to Beethoven's Pianoforte Sonatas*, page 170) thinks the distinction between wedges and dots in bars 93 to 100 (he uses a different numbering, starting from the *Allegro* instead of the *Grave*) are "purposeful", but he thinks that there is a dot in 99 and 100 and wedges elsewhere, while the first edition has only wedges, with a wedge in 99, and nothing in 100.

release with the first note of bar 5, and that implies a very slight diminuendo into that note. There is a similar relation between bars 6 and 7, and the first beat of bars 4 and 6 are given a slight initial attack, as well as the second halves of bars 5 and 7. The last five notes of bar 8 are marked by wedges, not by dots, as are the last two beats of 43, the detached bass notes of 48, 50 and 51 (but oddly not of 49 which has dots, as have 81 and 82 with a similar figuration; the final notes of bars 70, 71 and 72 have wedges, not dots, and this reasonably directs a sensitive execution of the detached notes). The left-hand slurs in the main theme are not placed in phase with those of the right hand, and the rhythmic counterpoint adds to the richness of the phrasing. Against our contemporary habits of performance, the endings of most of the phrases of the *Adagio* are short (bars 8, 16, 23, 36, 44, 58, 66, 68, 70, 71, 72 and 73), and in the second episode in A flat minor (bars 37 to 50) none of the notes in the left hand are longer than an eighth note except for the first, which is a quarter note to be released at once into a quarter note rest: this makes a significant contrast with the long-sustained bass notes of the outer sections. There is also an important contrast between the sustained melody of the first sixteen bars and the *parlando* style that follows and changes quickly into a simple vocal *coloratura*. Instead of decorating the last playing of the theme, now transferred from the tenor register to the soprano, a decoration that would have been normal at the time for an Adagio, Beethoven extends the increased triplet motion of the accompaniment of the second episode into the return of the main theme, altering texture rather than melody.

The Rondo finale does not attempt to sustain the fully serious approach of the first two movements. Although ending dramatically in the minor, it admits much more of the major mode than the first movement. Not until the "Waldstein" Sonata does Beethoven find a way to endow a rondo with significant grandeur. Nevertheless, the brief coda of the finale of the "Pathétique" manages to recapture some of the drama of the first movement.*

Two sonatas, opus 14
Composed by 1799

These two sonatas are considerably more modest than their predecessors, and were destined for use in the home. There are few technical difficulties. To the first three bars of op. 14 no. 1, Czerny indicated a crescendo with a diminuendo in bar 4: it is thought that he may have had the idea from Beethoven, but in any case it is a good one. It is legitimate to change the composer's directions if you can think of something better. By this time, Beethoven's sense of large-scale

---

* For a discussion of the indications of phrasing at the opening and closing of this movement, see p. 15.

phrase rhythm had become increasingly supple. For example, in bars 13 to 22 of the first sonata in E major, a two-bar phrase, accented at the opening, moves with a chromatic rise and a crescendo to an increasingly emphatic texture, displacing the accent to the middle of the bar. The most sophisticated detail is that the part of the repeating pattern that begins in bars 17–18 is inherently more expressive than the initial element in bars 16–17, yet the more expressive fragment comes with a sudden *piano* that magnifies both the lyricism and the sense of drama. This is an important structural point, which sets up the traditional half cadence on the dominant of the dominant.

The development, after four bars, is based entirely on a new theme in the subdominant minor, which lasts until the arrival of the dominant preparation for the return to the tonic. The new theme, broadly laid out and slow-moving, resembles the passionate new theme introduced similarly in the development section of the first movement of the Sonata for cello and piano op. 69. At the beginning of the recapitulation, the opening theme is played *forte* for the first time and is decorated by simple rapid scales over two octaves in the bass. A few bars later, these scales and the main theme return *pianissimo*, but in C major. This is the equivalent of the traditional subdominant harmony that the eighteenth-century composer felt obliged to refer to at this point (a good rule for deciding on whether remote harmonies are dominant or subdominant in character is to transpose the movement to C major; if the remote harmonies have flats in them, they are subdominant (from E to C would transpose as C to A♭)). The remote harmonies and the very soft dynamics make this brief passage stand out: it substitutes for the passage quoted above which accomplished the move to V. It is typical of Beethoven that his most salient inspirations should be placed over the basic moments of the large-scale structure.

The second movement, *Allegretto*, in the tonic minor, is in three-phrase minuet form. The first strain of 16 bars is not strictly repeated, but bars 9 to 16 are almost the same as 1 to 8, changing the half cadence on the dominant at the end to a full cadence on the tonic. The second strain, also of 16 bars, has two phrases, the second of which repeats the first, altering the cadence on the relative major, G, to a half cadence on the dominant with a fermata. The third strain starts as a recapitulation of the first, but enlarges the second phrase from 8 to 11 bars, by an insistence on the subdominant for 6 bars, which gives essentially a IV V I cadence. A ten-bar coda is added, which does nothing but repeat a cadence with a subdominant colour five times. The trio is in C major, also in three-phrase form. The first phrase is repeated, but the second and third phrases are played only once, modulating directly back to E minor. A coda after the da capo replays the last phrase of the trio, adding at the end three bars of unison tonic octaves, and a bar of rest with a fermata (the penultimate bar being the first of a strong/weak unit).

The amiable Rondo, *Allegro comodo*, returns to the tonic major. The first episode goes as expected to the dominant B major. The main theme is repeated, unaltered, and a middle section in G major is made up of brilliant arpeggios, conveniently easy to play. After our renewed acquaintance with the main theme, the first episode returns, but here Beethoven tries something new which nevertheless enhances an old convention. The episode does not come back in the tonic, but in the subdominant A major, and in a brief poetic moment at the end turns to A minor through a Neapolitan harmony. This is a charming and striking way of dealing with the traditional turn to the subdominant after the opening of the recapitulation, and of making something original out of it. The last appearance of the main theme is played first in a written-out *rubato* with the right hand always late. Then, *fortissimo*, this is reversed, the right hand is on the beat, and the left hand is late. The theme is now chromatically decorated, *pianissimo*, and the final cadence is accomplished forthrightly with unison octaves.

The opening of the Sonata in G major fools the listener for four bars into thinking that the bar line is in the wrong place. This is set right in bar 5:

Any attempt by the pianist to clear the matter up at once by emphasizing the first beats would be misguided. It would not only spoil the joke, it would ruin Beethoven's coda, when he decides to normalize the rhythm of the main theme, and make it no longer witty but expressive:

Now we are not only no longer puzzled by the beat, but we can see the expansive possibilities inherent in the motif. The original joke is in the style of Haydn, but the *cantabile* coda is Beethoven's own, even if he is indebted to Mozart for the idea of using the coda to set right the previous eccentricities of the material.

The first movement has a development section surprisingly long and elaborate for so modest a work, as long as the exposition, in fact, and includes a false reprise which fools no one since it is in E flat major. The cadential theme of the exposition, marked *dolce,* has a memorably popular character and is supported by an intensely expressive bass line.

The *Andante* slow movement is a set of variations in an ostentatiously simple style that recalls many of the modest sets by Mozart. The ending is a joke in Haydn's style, a sudden crash of *ff* after *pp* chords with rests (an ancestor, slightly less exaggerated, can be found at the end of the first movement of Haydn's Sonata in G major Hob. XVI/40, where soft staccato single notes are interrupted, *forte,* by a brusque arpeggiated seven-note chord).

The finale, a Scherzo marked *Allegro assai,* also opens by fooling the listeners as to the place of the bar line. It is in pastoral, even rustic style, with drone bag-pipe effects. Stylistically it is kin to some of the more humorous bagatelles that Beethoven wrote both early and late in life.

SONATA IN B FLAT MAJOR, OPUS 22
COMPOSED IN 1799–1800

Beethoven was proud of this sonata. It has never been popular, but it is, indeed, one of his most accomplished works, a demonstration of his compositional powers. In the first movement, in particular, Beethoven uses material of a neutral character; the themes have little intrinsic attraction, and they can seem unprepossessing. The interest lies almost entirely in what the composer does with the musical material, in the handling. The first movement is not picturesque, and neither tragic nor humorous, and it lays no claim to lyricism. It is content simply to be masterly.

The opening theme of the Allegro con brio is a simple motto, a rising and falling third: the Sonata op. 106, the "Hammerklavier", also in B flat major, begins with a very similar motto. The other principal theme of the exposition of both sonatas, the main theme of the second group, is made up almost entirely of falling thirds or the inverse equivalent, rising sixths. The correspondences of the two sonatas are striking. Opus 22, however, has none of the heroic ambitions of the "Hammerklavier". The character of the first movement is symbolized best by the closing theme, which consists of a simple scale in unharmonized unison octaves, fortissimo, which rises from the tonic an octave and a fourth, and falls back the way it came. This theme will be the instrument of Beethoven's most spectacular effect in the development.

The dominant of the relative minor, so conventional in a development, is dispatched at the opening. The bass rises from this dominant, D, through two fourths, G and then C, heard as the dominant of F minor. Moving to a B♭, the bass starts to descend step by step under simple arpeggios: A♭, G, G♭, F, F♭, arriving at E♭, harmonized as the dominant of A flat major. A variant of the closing theme of the exposition is introduced, starting on E♭, no longer fortissimo but piano descending to pianissimo. The theme is repeated starting on a low C, the foundation of a dominant minor ninth chord of F minor. Still pianissimo, the theme falls to the lowest note on Beethoven's keyboard, F, the basic dominant of the sonata: a dominant minor ninth chord built on it remains in place for 15 bars. (The minor dominant ninth harmony, which is a more dissonant and interesting heightening of the dominant seventh, is often used by Beethoven to prepare a return: e.g. op. 31 no. 1, op. 53 (finale), op. 57, op. 111, etc.) Throughout all this passage, a short arpeggio figure is quietly and unceasingly present. The extraordinary affective force and the mystery of this page lie in the descent from fortissimo to pianissimo that accompanies the slow descent into the lowest register of the piano, in the unremitting flow of the soft arpeggios, and in the neutral character of the theme, which has little expressive personality of its own, but can therefore be used as a building block that allows the elaborate harmonic progression with its final suspension of motion to speak for itself.

The *Adagio con molto espressione* in E flat major is often taken too slowly: the basic rhythmic element is not the eighth note but the dotted quarter. It is a sonata form, but in deference to the lyrical nature of a slow movement, the first theme is given a full close before the work moves on. There is even a double bar in the middle of the bar at this point (bar 12) to mark the end of the melody. What follows closely resembles the way the soloist picks up after a similar full cadence on the tonic that rounds off the first theme in the slow movement of Beethoven's Third Piano Concerto. The Adagio of op. 22 combines elements of concerto and opera. The development begins on the conventional dominant of the relative minor, G, and moves up a series of fourths, C, F, B♭, E♭, all interpreted as dominants in the minor mode. This conventional progression generally seems to have a logical urgency, and it is handled here with great poignance. The E♭, used as a dominant, brings us to the subdominant minor A♭, and the tonic minor and the return of the major mode and of the main theme are only a step away.

The minuet is completely regular: each of the three phrases is 8 bars long, and the second phrase obeys all the harmonic conventions: the relative minor preceded by its dominant, the dominant of the subdominant, and the supertonic minor, substituting, as so often, for the subdominant (it is, after all, the relative minor of the subdominant) – to sum up, V of vi to vi, V of IV to ii resolved by a half cadence on V to prepare the resumption of the main theme in the tonic. There is a six-bar coda, with echoes of the principal motif. The trio in G minor consists of two eight-bar phrases, both repeated. It impressed Schumann so much that he imitated it closely in one of the interior sections of his *Humoreske*.

The finale is the traditional Viennese rondo finale in the moderate Allegretto tempo. The first return of the main theme (bar 50) is prepared with remarkable ingenuity by repeating the opening seven-note motif over and over with a gradually accelerating rhythm: 4 to a beat, 6 to a beat, 8 to a beat, and finally 5 to a half beat; at the end, the arrival of the theme on an offbeat is a surprise in spite of the fact that we have been expecting it all along. The next return of the theme is given to the left hand in sixths, *subito piano* after a written-out trill with a crescendo, while the last appearance of the theme is richly decorated. Beethoven is perhaps the first composer to exploit the *subito piano* as a negative accent on a large scale. This finale employs it many times: bars 8, 17, 49 (a crescendo to *sforzando piano*), 128, etc.

Opus 22 demonstrates Beethoven's control of all the conventions of Viennese style. The works that follow are more openly radical. This sonata is his farewell to the eighteenth century.

Youthful Popularity
1800–1802

SONATA IN A FLAT MAJOR, OPUS 26
COMPOSED 1800

This was the sonata of Beethoven that Chopin preferred. It is the first of the thirty-two to have no example of what would later be considered a standard sonata form. The third movement, a funeral march "On the Death of a Hero", might imply a programme, but none, as far as I know, has reasonably been suggested. The four movements, all in A flat, are a set of characteristic pieces, as are the two sonatas that immediately succeed this one; on those, however, he attempted to impose a greater sense of unity. Opus 26 marks a significant progress in Beethoven's efforts to give an unmistakable individuality to each new work, as if he were not simply writing a new sonata but redefining the genre each time.

The exquisite lyricism of the opening *Andante con variazioni* may account for Chopin's preference even more than his natural interest in the funeral march. Offsetting the lyrical character, however, the *Andante* makes the most extensive use of the effect of a *subito piano* – that is, a crescendo followed by a sudden and unexpected drop to *piano*. From here on, this became a hallmark of Beethoven's style, and remained so through his last compositions. We find a *subito piano* in bars 8, 15, 23, 25, 27 and 33 in the theme alone, as well as in a few places in the variations.

The variations change character with striking contrasts. This has inspired performances with frequent changes of tempo. In particular, the variation in minor, no. III, is often played at a slower tempo, and no. IV played even faster than the theme. This is a misguided tradition, and there is no reason to think that any change of tempo is required in this movement. The third variation is exceptionally passionate, even with a certain violence, as we can see from the *sforzandi* that punctuate more than half of its continuously syncopated unwinding: a slower tempo only makes it sound unpleasantly insistent, and makes the passion sentimental. In the fourth variation the left-hand pianissimo staccato texture gains in transparency if we hold to the slow tempo, and the contrast with the articulated legato in the right hand becomes more telling. The second note of the omnipresent two-note motif in the right hand in this variation can be sustained for its full written value only by a use of the pedal which would be distinctly out of style in Beethoven: the note should not be very clipped, but it must be gracefully shortened and released before going on to the next note. Each appearance of this two-note motif is in another register, so the traditional eighteenth-century articulation is an advantage, technically as well as musically.

In variations II and V, Beethoven creates figures which place the notes of the original theme most of the time on the weakest beats: in II (starting with the third bar of the variation), on the second, fourth and sixth sixteenths of a 3/8 bar, and at the opening of V on the third, sixth and ninth of nine triplet sixteenths, with the second, fifth and eighth acting as *appoggiature*. For intelligibility these notes must all be delicately emphasized and appear with a constant effect of *rubato* imposed by their offbeat place in the pattern of figuration. When the direction of *piano dolce* is carried out, this effect is deeply poetic. It needs to be executed with a certain freedom. In this final variation, Beethoven introduces a written-out trill over the melody (in bars 179–86 and 197–204): he returned to this device in the last variation of the Sonata in E major op. 109. There is a fifteen-bar coda in which a new melody floats over a pulsating accompaniment and a bass that imitates pizzicato. In order to work, this requires a very sparing use of the pedal, a restraint all the more to be desired as there is a pedal effect in the last four bars, which needs a sonorous crescendo and a *subito pianissimo* on the last chord (on modern instruments, a discreet half change of pedal is necessary at the arrival of this chord, or the sonority will be muddy and thoroughly ineffective).

The accentuation of the Scherzo is very sophisticated.* In the opening phrases, the basic accent is on the first bar, but with a strong subsidiary accent on the second bar and an unaccented release of the fourth bar.† From bar 17, the accents are on bars 1 and 4 of the four-bar phrases, shifting to bars 1 and 3 at bar 29. An accent on bar 1 is relatively constant. Since, however, the scherzo proper ends on an odd-numbered accented bar, and the trio starts at once on an even-numbered bar, the accents continue on odd-numbered bars that are now always, in fact, the 2nd and 4th bars of a four-bar phrase, the 2nd bar acting in the trio as the downbeat of the phrase as a whole. Since Beethoven has shifted the beginning of the phrases from an odd to an even number, the first bars of each four-bar group in the trio function like an upbeat to the strong bar that follows. In short, Beethoven keeps the accents relatively constant, but varies the weight within the phrases, and changes from phrases that begin on the downbeat to phrases that start with an upbeat. The climax on the highest note of the trio is placed squarely

---

* For the phrasing in the autograph manuscript, see pp. 16–17.
† This is dealt with interestingly at length, but somewhat differently, by D. F. Tovey in *A Companion . . .*, pp. 96ff.

on the second (or strong) bar of its four-bar phrase (bar 85), but the squareness disappears soon after with the *sforzando* on an even-numbered (or weak) bar, 88: this is, in fact, bar 1 of the four-bar group. Beethoven's concern for a long line is nowhere more conspicuous than here: the opening of the trio is marked *sempre ligato*, and the second part of the trio is unified by a very long slur of 16 bars. Some modern editions extend the slur of the first part of the trio to the last note of the 8-bar phrase (bar 75), but the original edition clearly does this only in the bass, and indicates the last two notes of the melody as detached. This may be a revision of the composer.

The form of the outer parts of this scherzo is the usual three-strain pattern, enlarged astonishingly at the end of the second strain by stopping on a single harmony, the ultraconventional V7 of vi (accompanied by its sister harmony V9 of vi), and repeating over and over a single two-note motif $D\flat/C$ through sixteen bars, drastically suspending all movement.

The funeral march introduces the sound of tympani and brass in the trio: the muffled drum roll is with pedal, the brass interjections are to be played dryly. There is no tempo mark, and the idea that a funeral march is always very slow is a modern prejudice. The harmonic scheme of the march proper is very simple, original and effective: it rises by a minor third from A flat minor to the relative major, C flat; then, changing the mode to B minor, rises a minor third to the new relative major, D: placing a diminished seventh on the $D\natural$ leads naturally to the $E\flat$ dominant and back to A flat minor. The movement is laconic, sober and dramatic.

The final Allegro, in rondo form, opens with a sixteenth-note figuration in the right hand of two and a half bars to be played legato, and then the figuration continues non legato for three and a half bars while the legato line switches to the eighth-note descent in the left-hand tenor line. This contrast of detached and legato touch controls the entire movement. The return of the main theme is twice accomplished by a sudden piano without warning as the figuration continues and in the middle of a long slur. The movement ends pianissimo with a dose of subdominant harmony and an arpeggio figure that descends to the lowest region of the bass; Tovey correctly remarks that a ritardando or a lengthening of the final note would ruin everything.

The four movements of this sonata are all in relatively modest and unpretentious forms, and the work is pure chamber music rather than a grand public work. It is, nevertheless, neither modest nor unpretentious – indeed, it makes the more nervous styles of the *Pathétique* or op. 10 no. 3 seem small-scale. It achieves grandeur without recourse to any imitation of orchestral sound or concerto virtuosity. With this work, Beethoven needed only breadth of movement to achieve a large-scale rhythm in the relatively small forms.

TWO SONATAS, OPUS 27
COMPOSED BY 1801

Both these sonatas were entitled "quasi una Fantasia". They were printed separately, although by the same publisher. They went further than any previous work in a stylistic unification of all the movements of a sonata.

The Sonata quasi una Fantasia in E flat major op. 27 no. 1 runs all the movements together. Not only does each one start *attacca subito* from the preceding, but, for the first time in Beethoven's work, the movements are paradoxically well-formed independent movements in completely rounded structures that are nevertheless unintelligible played on their own. They interpenetrate each other. Works like Mozart's Fantasia in C minor K. 475, which serves as an introduction to the Sonata in C minor K. 457, could have provided a model for op. 27 no. 1, but not all of the sections in Mozart's work aspire to the status of complete forms on their own, while those of Beethoven give that illusion throughout.

Opus 27 no. 1 begins with a simple *A B A Andante*. *A* is in two parts of eight bars each, both played twice; on the return of *A* the repeats are written out and both are decorated (although the first phrase of *A* reappears initially with no decoration).* All phrases start pianissimo: only the second phrase has a crescendo, but it, too, ends softly. The *B* section repeats every one of these characteristics; it differs from *A* only in that it has a long-breathed cantabile melody in place of two fragmentary motifs returning in every bar.

The contrast with the *Allegro* in C major that follows is so great – in style, tempo, key and dynamics – that it is clearly an independent movement and not a trio section. (Nevertheless, the *A* section of the first movement surprisingly returns after the *Allegro*.) The 6/8 *Allegro* is in simple binary form of two 8-bar sections: the first section has one bar of brilliant arpeggios, forte and non legato, followed by a staccato motif *subito piano* one bar long, going from I to V, with the two-bar pattern repeated from V to I; then there are four bars of scale figuration (two bars of legato with a crescendo and two *subito piano* non legato). The structure is defined as much by the touch as by harmony or motif. The first half of the binary form ends on the dominant, G major: the first four bars of the second part act as a motivic development on a dominant pedal, while the last four bars recapitulate the end of the first part with a IV–V–I cadence. The form could not be more conventional, but the contrast of texture is exceedingly original and complex.

---

* This may be a stylistic principle of Viennese tradition. In Mozart's Rondo in A minor, for example, the decoration of the main theme becomes heavier and more elaborate as the work proceeds, but when the theme comes back only after the long interval of an intermediate episode, its opening is played unaltered for a few bars, the decoration only appearing at the end of the first phrase.

The return of the *A* of the *Andante* is not decorated, but the repeats are written out with the right- and left-hand parts interchanged. Double counterpoint at
the octave substitutes for decoration. There is a simple 8-bar coda. The opening
motif of the *Andante* had begun with two simple chords, the first played twice as
two quarter notes followed by the second as a half note: the coda eliminates the
half note and repeats the two quarter notes four times with an echo in the left
hand for three bars. Then the two playings of the chord are reduced to one, alternating I and V7 in each bar with a quarter rest in between, and finally the chord
appears only once in the bar on the tonic for two bars. The economy of means is
exceptional. I have described it in onerous detail to show that the reduction of
movement in the coda amounts to a written-out ritardando, so any further slowing down from the pianist would be redundant. The last bar has the chord of E
flat *pianissimo* as high on Beethoven's keyboard as was possible at that time, followed a beat later by his lowest E flat; this final bar is to be played with pedal –
senza sordino (for this to make its effect, one must be very sparing of the pedal
before):

The *Allegro molto vivace* in C minor that follows the *pianissimo* E flat major
and begins softly causes less of a shock than the previous irruption *forte* of the
Allegro in C major. The movement is swift, shadowy and mysterious. The outer
parts of this scherzo are in three-phrase binary form (16 bars repeated, and 8 and
16 bars repeated): the first phrase goes to the dominant minor, and the third
phrase takes it up again, resolving to the tonic. The second phrase goes simply V
of iv to iv, V of i to i. There is nothing remarkable about this, but the dynamics
and texture of the first phrase are typical of Beethoven: unremitting 3/4 quarter-
note rhythm with an articulation on each first beat, twelve bars of uninflected
piano, and then the shock of four bars of unprepared *forte* detached notes.

The binary trio is even more Beethovenian: the chords in the bass relentlessly
repeated over 14 bars going from A flat major to E flat major with a crescendo to
fortissimo, a fierce trill and a rapid descent back to *piano*. The second part of 18
bars (at the repeat it is reduced to 17) withholds the crescendo for 12 bars, but it
repeats the same chord (V7 of A flat major) in the bass for 16 bars, only descending to the lower register to get out of the way when the right hand cuts into
its territory. The first strain of the scherzo proper returns unaltered, but (as in

op. 10 no. 2) its repeat is written out as a *rubato*, the two hands out of phase with the right hand half a beat late until the end of the movement. The left hand is now staccato throughout except for one brief moment in the transition between the first and second strains: the right hand is always legato. The notation of the right hand at the beginning of the written-out repeat raises a question:

Beethoven ties the legato over the bar at first but then ceases to do so, and does not even repeat it when the same bars return at the opening of the third strain (bar 113). It is an effect difficult to realize throughout. He does take up the legato across the bar at the end in the last five bars of the movement, when it is crucial for the legato to be emphatic and continuous. Did he intend this effect only at these two places, or did he write it out once and continue with a notation less onerous to copy out and assuming that the intelligent performer would continue to take the hint? I do not know any way to decide this point. The phrasing at the opening of the movement implies a slight cessation of legato at the end of each bar, but too short a final note in each bar makes the delayed right-hand legato of the return of the material less effective. In addition, it is possible that the indication *sempre legato* over the right hand at this point may be intended to override the rests and to treat them only as a less precise way of notating the right hand. In any case, the contrast of legato and staccato throughout this page cries out to be executed so that it is immediately and effectively perceptible.

The *Adagio con espressione* follows without pause in A flat major. It stands midway between a separate movement and an introduction to the finale (and is, indeed, finally integrated more completely with the finale). The sonority is exceptionally rich, even thick, starting in the low register: the melody is often doubled in octaves. The dynamics swell continuously into *forte* only to drop back at once: a crescendo is found in bars 2, 4, 6, 10, 11, 12 and 14. The 8-bar melody is first rounded off with a half cadence, and followed by a new 8-bar theme at the dominant. The return of the opening melody now has a full cadence on the tonic, and then a swift scale in 128ths and 64ths moves to a written-out trill in 64ths and then another trill, this one unmeasured and presumably to be played even faster than the preceding. A brief cadenza leads directly to the *Allegro vivace*.*

---

* For a discussion of the phrasing and accent of the main theme of the *Allegro*, see pp. 40–1.

With this sonata Beethoven began an experiment, to which he continued to
return and develop through the years, of displacing some of the weight of the
work from the opening movement to the finale; the *Allegro vivace* is the most
elaborate movement of op. 27 no. 1. It is a sonata rondo with a fugal development, and with an elaborate return to the first theme (bars 139 to 168) that
closely resembles the returns in the later Haydn symphonies. Before the movement can end, however, the slow movement reappears, now in the tonic E flat
major, abridged down to the return of the first theme with its written-out trill,
completed this time by an even more expressive but less brilliant cadenza. A
Presto coda gives the main theme its final transformation.

The "Moonlight" Sonata is not only the most famous of the Beethoven sonatas,
but is a candidate for the most famous piece of serious art music ever written. Its
fame during Beethoven's lifetime ended by irritating the composer himself, who
felt that it unjustly overshadowed later works. Since the construction of pianos
changed radically during Beethoven's lifetime, the first movement soon ceased to
be heard with the particular sound that the composer can have imagined. This
did not affect its popularity: its sonority remained curiously fascinating even as
instruments changed and as performers disregarded Beethoven's instructions on
how to perform it.

"The Adagio", wrote Berlioz, "is one of those poems that human language
does not know how to qualify."[3] In the nineteenth century, several editions misprinted the time signature of this movement as C, and it is often taken at too
slow a pace. It is correctly in *alla breve*. Beethoven's direction, in Italian, at the
head of the score is "This piece must be played throughout with the greatest delicacy and with pedal [senza sordino, i.e. without the dampers]". The direction is
reinforced at the beginning between the staves as *Semper* [*sic*] *pianissimo e Senza
Sordino.* The accompaniment in triplets sounds alone over the bass for five bars,
and continues insistently without pausing for an instant until the penultimate
bar. At several points, indeed, it takes over the function of a melody. Each phrase
of the melody proper, characterized by Berlioz as a lamentation, is generally held
within the extremely confined space of a few notes.

The original nature of the piece is wonderfully defined by Berlioz:

> The left hand softly displays large chords of a solemn, sad character, and *the
> length of these allows the vibrations of the piano to extend gradually over each one
> of them* [my italics].

This is one of the first works to take account of the fact that the sympathetic vibration of the strings of the piano when the pedal is held down, the dampers raised,
is not instantaneous but grows with time, demanding a few fractions of a second
to become more audible and make its full effect. The extraordinary atmosphere
of the movement is based on this slight but perceptible delay in the vibration of

the open strings. Holding the pedal down on one of Beethoven's pianos took away the sharp definition of the beginning of each new harmony: even on his instruments there is a very brief moment of blurring while the previous harmony is still softly sounding, and the new harmony does not fully take over immediately but with a slight hesitation as the open strings respond to the new bass.

On today's instruments we cannot hold the pedal down unceasingly as Beethoven directs. However, if the execution is sufficiently delicate, the slight blurring of the older instruments can be reproduced by changing pedal a fraction of a second late, or by using half changes. Since every piano is different, a different pedalling has to be worked out for each instrument that one plays. With a little sensibility this is not as difficult as one might think. In bars 32 to 37, if the pianissimo is retained and the temptation of a crescendo is resisted through all the changes of harmony, I have found that the pedal need not be changed at all here. When the accompaniment is played with the delicacy that Beethoven asked for, the pedal need not be changed between the C sharp major and the F sharp minor harmonies of bars 53 and 54, for example, although some adjustment will be required on 55. The crescendo in bar 47, although starting at *pianissimo*, should be dramatic enough to allow the *piano* at 48 to be a *piano subito*.

The problem of the dotted rhythm of the soprano melody against the triplets in the alto is, of course, not to be resolved by identifying the soprano with the triplets: the problem lies in making the sixteenth note different from the triplet eighths, and yet not so short as to be trivial. The real difficulty is keeping the unchanging alto rhythm continuous without a hesitation at each point that the soprano becomes active. The tempo need not be inflexible – it can be accelerated or slowed for expressive effect, but the triplet motion should never be interrupted even fractionally to make way for sentimental effects in the melody. The triplets should be, as Berlioz said, relentless ("obstiné"). Their steadiness should be hypnotic. The difficulty is in making them unalterable but unobtrusive.

The harmonic plan of the first movement gives the impression of a free improvisation, but it is guided both by convention and by Beethoven's previous treatment of the minor mode. The first phrase of the soprano melody ends with a full cadence on the conventional relative major, E. As we have seen from op. 2 no. 1 and op. 13, Beethoven tried to replace the standard relative major by its own minor. That is what he continues to do in the opening movement of op. 27 no. 2. The E major is altered at once to E minor, and the change of mode is reinforced by going through a C major harmony to a cadence on B minor (bar 15). The B minor is immediately transformed into the major, but it would be a mistake to take the B major here as a point of rest, as it clearly functions ambiguously for four bars to suggest the dominant of E. This is resolved, however, not by a cadence on E but by a surprising move to the subdominant, F sharp minor, which is needed as a transition to set up a dominant pedal. Going from a tonic minor to its relative major coloured by its minor mode is a process we have already seen before, and the minor colouring is only reinforced here by the

momentary importance given to B minor, which turns back without delay
towards E minor.

The most unconventional aspect of the form is that bars 10 to 27 work at one
and the same time like a "second group" of a sonata by a concentration on the
relative major, and like a development as well, as the harmony drops a fourth
from E minor to B minor and another fourth to F# minor. Once this has been
attained, Beethoven loses no time in setting up at great length the return to the
tonic. The dominant pedal, which is reached at bar 27, is remarkably long for
this structure: it lasts for twelve bars and continues to influence the two bars that
follow. These fourteen bars take up, in fact, about 20 per cent of the whole 69
bars, and they demonstrate the unwavering attention that Beethoven continued
to give to the process of dominant preparation.

The recapitulation begins at bar 42: the first phrase goes as before to E, but the
second phrase now leads back to a full cadence on C sharp minor. The minor
mode now shifts to the major: as we saw before with the change from B minor
to B major, the shift of mode, reinforced by the Neapolitan cast, suggests that the
tonic major functions fleetingly as a dominant to the subdominant. The relationship is acknowledged with the affirmation of the subdominant in bar 55. The
most remarkable invention of Beethoven here is that the moment of greatest
intensity is not the chromaticism of bars 51 to 54, but the purely diatonic pressure on the second beat of bar 55:

The left-hand slur in bar 55 gives us the accent in mid-bar and imposes a diminuendo from 55 to 56: the F sharp minor chord has the paradoxical effect of
acting both like a downbeat that resolves the C sharp major chord and like a dissonance itself that needs resolution into the dominant seventh of E major, which
initiates the drive to the full cadence on the tonic C sharp minor that ends the

form on bar 60, rounded out by a nine-bar coda of threefold V–I cadences. Most of the compositional process of this movement is directly derived from eighteenth-century convention, enlarged by Beethoven's inspired colouring of the relative major through its minor mode: what is done with these conventions is radically original.

The *Allegretto* is to be played *attacca* from the *Adagio*. One should resist Czerny's contention that the movement needs a lively execution. Most musicians agree that his metronome marking of 76 to the dotted half note is too fast, and he himself admitted that humorous mirth is to be avoided.[4] Its grace displays a melancholy poetry. The three-phrase form is fairly regular (and absolutely regular in the trio): the first two phrases are each 8 bars long (the repeat of the first part is written out with decoration); the third phrase is expanded by arresting the movement after its sixth bar and dwelling repeatedly on the basic motif through four extra bars.

The finale is the longest movement, the most conventional, but also the most unbridled in its representation of emotion. Even today, two hundred years later, its ferocity is astonishing. It was as much too grand for contemporary instruments as the first movement is too delicate for modern ones. It must have been with music like this finale that Beethoven smashed the hammers and strings of his instruments, as he was reputed to do. The contrast between the opening and closing movements of this sonata exceeds anything else conceived for the keyboard until then.

A Mozartean model governs the form of the finale with a profusion of themes given to the secondary key area (G sharp minor) of the exposition. The more conventional relative major is completely rejected in favour of the dominant minor. Concentration on the subdominant is reserved for the opening of the development, and two of the principal themes appear there before the arrival of a long dominant pedal.* In the recapitulation, the closing theme leads back to the first theme and then to two fiercely arpeggiated diminished seventh chords, both with dramatic fermatas (the first edition correctly directs the first chord to be played without pedal, but mistakenly omits the direction for pedal that is clearly to be seen in the autograph for the second). A fermata in the middle of the coda recurs in opp. 31 no. 1, 53, 57, 78 (2nd movement) and 106. It is an attribute of the concerto that Beethoven transfers to the solo sonata.

The coda starts up again by going back to the eleventh bar of the development where the most expressive theme of the second group had been given to the left hand: that passage is now transposed from the subdominant to the tonic, and then the theme is given to the right hand in a rising sequence that leads to an elaborate cadenza, opening with arpeggios in strict time and ending with a trill and an unmeasured expressive scale arabesque that descends to the lowest region of the contemporary instrument. The regular closing theme returns and rounds off the form with further arpeggios fortissimo.[4]

* For a discussion of the phrasing and touch in this finale, see pp. 107–8.

SONATA IN D MAJOR, OPUS 28
COMPOSED IN 1801

This sonata was called the "Pastorale" by the original publisher, and with good reason. The first movement and, above all, the finale display characteristic elements of the pastoral tradition. The drone bass of the opening of the first movement is one of these elements. The repeated D does not cease for 24 bars, and it continues to be present for another 15 bars.* The dominant, A major, is established in the most traditional fashion by going to the dominant of the domi-nant of the dominant (the V7 on B of bar 46); this is even reinforced by the A# in bar 53, which together with the E and C# provide a hint of an F sharp major triad – that is, V of V of V of V. As the movement progresses, this is quietly con-firmed by the dominant seventh on C# in bars 63 and 65 and the flat dominant ninth chord on F# in bar 67. The final goal of all this movement towards domi-nant harmony is reached in bar 7 with the triad in root position of C sharp major – or V of V of V of V of V. For six bars this chord remains supreme and fixed, unchallenged except by adding the flat fifth D♮ to its own dominant, which immediately suggests the reaffirmation of the original dominant, A major. (As long as all these dominants remain subsidiary, as they do here by the continuous allusions to A major throughout, this was the proper way to give power to a modulation in the late eighteenth century, although the process was not often carried as far as Beethoven does it here. In the Sonata in B flat major K. 333, for example, Mozart establishes F major by brief and passing allusions to the chord of G major, which is the dominant of the dominant of the dominant of B flat major.) Most effective in this exposition is the tranquil atmosphere, an unpre-tentious air of quiet mastery, with which the harmonic movement is accom-plished.†

The main theme opens with subdominant colour (V of IV and IV are the first chords), and the development begins by exploiting that with an immediate move to G major. In this section, Beethoven mounts the circle of fifths – G minor, D minor, A minor, E minor, to the relative minor, B – and reaches the dominant of B minor, F sharp, choosing in this way the old-fashioned and even hackneyed device of going from the dominant of the relative minor back to the tonic. But he does this on a scale rarely seen, remaining on an F sharp pedal for 38 bars, for the last 30 of which the only harmony is an F sharp major chord. The end of this passage dies away to pianissimo, the quiet transition through B major and B

---

* For the phrasing of the opening theme in the exposition and the development with examples, see pp. 30–2.
† The break of the slur between bars 120 and 121 is an error found in some editions. In the original edition 120 is at the end of a system, and the engraver did not properly carry over the slur as it later appears in the parallel place in the recapitulation.

minor is soft with a subsidiary theme appearing as if from a long distance like a reminiscence; this ends in a brief Adagio, and the return of the main theme is not marked piano, as at the beginning, but pianissimo.*

The Andante is in the tonic minor and in ternary form, with the outer and inner sections in simple binary. It is in march tempo, with a scherzando trio. The outer sections contrast a cantabile melody with a staccato left hand. The sudden pianos after a crescendo (bars 4, 8, 9) are not so much lyrical nuances, as they were in the first movement of op. 26, but slight touches of the grotesque. This character is confirmed by bars 18 and 19:

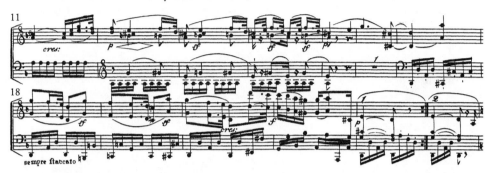

The *sforzandi* at the ends of a slur are intended as an angular surprise. It would be a mistake to add a crescendo before the *sforzando,* and an even worse mistake to begin a new phrase with the *sforzandi* as if the slur stopped on the third eighth note and started again on the fourth – as it does, however, in the next bar, 20. After each *sforzando*, there must be a very slight break for the idiosyncratic character to be effective. This touch of the grotesque makes the rewriting of the theme on the return with flowing arabesques so much more interesting (the staccato bass here is subsequently reformulated as *sempre legato*), and it sets in relief the new character of the coda, which commences (bar 83) with a more serious tone, still retaining the *subito piano* after a crescendo, and even repeating it twice dramatically with a fermata (bars 86 and 88). The scherzando middle section is quoted briefly, becoming sinister and dropping fiercely into the bass, and the movement dies away *pianissimo*.

The Scherzo is an example of Beethoven's humour of the kind that both exasperated and fascinated his contemporaries. The opening theme consists of nothing but four F sharps in descending octaves, followed by a light and simple I/ ii/ V7/ I cadence with a quirky motif repeated four times. There is no other material, except that the four single F sharps turn into four thirds, then into four sixths, and then (after the motif has appeared briefly with a more sensitive cast) four massive chords fortissimo.

---

*For a discussion of the end of the development, see my *The Classical Style*, new ed., New York, 1997, pp. 477–9.

The trio is decidedly a humorous tour de force. A simple four-bar phrase is played ending in B minor: it is then replayed, with the minimal change of only the last two notes so that it ends in D major. This is repeated. Then the same phrases are played again with new harmonies in the left hand, but in reverse order, first ending in D major, then in B minor (a crescendo from bar 1 to 3 and a decrescendo from 4 to 5 provide some relief). This is also repeated, rewritten, in fact, with no change whatever in the melody but with new harmonies in the bass and new dynamics, swelling to a *sforzando* in bar 5 and falling back to piano at the end. One must abstain from adding dynamics to the first part if the additions to the second part are to make their effect. As Beethoven's contemporary, the painter John Constable, said, making something out of nothing is the true work of the artist.

The Rondo, *Allegro ma non troppo*, starts out with a drone bagpipe accompaniment which continues for sixteen bars. The right hand breaks its silence with a simple two-bar motif in bars 3 to 4, and 7 to 8. It then commences a set of yodels:

This is very rustic. After a harp-like passage of arpeggios *molto legato*, a new motif descends imitatively from soprano to bass, and is followed by a second pastoral drone, which acts as a concluding theme. Following the tradition of the Mozart rondo, Beethoven adds a new theme in the subdominant after the return of the opening theme. Some elaborate and expressive three-part imitative counterpoint comes next, based, I believe, on the development of the Mozart rondo in the great Sonata in F major for four hands, one piano. An inversion of the concluding drone theme from the exposition ends the development with a pedal point on the dominant.

The recapitulation is straightforward, uneventful, but the coda is exceedingly original. The minimal use of the subdominant until now in this movement receives its compensation. The initial left-hand drone starts pianissimo in the subdominant G major, uninterrupted this time by any melodic motif, and continues on its own, punctuated only by offbeat harmonies in the right hand. After 8 bars with a crescendo at the end, a *subito piano* initiates a pedal point on the dominant which lasts for ten bars with a crescendo; a dominant seventh harmony continues for another six bars descending from *ff* to *pp*. After a pause, a *Più Allegro quasi presto* introduces some brilliant figuration in the right hand over the initial bagpipe drone bass played in octaves, a challenge to the amateur pianist. The movement closes with eighteen bars of virtuosity.

The Years of Mastery

THREE SONATAS, OPUS 31
COMPOSED BY 1802

Publishing important works of music in groups of three or six was a well-established tradition in the eighteenth century. Haydn's symphonies were commissioned by the half-dozen, as were some of his quartets: most of his later piano trios and the last piano sonatas came as triads. Except for the string quartets op. 18, Beethoven preferred three to six, and the piano sonatas that were grouped together generally appeared in triads: opp. 2, 10 and 31, as well as the quartets op. 59 and the piano trios op. 1. (The last three piano sonatas were clearly conceived as a set, but Beethoven must have considered it an advantage commercially to have them published separately.)

The publication of a set rather than a single work was a way of defining, and therefore publicizing, the individual style and the range of the composer. The structure of the set itself could be given greater intelligibility with three works instead of six: with, for example, Mozart's last three symphonies (intended, to my mind, as a unit, although not published during the composer's lifetime), each work was given a contrasting character that decisively separated it from the others. The last three symphonies of Mozart are respectively dramatic, lyric and majestic; the three sonatas op. 2 of Beethoven are dramatic, sociable and brilliant. In their contrasting character, the three sonatas op. 31 are even more strikingly set off from each other, particularly by their opening movements by which they are largely identified: comic, tragic and lyric.

The comedy of the Sonata in G major op. 31 starts with the first bar, even before the first bar, in fact, as the right hand enters a split second too soon before the bar line. The anomaly is making the right hand precede the left. Playing with the two hands out of phase but with the left hand slightly before the right is an established technique of keyboard style from at least the eighteenth century: at that time it was called *rubato* and classified as an ornament. We must remember that ornamentation, improvised or planned, was basic to the emotional expression of eighteenth-century music, and *rubato* has a considerable expressive charge. Abused or too mechanically overindulged by a few pianists at the beginning of the twentieth century, it was employed rather as a special effect in the eighteenth. The Italians, Mozart wrote to his father, were surprised when they heard him play *rubato*, so I assume that it may have been chiefly a feature of Central European performance practice. Playing the melody note in the right hand after the bass has already entered does more than imitate the breath that a singer might take before producing a note when momentarily overwhelmed with sentiment: it also causes the right-hand note to vibrate with the harmonic resonance already posed in the bass and makes its significance more immediately perceptible. The bass note establishes the beat as well as the basic harmony, and the momentarily delayed melody takes on a free and almost improvised character, entering comfortably into the harmonic and rhythmic frame which was set slightly in advance.

Playing the right hand before the left has the inverse effect. Of course, if the melody enters leisurely before the bass, it will sound like an upbeat, but the first note of op. 31 no. 1 comes in less than 1/16 of a second before the bass, and it is tied to the next beat, so it seems as if the two hands should have coincided with each other. The trick is then repeated ten times in the first nine bars, followed by two bars where the two hands finally get together to show what would have been correct and round off the phrase with a half cadence on the dominant:

If playing the left hand first has a comfortable feeling, reversing this and starting with the right closely followed by the left is disquieting, and the tenfold repetition does not, in fact, help by making it more familiar, but only increases the discomfort. That is because it makes us unsure where the bar line is – or, to put it less pedantically, where the weight of the accent is supposed to fall. This is an aspect of music to which we respond physically, and our reactions are repeatedly frustrated by Beethoven's humour. Traditionally the accent or the beat is defined by the bass, and for natural acoustic reasons the heaviness of the bass sonority allows a more convincing definition than the higher region, but throughout the first phrase of this sonata until bars 10 and 11 make the necessary correction, the right hand constantly encroaches on the authority of the bass: its too early appearance disturbs and arouses suspicion, but it does not completely convince. In short, the strange rhythm puzzles us, and it is even reasserted with a determined *forte* before bars 10 and 11 gently and softly (staccato and *piano*) assure us it was a joke by having the two hands play together at last. (Fooling the listeners about the place of the bar line was a trick of Haydn's, but I do not think he ever employed Beethoven's device.)

The opening phrase begins a second time in the key of F. The flat leading-tone is harmonically a remote area; immediately restating the opening phrase a whole tone down is a radical procedure that Beethoven will take up again in the "Waldstein" Sonata.* The harmony finally comes round again to the elucidating cadence with the hands together, now on the tonic. This conclusion is celebrated by a 16-bar monophonic burst of brilliant passage-work doubled at the octave, which reappears later almost like a *ritornello*, and which combines the functions of concerto virtuosity and an orchestral *tutti*. A counterstatement of the main theme begins, but quickly moves to a half cadence on the F sharp major dominant of B minor (V of iii), repeated four times, followed by a two-bar trill on F#. This is all that is needed to set up the mediant B major as a new area. Substituting the mediant for the traditional dominant at this point is an important innovation, but it is given a respectable preparation through its own dominant.

A theme of popular dance character in this key lasts in the major for only 8 bars, and it is then transferred to the minor mode and the left hand. This somewhat takes the edge off the daring of using the mediant as a secondary tonality, as B minor is harmonically closer than B major to the original G major. A 12-bar concluding theme alternates between B minor and major, beginning and ending in the minor and repeating a dominant/tonic cadence six times, making a firm ending to the exposition. That brings us by one laconic, unharmonized beat of modulation (second beat, bar 111) at once back to the beginning, with the repeat of the exposition, and also to the development section, which, for seven bars, exactly repeats the opening of the exposition before moving to the subdominant minor. Was this intended to have the comic effect of making the listeners believe that the exposition was about to be performed a third time? Beginning the development with the opening theme at the tonic was not uncommonly employed long before this work in the 1760s with sonata forms of much smaller dimensions, but almost completely disappeared from the practice of composition since that time. In op. 31 no. 1, the old form must certainly have seemed curious, but it was a device to which Beethoven returned in the more serious Sonata in E flat major, which is the third in this set.

Using the opening theme, with the right hand always a quarter of a beat in advance of the left, the development quickly rises through a series of fourths, G, C, F, B♭, each point being the dominant of the following. For the next 36 bars, the monophonic virtuosity of bars 26 to 40 provides the material. The tension is

---

* The device became almost an obsession in the later work of Prokofiev.

created by the unrelenting force, and a mounting sequence: B♭ major, C minor, D minor, each 8 bars long. The last group in D minor descends into the bass, and rests for 36 full bars on a D major chord, having reached the principal dominant of the movement. The extravagant length of the dominant preparation of the return is typical of Beethoven's style by this time.*

Having used the mediant, B major, in place of the dominant in the exposition, Beethoven was faced with the problem of a complex resolution in the recapitulation. He worked with the principle that the most effective agent of resolution in a sonata form is the subdominant.† But the resolution of a mediant is less straightforward, requires more work than a dominant, as it is a more dissonant element of structure. Accordingly, the main theme of the mediant section now reappears at length first in the submediant E major (which is the subdominant of the mediant), the submediant minor, and immediately afterwards in the tonic as well. (This is the solution that Beethoven was to reproduce in the "Waldstein" Sonata.) The concluding theme still contrasts the major and minor modes, but now, reversing the order in the exposition, begins and ends in the major, and this leads directly to the coda.

The coda opens for two bars exactly as the development – and since the development started by reproducing the opening of the exposition except for a more emphatic bass note, we find a rigid symmetry to the commencement of each principal section. It might also make the unwary listener think for a moment that the second half of the form, the development and the recapitulation, is about to be repeated. In place of this repeat, 14 bars of the exposition (bars 32–45) are replayed at once in the coda with no alteration, ending on the half cadence on the dominant: the coda consequently brings us back firmly to the first section of the exposition. The 30 bars remaining in the movement are devoted to an amusing play with the motif of the right hand's unnatural arrival before the left, combined with new motifs including an absurdly simple one of two tonic chords in a transparent texture filled with silences, and almost entirely *pianissimo*. Six bars from the end, however, there is an outburst of *fortissimo*, a bar of silence, the two tonic chords are echoed softly, and then there is a final bar of silence. The movement does not so much end as disappear. If a piano recital were not so desperately serious an affair, a good performance of this coda would make the listeners laugh: at best, we can hope that we have made them want to laugh even if the atmosphere of high culture is too intimidating. All this witty play with the motifs is an example of the grotesque humour that made contemporaries of Beethoven compare him to the serio-comic contemporary novelist, Jean-Paul.

The slow movement, *Adagio grazioso*, is in pre-Rossini, florid Italian opera

* For the use of the pedal in this dominant preparation, see p. 111.
† For this principle, see pp. 10–11.

style.* The key is C major, and the passage-work in bars 10 and 12 is inspired by the possibility of playing only on the white keys of the piano. The decoration gradually becomes heavier as the movement progresses, but it is already impressive from the outset. The touch demanded throughout is rarely a legato, except in the middle section, but either a *perlé* or a detached *cantabile* execution that ranges from *portamento* to staccato. The opening 8-bar melody is first rounded off at the tonic, and then repeated with a cadence on the dominant: the succeeding 10-bar contrasting episode that follows finishes with a cadenza that should not be executed too rapidly, and the 8 bars with the tonic cadence return with more elaborate ornaments. The middle section, particularly the long passage from bar 41 on, is less vocal and more orchestral in style. The written out *da capo* of the opening is varied by a faster-moving accompaniment derived from the middle section. The 22-bar coda has considerable weight, and quickly develops into an imitation of an operatic duet for two sopranos (bars 101–2).

The Rondo, *Allegretto*, has a typical rondo theme, with much interior repetition: the second phrase repeats the first phrase, changing only the last four beats; the third and fourth phrases are identical.[†] The entire theme is then repeated in the left hand, under an obbligato in triplets in the right. After a contrapuntal development, the main theme returns over a dominant pedal with broken octaves in the tenor. The final return of the main theme is fragmented, with silences every two bars and an alternation of *Adagio* and *Tempo I*, as if the movement were exhausting itself before picking up enough energy for the *Presto* coda, which develops the first four notes of the principal theme in whirlwind fashion. At the end, fragmented repetitions of the tonic chord going from *fortissimo* to *pianissimo* and interrupted by silences recall the last bars of the opening movement.

The opening of the Sonata in D minor op. 31 no. 2 is the most dramatic that Beethoven had yet conceived, with a contrast of tempos and motifs, and a radical opposition of mood:

The first music we hear suggests a slow introduction, but it turns out to be nothing of the kind. The opening motif, in *Largo* tempo, an arpeggiated A major chord (the bass is a C#, which gives the sonority a soft, unemphatic quality of a sixth chord) followed by a four-note theme tracing an A major chord, is a motto, and will govern the entire work. The harmony, when first perceived with the C# in the bass, could only be a dominant, and this is confirmed by the Allegro motif that follows, moving to D minor with an imitation violin figuration of a type fairly common in opera overtures. The agitated motif moves back to the domi-nant with a half cadence and a traditional ornamental turn, deeply expressive. The *Largo* and *Allegro* are related as question and answer. The double complex of motifs is now repeated, starting at the relative major, which was the usual goal of an exposition in the minor, but Beethoven will reject this in favour of the less fre-quent dominant minor. The next cadence is a full one on the tonic, and the opening motto is now played starting on the tonic note in the Allegro tempo, no longer a question but a decisive statement, completed by a new short motif, lamenting and supplicating. The harmony moves to the dominant minor, with the agitated string figuration in a new shape. (Beethoven is supposed to have claimed that this work came from Shakespeare's *the Tempest*; if so, he cannot have read anything beyond the title, but it gave this work its name.) The model for the first movement is derived from Haydn, and there is no clear separation in the exposition between first and second groups. In fact, Beethoven even inte-grates his closing theme seamlessly with what precedes.

The end of the exposition makes a transition back to the *Largo* tempo of the opening, with a long note that lasts two full bars. This suggests that the *Largo* is more or less twice as slow as the *Allegro*, and the proportion should be retained in place of the usual unmeasured or irrationally related exaggeratedly slow tempo for the *Largo*. At the beginning of the development, the Largo motto returns at the subdominant, and is played twice more modulating to an F# major chord. All three playings are marked pianissimo, and there is a fermata and a rest at the end of the first two, but only a fermata over the third with no rest: this implies that the last fermata should be longer than the others (it is over a whole note, not a dotted half), and that there should be no silence before the Allegro that breaks in fortissimo with a surprising change of mode, in F sharp minor. The version of the motto theme in the Allegro tempo with its supplicating answer rises over 20 bars in successive steps in the bass from F# to the tonic D (the use of a rising bass at moments when the tension must be heightened is indispensable to Beethoven starting with op. 2 no. 2).* The end of the development has 18 bars of a pedal on the dominant (A) of D minor, ending in notes that last a whole measure, returning us effectively to the slow tempo of the opening. A series of unison octaves in the bass suggests the dominant minor ninth chord that Beethoven

* See the remarks on the exposition, p. 125.

liked so much for the preparation of a return,* and the motto is heard again in its original slow form.

The Allegro is postponed this time for a dramatic recitative, certainly intended *pianissimo*, with the A major harmony held down throughout the entire passage by the pedal. The long pedal gives the recitative, marked *con espressione e semplice*, a hollow and even cavernous quality like a voice from the tomb. The original Allegro theme with its Adagio half cadence and expressive ornament is repeated, followed by the C major arpeggio that originally led to the relative major and back to the tonic – this time, however, the movement to F major is rejected and its dominant is sustained, *pianissimo* with an unchanged pedal, under a new recitative that changes the F major to F minor.† This recitative does not die away like the first one, but its last note is lengthened by a fermata on an A♭. The following harmony picks up this A♭ as a G#, harmonized by a chord of V of F sharp minor with E# in the bass.

Heavy muffled chords are repeated, punctuated by silence and succeeded by an arpeggio whose irregular rhythm suggests improvisation; they make a sequence that rises simply with a crescendo on E# F# G♮ and G#. The last two notes are harmonized with diminished sevenths, so that the following A is heard as a dominant. The recapitulation now omits any reinterpretation of bars 9 to 34 of the exposition, but repeats at the tonic what came after. A 10-bar coda in an unvarying *pianissimo* stays in the lowest region of the keyboard, with a 6-bar arpeggio figure that continually touches on an offbeat the lowest note on the contemporary piano. The pedal must be released four bars before the end although the tonic chord is sustained manually, and this clarifies the extraordinary thick sonority made softly by the bass arpeggio. The pedal is returned for the slow chords of the last three bars. No release of pedal is indicated at the end. Did the composer intend the final chord to last until the beginning of the next movement? That movement is closely related at once to the first, as it begins with a softly arpeggiated chord that recalls the beginning of the first movement.

The Adagio is in cavatina form (exposition and recapitulation with no repeats and no development) so frequent in Mozart's slow movements. The arpeggiated chord in the first bar does not simply set the frame: it is an integral part of the first phrase, and helps us to be aware that the strong accents should be placed on bars 1, 3, 5 and 7. This becomes idiosyncratically expressive, since bar 7 is a sudden piano after a *sforzando*. The main theme combines a short rising three-note motif (often decorated by an expressive turn) in the high or high middle register with two chords in the low register with a texture that recalls a chorale. The

---

* See pp. 111–12.

† If sustaining the pedal without change is too heavy in the modern piano, the left hand can hold down the lowest notes, and half or full changes of the pedal can be made during the recitative.

three-note motif has a characteristic rhythm with a double-dotted eighth note and a thirty-second note that runs through the movement:

After a statement of the first eight bars ending with a half cadence on the dominant, a counterstatement with echoes reworks the phrase and closes it on the tonic. A hymn-like theme, accompanied by a series of short, soft tympani rolls, dominates the next dozen bars and leads to the dominant, F major. A new theme, marked *dolce*, of a more popular nature, relates to the first theme by using the rhythm of a double-dotted eighth note with a thirty-second as its basic texture. To prepare the return to the opening theme, the melody with the drum-roll accompaniment outlines the dominant minor ninth chord that Beethoven found so useful for a reintegration of the tonic.

The return of the first theme is rewritten to include echoes of the three-note motif for the first eight-bar statement, and, for the second statement, the addition of an arpeggiated figure that descends from the highest note on Beethoven's piano, an F, to the lowest note, also an F. The transitional passage on a dominant minor ninth chord that went back to the tonic at bars 39–42 now reappears at bar 81 for a coda starting on the tonic, which brings the strong subdominant colouring traditional in the second half of a sonata form, and continues expressively for four bars before fragments of the opening theme appear with a play of different registers.

The various themes are tied subtly together. A new closing theme in bar 98 acts as a free inversion of the rising theme in bars 81–4. The scale figure that appeared as an upbeat to bar 6 is mirrored freely in bars 30, 34, 49, 72, 76, 89, 90 and 94. The last bar of the movement is largely monophonic but far from simple: it integrates a crescendo and a *subito piano* with a contrast of the highest and lowest registers of the contemporary keyboard.

The main theme of the *perpetuum mobile* which is the last movement (the steady rhythm broken only for a split second in bars 23 and 27 and their later analogues) has an *ostinato* A on an offbeat in the tenor which partly takes over the function of the bass:

This repeated A gives a syncopated impulse to the rhythm and plays an important role later in the movement; delicately emphasized it can have a hypnotic effect, but it should not be overdone. The allegretto tempo should be taken at a moderate pace so that the tenor *ostinato* of the A is audible without forcing. The belief that a *perpetuum mobile* is necessarily fast is responsible for misguided efforts to speed up this work.

Beethoven complained that in the first edition of these sonatas the dynamics were not well placed. A sure way of not realizing the composer's intentions, therefore, would be to follow the first edition faithfully. The autograph has unfortunately disappeared. A second edition with corrections appeared, but it is if anything less accurate than the first. Some editors move the *subito piano* on the first beat of bar 73 to later in the bar to conform with bar 301, but it seems obvious to me that 73 is Beethovenian and 301 is wrong.

The development section emphasizes the key of B flat minor extensively from bars 130 to 160, and then uses the B♭ in the bass as a large-scale structural *appoggiatura* to be resolved onto the dominant A. Returning in the recapitulation to the most unusual harmony of the development is a technique that Beethoven would repeat in the "Hammerklavier" Sonata, but he tries it out here first, and goes back briefly but explosively to B flat minor 28 bars after starting the return of the main theme: the B flat minor substitutes for a passage in the exposition that appeared in the tonic. The exposition of this movement is repeated, and after the recapitulation ends Beethoven appears to initiate a repetition of the second half but veers off after four bars and turns back to a final tonic appearance of the main theme. The preparation of each return of the theme is modelled on the technique learned from Haydn of repeating a short figure several times in an unchanging rhythm until the principal motif suddenly and often surprisingly appears to spring from it. The final appearance of the theme is the most jolting:

The unrelenting pedal on the dominant is played for sixteen bars, swelling and diminishing with a final drop to *pianissimo*. Then the theme reenters with an unexpected *fortissimo* (bar 350), and the inner pedal in the tenor on A is now joined by a new one in the soprano, insistently set in relief by eight *sforzandi* (added to the previous bass pedal, this adds up to 24 bars of accents on the dominant).

The two brief arrests of the perpetual motion in bars 23 and 27 were omitted from the recapitulation, but they are brought back now, with a third one added, the cessation of motion is lengthened, and the dynamic is now *fortissimo* in place of the simple *sforzandi* of the first time. This brings the piece to an end except to confirm the closure: a V/I cadence played four times, a four-bar crescendo on a tonic chord, and a descending tonic arpeggio *subito piano* to the lowest D on the contemporary keyboard. All three movements of this sonata end quietly, as do all of the movements of the first sonata of this opus. It is astonishing how often Beethoven, compared to his contemporaries and predecessors, preferred a delicately soft ending to an emphatic final chord. These soft endings, however, are not modest, but more pretentious than the standard closures. They prolong the atmosphere beyond the final chords.

The first bars of the Sonata in E flat major op. 31 no. 3 are emotionally the most unsettling that Beethoven had written. It begins as a repeated question, and continues with increasing urgency as the initial harmony, with a rich, compressed spacing in a low register, is further repeated, rising chromatically in a gradually slowing tempo that makes each chord more emphatic; a tonic chord is not reached until the sixth bar, at which point the music is briefly halted. The answer to the questioning pressure, when it comes in bars 7 and 8, is a shock after the unprecedented opening: it is simply a conventional cadence, sociable, courteous and deflating.

It is characteristic of Beethoven's art that he should juxtapose the most original and the most conventional musical ideas, and that he should exploit the conventional to create both a dramatic contrast and a splendid touch of irony. The cadence is there just because it is conventional: anything more interesting would spoil the conception. The unusual combination of intense lyricism and humour gives this sonata its individual stamp. Technically, the opening is a lesson in craftsmanship: how can one define a tonality while withholding the tonic chord?

SONATA

Although the tonic is not reached until the sixth bar, no simple resolution except E flat major is justified after the opening harmony (the relative minor, C, is a more remote possibility, and Beethoven works this solution out at the opening of the development). The progression, mysterious and unsettling, is also inevitable. The first chord mixes the allied harmonies of IV and ii (A flat major and F minor, subdominant and supertonic). In a IV–V–I cadence, which is essentially what we have here, ii can substitute for IV. Beethoven prolongs the cadence by interpolating the diminished seventh on A♮, which allows the bass to rise more expressively and more convincingly with the smooth chromatic move-ment of A♭–A♮–B♭. In the first chord, it is the E♭, the tonic note, which must be treated as a dissonance, and resolved to the D: Beethoven prolongs this note for six bars in both treble and bass, and the resolution to D takes place in the sev-enth bar – and this is the point where the conception moves not only from the chromatic to the diatonic, but from the intensely original to the politely conven-tional. Making the conventional a stroke of humour justifies its existence, gives it a new significance by integrating it into a scenario. The opening of the sonata is a dialogue, opposing passion and ironic mockery.

The repeated chords in bar 3 are further intensified in bars 33 to 42 by being transformed into the minor mode. At the end of the exposition, the opposition of the original and the conventional is resolved by the closing theme, an abridged version of the main theme:

This is a synthesis that combines the harmony of the supertonic (ii) (bar 84) with a conventional cadence, abridges the repeated descending motif of the first two bars into one graceful dip, slightly simplifies the conventional cadence, and com-presses the eight-bar opening phrase into four, erasing most of the contrast. The original shape, however, is clearly recalled, and there are traces of the initial sig-nificance.

The exposition follows a Mozartean model with an elaborate and decisive cadence on V of V (bars 44–5), followed by a lyrical new theme in the dominant B flat major and, as almost always in Mozart, some virtuoso passage-work to round off the various themes of the second group of the exposition before intro-ducing a concluding theme. At one point the passage-work speeds up to 12 notes per beat, impossible to execute in strict time, and necessitating a controlled *rubato* in that bar (54) so that it does not sound as if there was an entire extra beat. The rounding off is expansive: Beethoven prolongs a B flat major chord with not even the suggestion of another harmony for six bars (72–8).

As in op. 31 no. 1, the development returns to the first bars of the exposition, but it is presented unaltered only for two bars:

In bar 3 of the theme, the soprano is now doubled at the lower octave, making a deeper and more forceful sonority, and in bar 4, the A♭ in the bass is no longer moved up to A♮, because it will now descend to G and then to F# in order to impose the relative minor, C. The A♮ is shifted to the soprano, so that it can descend through A♭ to G, the dominant of C minor. This is the most conventional key for a development, and Beethoven not only gets it out of the way at once, but changes the mode without delay to C major. From C, the bass rises with an accelerated motion over a series of fourths, each successive step used as a dominant to the next: that is, C, F (bar 116), B♭ (124), E♭ (126), A♭ (128). The A♭ is harmonized as an F minor sixth chord, which was an element of the harmony of the opening bar of the main theme, and this chord is prolonged with reiterated arpeggios through seven full bars until it finally produces the opening theme. The principle is a simple one, grandly exploited for many decades by Haydn: repeat a single detail insistently over and over again, and listeners will be persuaded that what follows was inevitable as long as there is some reasonable continuity.

The recapitulation is straightforward. No attempt is made to introduce the traditional subdominant colouring, and none is necessary since the main theme contains the harmony of the subdominant as an element of its first chord. However, Beethoven evidently felt the necessity for more of the subdominant in its role of resolution, and begins the coda by restating the principal theme at that level, starting the theme with the chord of D♭ major (bar 220). This time the chromatic rise from bars 3 to 6 of the theme does not stop at going from B♭ to C♭ and then to C♮, corresponding to the rise from F to G of the opening, but continues step by step all the way up back to G, reproducing at the end of this road the pitches of bars 3 to 6 of the original theme and so returning to the tonic. The music naturally continues with bars 7 and 8 of the first theme, and then restates the whole theme, shifting successive members of the phrase into a different octave, with the fermata of bar 6 now composed out into a length of three bars repeating the final chromatic step and completed by an interesting arabesque. The material for the end of the movement comes somewhat ironically from the passage used in the exposition to start the movement towards the dominant (bars 25–32): it is now used again to confirm that we remain in the tonic. The use of the same material in the service of opposing significance and function was the glory of the tradition in which Beethoven was raised, and he continued to exploit the effect for the rest of his life.

The second movement is a scherzo in A flat major, *Allegretto vivace*. The tempo should not be so quick that the 32nd notes of bars 43 further and elsewhere cannot be distinguished from the 16ths, and they must also sound staccato in bars 42 and 46. These 32nd notes determine the character of the piece. They are introduced in bar 10 before a *ritardando*:

The 32nd notes are so idiosyncratic here that when the *ritardando* arrives, they should, I believe, remain invariant. The tempo slows down briefly, but the 32nd notes should not change: they must retain their personality.

This is one of the most humorous of all Beethoven's scherzos, and its many passages of light rapid staccato texture make it a forerunner of the Mendelssohn scherzo. The dynamics are extreme, however, going from *pianissimo* to *fortissimo* as early as bar 35. After the first eight bars, the main theme concentrates on the harmony of the dominant of F minor (V of ii), perhaps recalling the importance of the F minor colouring of the main theme of the first movement. In this scherzo, changing from F minor to F major inspires Beethoven to the most dramatic detail of the exposition: the F major *fortissimo* crashes in bars 34 to 35. While astonishing, this is simply the magnification of a traditional eighteenth-century technique. To establish the E♭ dominant from an A♭ tonic, it is normal to approach it through a half-cadence on B♭, the dominant of the dominant. This can be made more effective by a suggestive glance at the dominant of the dominant of the dominant, F. Beethoven opts here for much more than a glance: he imposes an unprepared *fortissimo*. He cuts to the heart of the standard technique, and displays it enlarged for all to appreciate. This is classical craftsmanship stripped naked.

Perhaps stimulated by this effect in the exposition, the development opens with the principal theme played in F major. The work is full of odd, light-hearted ideas: powerful offbeat accents, surprising changes of mode. The most novel is the exploitation of the very rapid quintuplet in 32nd notes first heard in bar 19 as an upbeat to the counterstatement of the main theme. It returns in the development at bar 86, becomes a sextuplet in 88, and is then heard as a quadruplet twice in every bar from bar 91 to 96. The rhythmic impact is percussive and very strong, and it sets up the preparation for the return to the main theme. The presence of Haydn as an inspiration in this humorous work is confirmed by the addition of a counterpoint to the main theme in an inner voice that consists only of repeated notes (bars 125 to 130), a device typical of the older composer. The last eleven bars of the piece are entirely monophonic with octave doublings, all staccato, mostly *pianissimo* (there is a brief crescendo swell of two bars), and requiring an unyielding execution of metronomic precision.

The third movement is the only minuet in the three sonatas of the opus. This is a slow minuet, three strong beats to the bar instead of the one to the bar in all the other minuets we have seen in the earlier sonatas; it is marked *Moderato e grazioso*. The outer part is in two-phrase form, not three, and the repeats must be played again at the *Da capo*. The trio is in three-phrase form, the second phrase consisting of absolutely nothing but a steady reiteration of a dominant minor ninth chord (or an unharmonized dominant bass note alternating with the diminished seventh that produces the dominant minor ninth harmony). The first and third phrases of the trio play with transferring chords from one octave register to another.

The outer part of the minuet, in appearance simpler than the trio, is one of Beethoven's most sophisticated lyric inspirations. As it proceeds, it grows more intense. One sign of this is the indications of phrasing: for the first phrase and for the first four bars of the second, the slurs are never more than a bar in length, but the last four bars, which begin by rising to forte, are united by one grand slur. This calls for a *cantabile* style at that point that overrides all the articulations to the end, and carries out a surge of lyrical power. After the return of the minuet, an 8-bar coda with Neapolitan harmonies compresses all the melody into three contiguous notes (D, E♭, and F♭), and into only the first two of these in the last four bars.

The *Presto con fuoco* finale is a tarantella. As with so many tarantellas, it requires a good accent on the second half of the bar as well as on the first – above all in this case, as the beginning of the second half contains the most dissonant note of the accompaniment (in the left hand alone):

There are two bars of accompaniment alone, and then a four-bar theme – or, rather, a two-bar theme repeated at the lower octave. The accompaniment begins to manifest further its independence toward the end of the development; by the beginning of the coda it is self-sufficient, and needs no help from a melody to provide musical interest on its own. The B♭ on the first beat of the accompaniment makes the dissonance of a fourth, but it is part of the E flat major tonic chord;

the D at the opening of the second half of the bar is a dissonance within the basic tonic harmony, and it adds spice to what would otherwise be a banal accompaniment figure. When the harmony is a dominant seventh on B♭ (bar 3), a dissonant E♮ begins the second half of the bar. Both dissonances require emphasis. This accompaniment figure sustains a continuous level of dissonance and gives the movement its characteristic sonority. The brilliance is steady throughout.

The development begins as a surprise in the key of the flat mediant, G flat. The recapitulation takes the unusual course of bringing back in this key all the material originally presented in the dominant, returning to the tonic only at the last minute – the tonic minor, in fact, since that is closer to G flat. This is not the first time – and it will not be the last – that Beethoven's recapitulation continues a process initiated in the development. The coda exploits an opposition of legato and non legato touch (bars 271 and 274 on), and presents the main theme in fragments, with some acrobatic crossed-hand virtuosity. The lyricism of the first and third movements and the humour of the second are replaced in the finale by rough energy and exhilaration.

Two sonatas, opus 49

Opus 49 belongs with the eighteenth-century sonatas, and the two works were written several years before they were printed. Beethoven had no intention of publishing them: they were sent to the printer by his brother without his knowledge. Both of them are easy pieces in two movements for the inexperienced pianist, and they must have circulated privately among Beethoven's friends for the benefit of their children.

The first one, in G minor, is nevertheless a deeply affecting and distinguished work. The opening Andante welds the opening theme in one continuous movement to the quicker material in the relative major, B. The initial 2-bar motif of the B flat major section, marked dolce, is simply repeated twice at the end of the exposition as a closing theme, and it also provides much of the inspiration of the development. This begins forcefully with a move to the submediant E flat major. A 4-bar phrase of new material, graceful and expressive, is introduced and at once repeated with traditional decoration. The 2-bar motif returns and leads to a pedal point on the dominant that prepares the recapitulation with a restrained dramatic force.

The recapitulation follows a Mozartean model (see, for example, the first movement of the Sonata in A minor for Piano K. 310) in which the opening theme, after a playing of the initial eight bars, is restated in the bass with a new counterpoint in the right hand. The material originally in the relative major returns in G minor and is altered forcefully as it proceeds. Beethoven transfers the closing 2-bar motif deep into the bass, and it is followed in that region by an 8-bar pianissimo coda. Young pianists who start their experience of Beethoven

with this movement can learn a great deal about his handling of rhythmic continuity and his economy of motivic form.

The second movement, a Rondo, Allegro, in G major, has an elaborate middle
section in which a G minor theme first has an initial cadence in its relative major
B, and returns – after a conventional binary form of 32 bars in that key – to
cadence in G minor. In this way one simple binary form is a frame for another,
and in turn it, too, is framed by the G major opening theme. This is made more
complex by a reappearance later of the B flat major section in G major, as if it
had been the second part of a sonata exposition. The opening theme comes back
at the end and is made the basis of an elaborate coda. The form may be summed
up for convenience:

Theme A: 16 bars   G major
Theme B: 10 bars + 4   G minor   B flat major
Theme C: 32 bars   B flat major
   Phrase 1: 8 bars   cadence on F
   Phrase 1 repeated: 8 bars   cadence on B flat major
   Phrase 2: 4 bars   transitional development
   Phrase 1: shortened: 4 bars   B flat major
   Repeat of phrase 2 and shortened phrase 1: 8 bars   B flat major
Theme B: 10 bars + 2   G minor
Theme A: 16 bars   G major
Subsidiary development: 8 bars (theme A) with traditional move to the sub-
   dominant
Theme C: 32 bars   G major
Coda: 30 bars

This is an ingenious and original adaptation of various conventional devices.

Opus 49 no. 2 in G major is less personal. Beethoven obviously took little trouble
over it; there are almost no dynamic markings. The two eighteenth-century conventions of ending the development on the dominant of the relative minor and
introducing the subdominant with the second phrase of the recapitulation in
order to reaffirm the tonic are dealt with in the first movement with almost per-
functory efficiency. It is a perfectly competent work. The second movement is
the famous minuet of the Septet in E flat major that was Beethoven's most popular piece with the "Moonlight" Sonata. It is as easy to construe as one of the simpler pieces of Boccherini.

SONATA IN C MAJOR, OPUS 53, CALLED THE "WALDSTEIN"
COMPOSED BY 1804

No previous sonata by Beethoven had a first movement with so powerful and so unremitting a drive. The tempo mark, *Allegro con brio*, is an apt description. The opening paragraph follows the scheme used just previously in the Sonata in G major op. 31 no. 1: the first four-bar phrase is repeated at once a whole tone lower, starting with the chord of B flat major. The scheme is tightened, however: the arrival at the flat leading tone took twelve bars in the earlier work and only five in the "Waldstein". The voice-leading is also much smoother now: in the first phrase the bass moves chromatically down from C to B (giving the harmony of tonic to dominant), and then repeats this a whole tone lower from B♭ to A (making flat VII to the subdominant), and then descends simply from A♭ to G, providing a half cadence on the dominant. The greater mastery is evident when we compare this with the earlier sonatas. With all the complexity of harmony, this opening defines C major sufficiently for Beethoven to continue with more interesting matters. This is the initial statement, and the beginning of the counterstatement with its extraordinary rewriting of the pulsating opening as a tremolo:

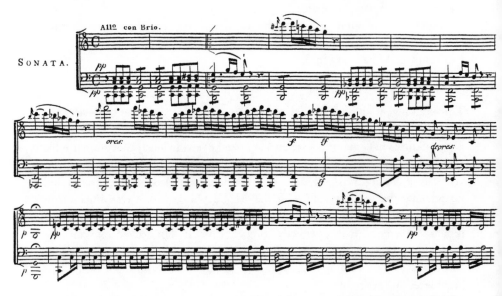

Also developed from op. 31 no. 1 is the replacement of the dominant (G) by the mediant (E) as a secondary tonality in the exposition, but the transition is more powerful and more integrated. Of course, in the "Waldstein", Beethoven is no longer trying for comedy. To set up the mediant the main theme starts once more an octave higher with an imitation of a string orchestral tremolo. The first four bars are repeated as before, but this time not a whole tone down but a whole tone up, with the bass now going from D to C, harmonized as D minor and A minor (ii to vi). This puts the C in place for an easy and natural resolution down to B, the resolution being forced by the appearance of an A#, and the B remains absolutely fixed as the bass for 8 bars and understood for 4 bars more as the fundamental harmony. This is enough to establish E major firmly (in the 12-bar dominant preparation, we appear to be moving towards E minor, but at the end E major is the goal). There is little attempt as in op. 31 no. 1 to mitigate the tension between tonic and mediant (C major and E major) by using the mediant minor. The major mode governs throughout until bar 74 of the exposition. The change after that point to E minor makes a warmer, more expressive concluding theme for the exposition, and it also facilitates the return from the mediant to C major when the exposition is repeated.

New in Beethoven's style as well is the economy: so much of the rich and varied thematic detail of the entire movement is implicit at once in the opening bars. Here we must take care not to confuse unity of texture and harmony with the return of a motif. It is one thing for a new theme to recall an earlier one, another for two themes to be constructed out of similar elements so that they belong happily to the same piece. The danger of this confusion was already understood by early admirers of Beethoven, like E. T. A. Hoffmann, who remarked that a work of Beethoven often seemed to be constructed out of one small cell, but that this was difficult to grasp even for musicians, who could hear thematic relationships easily only if the two themes followed each other immediately or if they were both harmonized alike.[5] If the return of a theme or a motif is difficult for the listener to recognize, then it would be a failure on Beethoven's part if he expected that recognition. If what he expected, however, was a sense that all the parts of a work fit together convincingly, then even a subliminal perception of that relationship by listeners must be accounted a success.

The "Waldstein" has a sound unlike any other work of Beethoven. It comes largely from the use throughout the first movement of themes that all move stepwise, alternating harmonies of perfect triads with dominant seventh chords. The constant presence of the dominant seventh chords makes for a certain neutral harshness, which admirably complements the driving rhythms. The alternation of triads and dominant seventh chords is found at the opening in a rising motif. The principal new theme at the mediant, a soft and expressive chorale-like melody marked *dolce e molto ligato*, presents the same harmony of alternating perfect triads and dominant sevenths, first descending and then rising (it might be noted here that the *sforzando* in bar 38 applies only to the B in the alto, which then descends to take over the soprano line in the lower register):

This should not be considered a thematic recall of the opening: they are two different themes that cohabit ideally.

The traditional virtuoso figuration that rounds out the new theme displays the same stepwise movement with the same alternation of triad and dominant seventh:

And so do both halves of the concluding theme:

The dominant seventh chord saturates this passage, as it did the earlier ones, but it is the alternation with perfect triads that gives them all their family likeness. The descending figure of bars 82–3 is set in relief by the *subito piano* which starts bar 83 in the middle of a longer slur. Even before the "Waldstein", Beethoven had imagined an individual sonority for many of the works, but the consistency with which he carried it out has become more striking here. For example, hammering out twelve A major triads in the bass fortissimo against some brilliant passage-work in the right hand (bars 62ff.), and continuing with twelve even harsher inversions of a dominant seventh chord, produced a sonority revolutionary in piano music that is derived from concerto style, but exceeds anything from contemporary concertos in massive power.

Besides the alternation of triad and dominant seventh, two other motifs, closely related to each other, are presented in the opening bars quoted above: the four-note motif in bar 3 with a characteristic rhythm of two sixteenths, and the motif that clearly springs from this in bar 4, with an initial *acciaccatura* and an expansion of the two sixteenth notes into a descent of a fifth. Both of them dominate the development: the first is found in bars 92, 94, 96, 97, 98, 100, 101, and from 104 to 112; the second in 93, and from 95 to 103. Both motifs return for an important role in the coda.

The development begins by repeating the short concluding theme and then the main theme at the subdominant, and the effect of stepping backward into this more relaxed harmonic region is to allow a new wave of tension to build up for the rest of the development. After the concentration in the development on the two motifs of bars 3 and 4, Beethoven turns to the theme of rising arpeggios that first appeared in bar 30 onward,* and works them into a virtuoso sequence of 29 bars. The influence of concerto form becomes even more evident. A long sequence of arpeggios was almost obligatory in the 'second solo' (or development section) of a concerto at that time. Beethoven never failed to write one in his concertos. Earlier composers during the 1760s would merely indicate the harmony and allow the pianist to work out his own realization with arpeggios. This implied a certain freedom of execution reminiscent of improvisation, and the style demands that we avoid the impression of mechanical virtuosity and recapture some of that sense of improvisation in the arpeggios of bars 112 to 142. The long sequence finishes with the harmony of G major, explained by the context as the dominant of the tonic minor, and the arpeggios descend to the lowest region of the bass.

Fourteen bars of dominant preparation of the return of the main theme and C major follow. It starts *pianissimo*, and the lowest G on Beethoven's piano never ceases to be sounded throughout the entire process with the three sixteenth notes (C, B, A) plus G of the motif from the fourth bar of the opening theme played 32 times in the bass. Their inversion is heard in the right hand, and this motif, punctuated with silences, gradually outlines a G major chord and rises with a crescendo to F, the highest note of the keyboard. The F is heard nine times starting *forte* and ending *fortissimo*, making an extraordinary insistence on the dominant seventh chord that it forms with the G in the bass, which has continued the

* Quoted above, p. 182.

four-note sequence (C, B, A, G), but with the C rising to C# and finally to D. The two hands play the motif simultaneously in contrary motion, rising and descending twice, emphasized by *sforzandi*. A descending scale from the top of the keyboard coincides with a rising one from the bottom, and the two hands meet in the centre on the tonic harmony, followed by an immediate *pianissimo* as the first theme returns. I give this detailed description only to show how little material Beethoven needed to work with, a four-note motif and a single harmony. Reiteration, the expansion of the register, and a crescendo are the tools. When it was first published, this was the most dramatic return ever written in the history of music. Since then, the effect has been made louder and longer, but never more efficient or more exciting.

In the recapitulation the first bars of the theme are replayed unchanged up to the fermata in the 13th bar, which now provides a shock: the dominant G is altered to an A♭, and 5 new bars are interpolated *pianissimo*:

This is the place for the traditional injection of subdominant harmony that the eighteenth-century musician felt necessary at the beginning of a recapitulation. For the subdominant, a harmony characterized by the flat direction, Beethoven substitutes more remote harmonies with flats (D♭, E♭), making a more exotic but even more effective subdominant tone. At the end of the interpolation, the music takes up where it had left off in the exposition.

The move to E major cannot be resolved simply into the tonic like a dominant, but needs more elaborate resolution. The theme first heard in E major is accordingly first played in A major, its subdominant, for four bars, then in A minor, bringing it closer to C major, and finally in C major. (This repeats the technique for resolving mediants that Beethoven had worked out in op. 31 no. 1.) The rest of the recapitulation proceeds in parallel to the exposition until the closing theme. This starts correctly in the tonic, but then moves to the subdominant, F major, as if Beethoven were going to go back to the development and repeat the second part of the movement as well as the first (an aborted threat he had also tried out in op. 31 no. 1). The end of the exposition, however, moved up from E major a half step to begin the development. It is this that Beethoven finally decides to reproduce, taking the end of the recapitulation in C major up a half step to D flat major to initiate a substantial coda.

The coda starts with the motifs of bars 1 to 4, working them up into a grand climax on a 6/4 chord with the utmost virtuosity of concerto style. Two fermatas on dominant sevenths, each followed by rapid scale descents, lead to the second theme. This brings on the soft chorale theme, no longer phrased with two-bar slurs, but with the greater unity of a four-bar slur. The second phrase of the theme cannot bring itself to end, but plays its penultimate bar three times and is always halted by a fermata, the second time with a chromatic alteration, and the last two in a tempo twice as slow with a *ritardando* added as well. The melody of this penultimate measure is simply an approach to the tonic: G A B. This is similar to the rising third (E F# G) that forms the basis of the opening theme in bars 1 to 3, and it is similarly harmonized with a dominant seventh and a triad (the latter in a 6/4 inversion, however). Nevertheless, this is not quite a thematic recall. The rising third of the opening theme is resolved on the third note: the threefold playing of a rising third in the coda aspires each time to the fourth note, C, but remains incomplete until the last fermata is released.

There is a final, truncated appearance of the opening theme. The right hand rises to the F and the left hand falls to the G at the limits of Beethoven's keyboard; a scale like the one at the end of the development simultaneously falls and rises into the centre. Four staccato chords *fortissimo* end the movement brusquely.

Beethoven originally composed a decorative, even florid, Andante for this sonata, but published it separately (it is the "Andante favori"), and wrote the *Adagio molto Introduzione* in its place. In form, it is an *arioso* (half cantabile aria, half *parlando* accompanied recitative) with an orchestral prelude and postlude. The prelude is nine bars long, and presents two motifs at once:

The *tenuto* on the third beat merely directs us to hold the note for its full value. At that time, a note before a rest would be released after half its value had elapsed.* The editor of the Henle edition points out that Beethoven would surely have wanted the left-hand octaves in bar 2 to sound an octave lower, but he did not yet have the low E on his piano. Adding the lower octave certainly improves the passage and does no harm to the conception of the whole piece.

As in the opening of the first movement, the bass of the first nine bars of the *Introduzione* descends chromatically from tonic to dominant. No profound con-

---

* See pp. 25–7.

clusions about organic unity can be drawn from this. Most chromatic basses from 1650 to 1825 descend from tonic to dominant. What is remarkable about the first paragraph of this introductory slow movement, however, is the very moving contrast between the firmness of the bass line and the supplicating hesitancy of the melody.

With the *rinforzando* of bar 9, the vocal soloist takes over. Many of the notes are detached for expressive emphasis, and so are the notes of the accompanying instruments in bars 11 and 13, marked *piano*. The dynamics and phrasing of the *arioso* melody are carefully indicated by Beethoven. An accent on an offbeat note was also called rubato in the eighteenth century, as well as delaying the right-hand melody note. The *sforzando* at the end of bar 14 is an example, and requires a liberty of tempo. Playing it in strict time would be unacceptably brutal, and it must be lingered over.

This blurs the distinction between vocal line and accompanying instrument which has been so effectively established by tone colour, but the disappearance of the vocal cantabile is deeply affecting as we move back into the hesitancy of the instrumental opening. The return of the first bars of the prelude as a postlude brings on a powerful development; then an insistent climactic reiteration of the highest note on the keyboard serves dramatically to return the music to C major before falling back exhausted. The imitation of a voice surprisingly surfaces again at the end in bars 26 to 28, but it is now not a tenor but a soprano.

This is the first impressive example of Beethoven's substitute of a brief Adagio introduction to the finale in place of a slow movement. It gave him the possibility of an unusually compressed expression of great intensity. Other affecting examples are the slow introductions to the finale in the Sonata in A major for cello and piano op. 69, the Sonata in C major for cello and piano op. 102 no. 1, and the Sonata in A major for piano op. 101. A related project was Beethoven's attempt to tie a complete slow movement directly to the finale. The first example of this in the piano sonatas was seen in the Sonata in E flat major, *quasi una fantasia*, op. 27 no. 1, but there were many examples to come, including the "Appassionata" Sonata, the "Les Adieux" Sonata, and the "Archduke" Trio, where the slow movements are followed *attacca* by the finales. This turns the slow movement in each case essentially into an unfinished or open-ended form.

The Rondo finale, *Allegretto moderato*, is the most massive and elaborate of the three movements of the "Waldstein", and it is also essentially the most simple. The melody is not only repeated several times in the work, but it also, like all rondo tunes, repeats within itself. The second phrase repeats the first, only leaving out the last note. The rhythm and shape of the third phrase, although not the exact pitches, repeat the first. The fourth phrase repeats the third phrase, changing only its third bar from major to minor; the last member of the fourth phrase is played twice, and then the last note of the phrase is played seven times. The tension found in the first two movements is reduced, and we end up with a much looser and more amiable structure.

As if to compensate for less complex demands on our attention, the rondo has exquisite and even radical contrasts of tone colour. The first note in the left hand is part of the melody, and the left hand crosses at once to leap three and a half octaves. The first note has a dual role providing a rustic drone bass as well as the start of the melodic line, and it must be held down by the pedal throughout the phrase; this gives, even on Beethoven's instruments, an exquisitely cloudy, semi-transparent atmosphere that enhances the pastoral mood of the melody. Throughout the first playing of the melody, the dynamic is pianissimo. Starting at bar 23, not only does the cloudy sonority of the pedal vanish, but all the voices except the soprano disappear as well, leaving only an eight-bar arabesque that rises and then falls back into a replaying of the theme. The contrast of tone colour could not be greater: the whole eight bars are covered by a long slur that directs an unbroken legato, but any use of the pedal here would only disturb the extraordinary new sonority. The opening melody is now played in octaves and a more elaborate accompaniment with full pedal. The opening is still *pianissimo*, but changes of dynamics begin to be introduced after 16 bars, and the pedal is lightened and clarified after 11 bars. The last eight bars of the theme are *fortissimo* over a trill and scales that rush rapidly upward but descend with an emphatic staccato.

The form of the rondo is not complex. It can be summed up:

I: Principal theme A and counterstatement
II. 1st Episode: Theme B1 Tonic (Bar 62)
  Theme B2 Relative minor (A minor) (Bar 70)
  Transition back to C major. Theme A
III Complete return of Theme A and counterstatement. (Bar 114)
IV 2nd Episode in C minor. Theme C. (Bar 175)
  Development of theme A. Bar 221. A flat major. D flat major
  12 bar episode (Bar 239)
  Further development of A. (Bar 250). From F minor leading back to C minor (Bar 277).
  Dominant pedal beginning on bar 279, but fixed and unvarying (Bar 295)
V Return of A, counterstatement alone, fortissimo.
VI Return of B1 24-bar extension.
  24 bars on the dominant, based on opening motif of A
VII Coda *Prestissimo*. A played at quadruple speed. Written-out cadenza in tempo.

The form for the most part has precedents in eighteenth-century finales. Attaching a development section to an episode in the subdominant is Mozart's general practice; the tonic minor lies in the flat or subdominant area, and is therefore a reasonable substitute. A coda in faster tempo is common enough in finales. Slightly more unusual is theme B1; beginning a new theme after the rondo theme has been completely displayed, and using it to move away from the tonic is perfectly canonic. In texture B1 resembles B2; remaining in the tonic allies it with A. Before the coda it is only B1 that is brought back, and it is the occasion of a virtuoso development.

The voice-leading of the return of B1 is complex. Most pianists bring out the soprano voice offbeat for the first eight bars and then switch to the alto on the beat for four bars. However, the end of the phrase in the alto from bar 355 to 356 is not convincing, and I now believe the emphasis should remain in the soprano, even though this consists mostly of one note repeated: CCCCCCBC. The repetition is Beethovenian, the end is convincing, and the alto voice melody will make itself heard as a subsidiary voice without bringing any emphasis to it. A similar point applies to bars 361 to 364 and beyond. This means, however, interpreting the *sforzandi* in these bars as applying not to the single note under which they stand but to the whole triplet, though in bars 362 to 363, for example, it would seem evident that the principal melodic line is from the offbeat note A to G, not from the alto F to D. The lack of a sign that would apply an accent not simply to one note but to a small group of two or three notes would disturb Liszt thirty years later, and he invented such a sign in his earlier publications, but later abandoned it because it never caught on with anyone else. I think this was already a notational problem during Beethoven's lifetime,* and that the successive signs in this section of *sf* should be considered as applying to the three-note group, and that for most of the passage the soprano should retain its supremacy.

If the opening note of the Rondo in the bass is not played from the beginning as an essential part of the main theme, the entire development section from 251 on will make little sense, as it is based largely only on the first three notes of the theme. In bar 257, the manuscript reads *sempre pianissimo*, the first edition *espressivo*. I do not like to believe that this is a misreading as editors have suggested, but it is certainly possible: I prefer to think the *espressivo* is a revision. The sonority of the whole section is magical and depends on exceeding care for a soft tone quality. Beethoven directs *pp* in bars 269, 271, 273, 275, 277 and 279, so he was clearly concerned. In no other work, not even the first movement of the "Moonlight" Sonata, was Beethoven as inventive with sonority. The variety of sound effects and technical display in the *Prestissimo* is astonishing: octave *glissandi*, trills that are almost forty bars long, a double trill, trills played with the thumb and second finger and the melody with the fourth and fifth, and fifteen bars of heavily pedalled pure C major at the end. Never again in his career did the composer try to find so many tone colours and technical inventions for the pianist in one work. This is set out in the first page of the first movement, when the pulsating opening is reconceived as a measured tremolo.

---

* I have pointed out a passage in the finale of op. 7 where the *sf* makes sense only if applying beyond the note under which it is indicated. See p. 134.

SONATA IN F MAJOR, OPUS 54
COMPOSED IN 1804

This has never been a popular sonata. Its style has seemed drab, its expression unforthcoming. Many musicians, like D. F. Tovey, have claimed it as exceptionally beautiful, and correctly so. It has a hidden poetry that will not reveal itself easily, but that will withstand a challenging examination.

The first movement, *In Tempo d'un Menuetto*, may dismay by an exaggerated economy of means, but that is one of its greatest virtues. The minuet proper has only two phrases. The opening phrase, which is repeated, has an F major chord at the beginning of every bar. The second phrase has only three cadences, all on the F major tonic.

The four F major chords of the 4-bar first phrase are in root position, first inversion, second inversion, and root position. The first three chords rise successively through three octaves. The second phrase, which is twice as long as the first, also rises through three octaves. The proportions of the first phrase are 1 + 1 + 2 bars: the melody of the first two elements is identical, although the second is transposed up an octave. The proportions of the second phrase are 2 + 2 + 4: transposed up an octave, the second element is exactly the same as the first, and the third element begins similarly before it extends the motif. Every element of every phrase ends on a short, unaccented note. The sobriety is almost wilfully ostentatious, the simplicity dogmatic, but each element of each phrase has exceptional grace.

The trio is anything but graceful. It is a rustic perpetuum mobile in triplet octaves and sixths, with two imitative voices, *sempre forte e staccato*, often brutally punctuated by *sforzandi*. The phrase structure of the two hands is out of phase, since one starts a bar later than the other but imitates it, and is made more complex by the intermittent injection of hemiola. The first paragraph is 14 (or 4 + 10) bars long, the second 16 (or 4 + 12), overlapping with a 15-bar coda (2 + 2, overlapping with 5, overlapping with 5, overlapping with 4) of which the last 8 bars are a dominant pedal preparing the return of the minuet. A drastically abridged version of the trio (12 bars) separates two returns of the minuet with all the repeats still carried out.

The returns of the minuet are more and more heavily ornamented as they proceed, although Beethoven follows the classical principle* that the opening of each return appears in its original undecorated form. The ornaments in this work are not simply decorative, but generative. They create movement and they expand the phrases. The end of the second return of the minuet is dramatically extended for eight bars, the florid arabesques eventually transforming themselves into a short cadenza, the inspiration for which comes entirely from the increasing energy of the lavish ornamentation.

---

* See the remarks on Mozart's Rondo in A minor K. 511 on p. 153.

An 18-bar coda completes the movement. A 4-bar theme is introduced, of a new lyrical and even popular cast, but clearly related to the opening of the minuet in style, rhythm and character: on the first beat of every bar is a tonic chord. This is repeated with ornaments that are similar to those at the end of the first return of the minuet. A swell to *fortissimo* and a fall back to *pianissimo* close the movement with a feminine cadence.

The *Allegretto* finale, marked *dolce* for both left and right hands in the first and third bars, is a perpetuum mobile.* The two indications of *dolce* need to be given full weight. The finale can either appear to be heartless or to develop a wonderful poetry out of almost nothing. As in the minuet, the material is radically minimal. There are two initial motifs. The first consists of one beat of a tonic arpeggio followed by broken sixths rising, and it provides the unstoppable motion. The second appears in two odd guises: a sixteenth note on the beat with a *sforzando* offbeat that lasts for 3 and 3/4 beats; or two sixteenth notes followed by a *sforzando* that lasts 3½ beats. After three sets of two-bar slurs, a four-bar slur imposes a longer line. Then the offbeat *sforzando* on the second sixteenth note of the beat appears at first once a bar in bars 13–14, and accelerates to twice in a bar in 15–16, an acceleration that serves to confirm a half cadence on the dominant. The whole section of 20 bars is repeated. The contrast of the flowing initial motif with the quirky accents of the second is striking.

At the end of the repeat, the key switches without warning or preparation to A major. The preceding trill on a B♭ suggests that the A major is a dominant of D minor, and so it turns out six bars later. There is a considerable chromatic development of the two motifs, alternating loud and soft (*f* and *p*, or *ff* and *p*), first in two-bar groups, accelerating to one bar and then to accents at the half bar.

At bar 75, on the dominant of D flat major, a new 4-bar theme is displayed, twice marked *espressivo* in bars 79 and 83. The repeated *appoggiatura* is unusually eloquent:

* For the tempo, see pp. 88–91. The 2/4 *Allegretto* should be the same as the finale of the Sonata op. 22, the *Allegretto* of the Piano trio op. 70 no. 2, or the *Allegretto* of the 7th Symphony. Any much faster tempo will destroy the poetry, and ruin the contrast with the final *Più Allegro*. I repeat here that the distinction in Beethoven between *Poco più allegro* and *Più allegro* is very marked.

This adds a new depth of sentiment, and develops sequentially around the circle of fifths, becoming more rapid as it proceeds: V of D♭ (bar 84), V of F# (87), V of B (89), V of E (90), V of A (91), V of D (92), V of G (93), V of C (94), V of F (95), bringing us back at last to the tonic. A dominant preparation begins three bars later at 99, and is sustained for 16 bars. A recapitulation of the main theme with a much grander sonority and a pedal on the tonic starts at bar 115.

We have here, so far, extremely odd proportions: a 22-bar exposition and a 93-bar development. This, however, underestimates Beethoven's power of experiment and takes no account of the new theme at bar 75. Beethoven now interprets the development as if it had partially retained the function of exposition. After 6 bars of recapitulation of his first motif on a tonic chord, he turns to the harmony of the subdominant, traditional at this point, and this leads him to the tonic minor at bar 130. Here he begins a 4-bar passage that echoes bars 37 to 43 of the development, and then a long section with an intense chromaticism reminiscent of both the harmony and the repeated *appoggiatura* of the *espressivo* passage at bar 75:

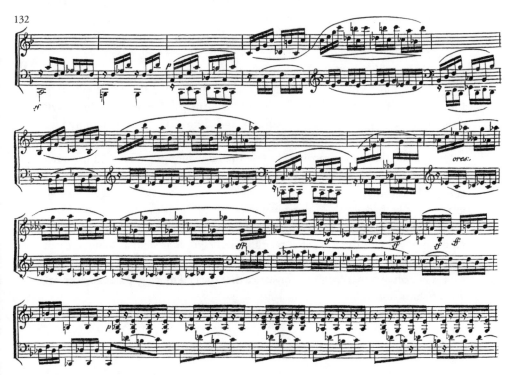

Ten bars of a dominant pedal with an intensely expressive repetition of the *appoggiatura* motif lead back to a repeat of everything from bar 22 on, and then to a coda in a much faster tempo *Più Allegro*, ending with a dazzling and even ferocious and percussive brilliance. (The tempo of the final page should be about 152–60 to the quarter.)

The experimental nature of this work, the radical simplicity of the means employed, needs an exploitation of the repeated *dolce* at the beginning and the repeated *espressivo* at the centre to bring out the implicit quality of the motifs, and it also demands an exploitation of the variety of textures created by Beethoven with such slender material in his perpetual motion. This is an essential work in the development of Beethoven's style. It is his first attempt to repeat a very long second half (140 bars) with a first section less imposing by comparison (22 bars, or 44 when repeated). The experiment was tried again immediately afterwards with the finale of the "Appassionata", where the repeat of the first section was omitted and that of the second required.

SONATA IN F MINOR, OPUS 57 ("APPASSIONATA") COMPOSED BY 1805

For musicians and public alike, this sonata has remained, with the C minor Symphony, the archetypal example of Beethoven's heroic style. He was proud of the work, but he did not like the popular nickname it was given by the publisher, and which has remained attached. The term "appassionata" does not render the tragic character of the work, evident at once with the opening page.

The handwriting in the autograph manuscript betrays the emotional turmoil of the piece, but there are very few places where there is the slightest doubt as to the composer's intentions. The phrasing of the principal themes is not consistent either in the autograph or the first edition, and almost all editors have opted for normalizing all the appearances. There is no reason for this. The articulations and accents of the themes are capable of more than one interpretation, and it is even possible to realize two different phrasings simultaneously. The opening theme is covered by Beethoven in one long slur of four bars, and also divided into two groups of two bars: both of these make sense, and both can be embodied in a single performance. The best edition would simply reproduce the phrasing of the autograph and give the few variants of the first edition as well, as some of them may stem from the composer's revisions rather than the engraver's fantasy.

It is not often remarked in performance that the end of every phrase before bar 16 is a short note:

Beethoven goes out of his way in bars 4 and 8 to write a quarter note with an eighth rest followed by two rests of a dotted quarter. It is evident that he did not want a note of a dotted quarter or more, which is what we always hear. In addition, there are no dynamic indications beyond the opening *pianissimo* until bar 9. The low C in bar 10 is marked staccato. There is no staccato mark on the low Cs in bars 12 and 13, and perhaps Beethoven intended them to be similar to bar 10. The dots on the low D♭s in bar 13 are missing, although they are present in bars 10 and 12, and there is little reason to think that a different touch was intended here. In any case, none of these notes are long, and all demand an almost immediate release. This is important because it imposes a reserved, sober and almost dry sonority on the opening, which renders the arpeggio and the *forte* that follow more effective, and makes the *fortissimo* counterstatement of the theme all the more astonishing. The sobriety is consonant with the extraordinarily lean texture of this first page, with a monophonic opening, and a large proportion of silence.

In notating rhythm, Beethoven now works in the "Appassionata" toward a greater precision: in bars 32 to 34, for example, the chords are first quarter notes and then dotted quarters, and the distinction makes musical sense. None of them, however, should be lengthened, as the contrast with bars 35 to 45, where every chord is sustained, would be undone.

This work resolves two problems that Beethoven had with movements in the minor mode (although they do not seem like problems until they are re-examined in the light of the "Appassionata"). The first is the effective incorporation of the traditional relative major as a secondary key area while sustaining the tragic possibilities of the minor mode throughout. The second problem is related to the first, and forms part of its solution: that is, how to unify the extreme contrast of emotions needed for the tragic genre. In the Sonata in D minor op. 31 no. 2, a disunity is accepted, with a contrast of tempo, and the use of an operatic recitative. Op. 57 is more sparing: the *poco ritardando* and the fermata on the first page are the only things that hold back the inexorable rhythmic sweep of the whole movement. The fermata will recur at the beginning of the recapitulation, and there is both *ritardando* and a fermata in the middle of the coda before the final *Più Allegro*: otherwise fluctuations of motion are controlled within a steady beat. Any slowing down, as in bars 41 to 47, is written out and measured by the composer.

The efficient agent of this controlled rhythm is the repeated notes, which appear in the motto at bar 10, and dominate many sections, starting first at bars 24 to 34 where the minor mode of the relative major A♭ is introduced, and recur throughout. The steady beat set up by the repeated notes makes it possible to extend the same eighth-note rhythm to the accompaniment of the new theme *dolce* at the relative major at bar 35, an accompaniment that grows directly out of the repeated notes. As in op. 2 no. 1, the new theme at the relative major is perceived as a variant of the opening theme, but the minor mode is not reimposed until the end of the theme, dramatically in bar 42. After the measured *ritenuto* of bars 41 to 46, the steady eighth notes are given a monophonic scale descent from the high treble into the bass, and lead to the unleashed storm of the double speed, the sixteenth notes of the A flat minor theme, a rhythm which does not vary until bar 65.

The steady beat which controls so many different levels of rhythm unifies the contrasts of harmony and of mode. Another agent that synthesizes major and minor modes is the Neapolitan relationship that is not only displayed immediately at the opening with the main theme played in F minor and in G flat major, but is also reflected at all levels of the material, from the motif in bar 10, with the repeated D♭s and C, to all the related reiterations of the minor second throughout bars 25 to 32, 44 to 47, and 53 to 64. The Neapolitan (which characterized Beethoven's conception of the tonality of F minor throughout his career) contains within itself the contrast of major and minor modes. Along with the controlled rhythm, it enables Beethoven to encompass in one form the radical contradictions of the sober *pianissimo* opening, the *fortissimo* counterstatement, the new *dolce* theme in the major, and the ferocity of the closing section of the exposition.

The tension is carried further at the opening of the development with the change from E major to E minor, making the most radical contrast with the principal key. It is this part of the key structure that brings the "Appassionata" so close to the generation of Chopin and Schumann. Chopin, for example, achieves his most radical modulations by mediant relations (modulations by thirds) and by changes of mode from major to minor. Beethoven moves in the exposition from A flat major to A flat minor, shifts to a mediant, E major, at the beginning of the development, and then changes the mode to E minor, harmonically as distant from the tonic F minor as possible. The composers of the 1830s found themselves at home with these procedures.

The arpeggios that follow are adapted from the concerto genre, but are now better integrated, as they come out of the broken thirds at bars 79–80, which are a new synthesis of the repeated notes of the exposition with the sixteenth notes of its final section. The development begins by concentrating on the first theme and the bass descends by thirds from E to C to A♭. The minor second relationship of A♮/A♭ transforms this into a dominant, and attention is turned to the transitional theme with the repeated notes first displayed at bar 24 and then to the *dolce* theme. All sections – exposition, development, recapitulation and coda – take up the themes in the same order – and all four sections are approximately the same length, which gives the form a rigid symmetry that only enhances the violence of the passion. The rising bass on which Beethoven had taken out a patent in op. 2 no. 2 has its greatest hour of glory and fame here, starting at bar 109, ascending through two full octaves from the low D♭. Reaching a diminished seventh on D♭, the bass continues to rise for two more octaves and then descends down this harmony into the lowest region of the keyboard, and with the D♭/C motto repeated eight times (four times first on D♭ alone) accomplishes the transition back to the tonic F minor.

The shock is that the low tonic F is refused, and the bass remains on a repeated dominant C as the recapitulation commences. No return to the tonic and to the main theme had ever before been invested with such tension, allowing the drama of the development to invade the resolution. The dominant pedal is prolonged for seventeen bars until the fermata at bar 153. The return of the *fortissimo* explosion first heard at bar 17 is now in F major, and the passage that follows is rewritten with greater dissonance and passion to return to the tonic minor. The rest of the recapitulation follows symmetrically.

The coda takes up both principal themes, and then a measured cadenza-like structure presents a rising bass once more, two octaves and a third from a low B♭ to a D♭. Virtuoso arpeggios finish with a pedal on the dominant, over which is played the motto theme with the D♭ blended with the C, *sempre Pedale,* and the tempo slows down to an Adagio and halts. The *Più Allegro* starts with the rhythm of the motto heard resolved for the first time in the movement, going from tonic to dominant (this is often performed with a slow emphasis, but should already be at the new quick tempo). This final section, beginning with the *dolce* theme for the first time in the tonic minor, rises to an exceptional violence with antiphonal chords *fortissimo*. Six bars before the end, the left hand plays the lowest octave on Beethoven's piano *fortissimo*, followed instantly by a *piano* and *diminuendo*. The low F must be held by the pedal until the end of the movement: on a modern instrument this effectively drowns out the initial notes of the soft melody of the main theme (the effect of the old instruments can be achieved on the new ones if one quickly changes pedal for a split second immediately after striking the octave with full force, enough to remove most of the sound but still leave the bass note vibrating). The dynamics descend to *ppp*. Hans von Bülow remarked that no *ritardando* is necessary or desirable at the end, as Beethoven has written out a measured one.

The variations of the *Andante con moto* double the speed and rise to a higher octave with each variation. The chorale-like theme, a short symmetrical binary form with repeats, reserves most of its movement and all of its agitation for the left hand. The melody of the first four bars uses only two notes A♭ and B♭, the next four bars only D♭ and C (the A♭ and B♭ are now hidden in the alto). The rhythm moves in quarter notes. In the first variation, still in a low register, the left hand is invested with a cantabile legato off the beat, while the right hand on the beat plays the melody only in detached notes: the contrast of touch here should be marked; the rhythm moves basically in eighth notes. A continuous sixteenth-note rhythm appears in the second variation, which has moved to the middle register.

The third variation, the repeats written out, ascends to the high register and quickens to thirty-second notes. For once, Beethoven has somewhat unclearly specified the dynamics. There is a forte at the second half of each phrase, and this implies that the first half is always piano – that is, the accompaniment is *piano*, but the melody notes, offbeat, are each marked *sforzando*. (To make sense of this, one should return to *piano* in bars 52, 56, 60 and 64.) This last variation rises to a *fortissimo* with a scale in the right hand that descends from top to bottom of the piano, and brutally short accented chords in the left (staccato sixteenth notes followed by rests). The final variation, the two halves not repeated, is a synthesis that combines the low, middle and high registers, and the slowest rhythms with sixteenth notes at the end of the phrase. In place of the final tonic chord, there is a pianissimo arpeggiated diminished seventh chord on B♭ with pedal, and a fermata; and then a second diminished chord, fortissimo, only the left hand arpeggiated, and another fermata. A diminished seventh chord on B♭ repeated twelve times opens the finale *Allegro ma non troppo*, and the first twelve bars are confined to that harmony. The *ma non troppo* should be taken sufficiently seriously so that the *Presto* at the end can be almost double tempo.

This perpetuum mobile is in sonata form and in rondo style. The structure, like that of most finales of the time, is much looser than that of the first movement. The four-bar periodic rhythm is occasionally varied by an extra two bars, but there is little irregularity, and none of the suppleness of the first movement. The themes are square and full of interior repetition. As in the first movement, the opening motif is repeated at once a half step higher in G flat major. The 8-bar main theme is played a second time with an obbligato in the left hand crossing over the right. There are only tonic cadences in the opening pages (bars 20, 28, 36, 50, 64) and then a move to the dominant minor is achieved by bar 72. At bar 76 a new theme with Neapolitan harmony continues the steady sixteenth-note rhythm. A variant of the main theme is played in two-part imitative counterpoint (bar 96) followed by insistent chords to initiate a closing theme that ends on a diminished seventh chord on a G♭.

"The second part to be played twice" is written in large letters in the autograph. A glance at the manuscript will show that Beethoven was very serious about the matter. This insistence on the return gives the form some of the character of a rondo, particularly since the main theme appears at the tonic, the dominant, and the subdominant. The second part begins with the main theme at the subdominant, remaining there for 32 bars (a large dose of subdominant harmony in a finale is standard late eighteenth-century practice), with a contrapuntal development. A new 8-bar theme is introduced in the subdominant at bar 148, first played *piano* with strong offbeat accents, and then repeated *forte*. These sixteen bars are then transposed to the tonic, and followed by a variant of the main theme in close two-part imitation. The emphasis on the tonic in the development section distinguishes the form from a first-movement form, where this would be avoided. The steady sixteenth-note motion breaks down with arpeggios on the flat supertonic and the dominant. A long slow arpeggio on the diminished seventh that opened the movement rises and then falls onto the lowest G. Six bars of V7 reintroduce the main theme at the tonic.

The recapitulation borrows a device from the same place in the *Allegro maestoso* of Mozart's Sonata for piano in A minor K. 310, where the main theme is presented in its original form, and then repeated at once in the left hand (the repetition is more literal in Beethoven, who also adds an obbligato motif in the treble). The second ending of the second part of the finale is marked *sempre più allegro*, and leads to the *Presto* coda. This begins with new material, a simple two-phrase binary form with repeats. It continues with the main theme in the new, much faster tempo, with the added excitement of a *sforzando* on the weak beat of every bar. The sonata ends with a torrent of descending arpeggios, heavily pedalled. The sonority of the last bars is brilliant and intense.

SONATA IN F SHARP MAJOR, OPUS 78
COMPOSED 1809

Although only two short movements, this sonata is not a modest work. The four-bar *Adagio cantabile* that opens the work is like no other introduction – or, rather, it is not an introduction at all, but a fragment of an independent slow movement. It is a fragment only because it is too short to exist on its own, but it is, indeed, complete. In fact, that is why it is not an introduction: in an eighteenth-century classical form, an introduction is never complete. There are no models or precedents for these opening bars, and they have never been successfully imitated.

The *Allegro ma non troppo* is one of Beethoven's rare works that depend entirely on lyrical charm. He developed new stylistic methods here. The first three phrases (bars 5–8, 8–11 and 12–16) all outline the same contours in a different way:

This is not the traditional motivic technique that Beethoven had learned from Sebastian Bach and Haydn, but a more novel and fluid procedure, foreshadowing the later work of Schubert. The melody seems to be improvised as it proceeds, to grow naturally. A trace of the more orthodox treatment of motif is the way bars 9 and 10 seem to develop from the last notes of the *Adagio cantabile*. Otherwise each phrase seems to recall the contour of the previous one, either to dissolve it into a lightly conceived arabesque or to expand it towards a more intense expression.

The move to the dominant C sharp major is orthodox, except that Beethoven substitutes a V7 chord on A♮ instead of the more orthodox V of V of V (D sharp major) to resolve into the G# dominant of C#. In so doing, he spells the right-hand harmony with F double sharp and the left hand with G natural, showing that he had no interest in a harmonic theory based on natural intonation. This is not simply because such a notation is senseless on the piano; the same inconsistencies show up in his string quartets. Whatever expressive adjustments of intonation he expected of his string players, he composed always with a basic system of equal temperament.

The development is condensed, concentrating largely on the minor mode for a more urgent expression. From bar 47 the harmony descends: D sharp minor, C sharp minor, B major. Under the B, a C# is implied from bars 52 to 54, and finally arrives in 55 to form the dominant seventh of F sharp major.

Only a few bars into the recapitulation, bars 10 to 16 of the exposition are reworked spectacularly to introduce the subdominant area (bars 61ff.):

The rewriting goes first to E major, the subdominant of the subdominant, working through the flat relations of the tonic minor to the subdominant B major, and exploits the old convention with great power. The short coda is incorporated into the repeat of the second half, and is exceptionally interesting. Fragments of the main theme appear at the tonic in a kind of stammer over a flowing left-hand line.

The finale, *Allegro vivace*, is eccentric, and makes no attempt to sound normal. It begins on an augmented sixth chord, and there is a series of jerky, two-bar phrases. Bar 2 is an eighth note followed by two eighth rests. After that, in bars 4, 6, 8 etc., Beethoven writes quarter notes with one eighth rest. It may easily be that he intended all these to be slightly longer than the first chord in bar 2, but he writes a quarter note in the return of bar 2 when the main theme comes back in bar 32, and there is no musical reason to think that bar 33 is any different from bar 2. It is up to the pianist to divine Beethoven's intentions, but in any case, all these notes at the ends of the two-bar phrase are quite short.

It is immediately clear that the end of bar 1 is the dominant; the tonic is not reached until bar 10; but there is not the slightest ambiguity about where the tonal centre is from bar 1 on. It is finally affirmed by a new theme at bar 12, and the little groups of two sixteenth notes dominate the texture of the whole movement:

The first chord of the movement, an augmented sixth, is the major influence on the large structure. It is incipiently the dominant seventh of G major, a V7 on D♮. The last appearance of the main theme in the rondo is introduced with a *ff* crash on that chord, and that harmony without any alteration is made to last 18 bars (133–51), when it becomes the opening harmony of the theme. This accounts earlier for a similar passage working out the harmony of V7 on G♮ (bars 74–89): that can be resolved to the V of IV, just as the first chord resolves to the principal dominant. These are the longest sustained harmonies of the movement. The eccentric rondo form can be summed up:

I Main theme (Bars 1–11)

II Second theme in the tonic (Bars 12 –21) Move to V at bars 20–1

III Episode on V (two sixteenth-note figure antiphonally divided between the hands)

IV Main theme at the tonic (Bars 32–40)

V Second theme at tonic Bars 42–50, move to V of vi (D sharp minor)

VI Theme 3: arpeggiated alternation of D sharp major/minor, *subito FF/subito P*

VII Excursion on V7 of C major (Bars 74–88)

VIII and IX Sections I and II transposed to the subdominant

X Theme 3 at the tonic

XI Excursion on V7 of G major

XII Main theme in the tonic, bars 3–4 and 7–8 now played legato

XIII Coda based on bar 11 of main theme leading to a fermata, brief cadenza, and final 6-bar cadence.

The hand-crossing makes for some dazzling pyrotechnics, and so do the alternations of *fortissimo* and *piano*. The unexpected transformation of parts of the theme to a legato invest its last appearance with a charming lyrical sense, a warmth of sentiment which is extended at length into the opening of the coda.

SONATINA IN G MAJOR, OPUS 79
COMPOSED IN 1809

This was undoubtedly meant to be an easy piece, but the opening movement, *Presto alla tedesca,* is exceedingly tricky. It is an early form of the waltz, a development of the *Ländler.* In the late eighteenth century, the form was called an Allemande or a Teutscher (translated by Beethoven's *alla tedesca,* or "German Dance"). This is a Haydnesque work (several of the Haydn piano sonatas and piano trios have German dances for a finale), and the form of the exposition is decidedly derived from Haydn: short tonic section (bars 1–12), move to V with long development (12–46); short closing (46–47). After stating the 8-bar first theme with a 4-bar postscript, the entire exposition is devoted to the modulation to the dominant. One must not think that the dominant reaches the new status at bar 12, even though it is attacked by its own dominant: it is still only a dominant, and has not yet been raised to a higher level of power. That does not take place until bar 20, with the use of V of V of V. When the dominant is finally established to Beethoven's satisfaction so that he can permit a full cadence on it, there are only four bars of exposition left, two of them a modulation back to the tonic. The style is alternately light and boisterous.

The development starts in E major, and produces a rustic theme with offbeat accents and crossing hands *forte,* repeated *dolce* and *piano* in E minor. This new theme is nothing but the first bar of the main theme played over and over again. After the postscript to the main theme, the rustic theme returns *forte* in C minor, and then *piano* in E flat. Finally, with a crescendo and hemiola over a dominant pedal, it introduces the recapitulation, which merely adds a touch of subdominant to the exposition in order to end in the tonic. Both halves are repeated. The coda starts the main theme in the left hand and continues in the right to round it off more squarely than at its first appearance. This is replayed with some rustically humorous *acciaccature,* and then 10 bars of arpeggios *leggiermente dolce* allow the piece to disappear into thin air.

The last two movements are indeed easy to play. The *Andante* in G minor is a barcarolle, presented like so many barcarolles by Rossini (and one by Chopin) as a duet for two sopranos. The central section in E flat major is a solo. The style of Italian opera is very much in evidence.

The final *Vivace* is in a style reminiscent of Beethoven's earliest work, but with more sophisticated transitions. At bar 94 there are some humorous delaying echoes. After a crescendo, the final short chords *piano subito* are a great surprise and a joke.

SONATA IN E FLAT MAJOR, OPUS 81A
LES ADIEUX
DAS LEBEWOHL [THE FAREWELL]. *VIENNA, 4 MAY 1809, ON THE DEPARTURE OF HIS ROYAL HIGHNESS, THE ESTEEMED ARCHDUKE RUDOLF*
COMPOSED IN 1810

The Farewell begins, *Adagio,* with a horn call, a symbol in poetry well established by 1810 of distance, isolation, and memory. The three notes of the horn call are a motto. They are also the kernel from which the movement grows: along with the motif of a rising fourth that follows, they provide in one way or another most of the important themes of the piece. Bars 3 and 4 express a sense of yearning, regret and melancholy. The introduction goes first to the relative minor, returns to the tonic and changes the major to the tonic minor. Bars 12 to 16 invert the three-note motto into an expression of desire.

The *Allegro* begins without pause on the chord of the subdominant, and an octave A♭ in the soprano. The *tenuto* on the G at the opening of the second bar allows us to hear that this is the beginning of the motto, G F E♭, and that the opening bar with the A♭ must be considered as an *appoggiatura*. The bass from 21 to 24 inverts the treble line of the opening bars of the Allegro, A♭ G F E♭, and bars 25 to 29 repeat this and rise through A♮ to the B♭ dominant. A rapid passage that confirms the dominant in double- and triple-note scales descending and rising in the right hand is the terror of most pianists. It introduces the new texture at the fast tempo without warning, begins legato and turns into staccato, and the physical impetus for the performer is disturbed by the fact that two of the chords are played twice. The motto, now in the minor mode, is played simultaneously inverted in the right hand and right side up in the left. The harmony insists constantly on the degree of the flat sixth (G♭ in the key of B flat major), colouring the dominant with an expressive and even painful dissonance.

The motto is played (bar 50) at the original tempo (that is, the note values are twice as long as they were in the *Adagio*, but the *Allegro* must be more or less twice as fast). Beethoven continues to insist on the dissonant G♭, adding to it a C# and an E♮. A concluding theme of four bars (bar 62) uses the motto eight times as fast as the original in a descending imitative sequence. The motto is present throughout the exposition in all forms and all rhythms: it is the tissue out of which the cloth is woven. The nervous rhythm, the growing dissonance, and the constantly changing texture represent the agitation of the departure and the anxiety of the coming absence.

The harmonic scheme of the development is, in its large outline, the most conventional one, beginning and ending with the relative minor, but the details are surprising. The three-note motto is first reduced to two notes, unharmonized, played four times, and punctuated by the bustling motif at the opening of the *Allegro*. The harmony goes to the tonic minor (bar 88), to its relative major G♭ (bar 92), and immediately back to C minor, and the soprano descends from A♭, down an octave to an A♭ sixth chord, every note held for a full bar (the pianist can suggest by touch that the motto has been reduced from two notes to one here) and the last A♭ played *pianissimo* six times. An A♭ sixth chord is the first chord of the *Allegro*. After the chord has sounded six times, it would seem only logical to start the recapitulation. Accordingly, a crescendo for two bars in broken octaves on the A♭ sixth chord brings back the main theme (the harmony is subtly rewritten, and there are longer slurs to make the return more intense). To stay in the tonic instead of going to the dominant, Beethoven has only to rewrite the virtuoso passage in double notes.

He does not introduce the subdominant harmony traditional at this point, since the principal theme of the *Allegro* begins with the chord of the subdominant, and the recapitulation was introduced with eight bars of unrelieved subdominant. Nevertheless, the coda begins by transposing the main theme to the subdominant (the process is different from the one in the "Pastoral" Sonata, which also opens with subdominant harmony but transfers the major use of the subdominant from the recapitulation to the beginning of the development – it would seem as if a certain amount of subdominant in the second part of a sonata was necessary to the harmonic sensibility, at least to a composer like Beethoven, who follows Haydn in his sensitivity to these questions of balance).

The coda is the most picturesque and programmatic section, representing the sense of distance and departure, with the motto appearing unharmonized in dovetailing imitations, first in single notes. Then the original sonority of the horn call is restored (bar 197), and played with a running motif that goes from the lowest to the highest part of Beethoven's keyboard. From bars 223 to 243, the horn calls dominate, played at the original tempo (a whole note), and then four times as fast, overlapping with each other so that the tonic and dominant blur.

In the bass (bar 243), whole notes derived clearly from the rhythm of the horn call descend a scale into the depths *pianissimo*, while a right-hand scale eight times as fast rises as far as it can go, as if following something disappearing into the distance and itself disappearing. (In the Credo of the *Missa Solemnis,* eternity ("world without end") is represented by rising scales that also seem to disappear in the distance.) At the end in the autograph there is an impossible crescendo on a single octave C going to a B♭, as if straining to see what is no longer there. The dynamic indication is not in the first edition. Did Beethoven or the engraver decide it was too eccentric?

The Absence (*Andante espressivo, In gehender Bewegung, doch mit viel Ausdruck*) starts with a motif that recalls the rhythm that enters with the third bar of the introduction of the first movement (and it acknowledges that the introduction represents the premonition of absence). We hear first the chord of C minor, but when it is succeeded by a diminished seventh on F#, it does not sound like a tonic but like the subdominant of G minor. In the third bar the diminished seventh is resolved not to G minor but to G major, which is therefore a dominant (the E♭ prevents acceptance of G major as tonic), and C minor is, after all, the tonic. This is confirmed immediately by the next phrase, which repeats the first phrase transposed a fourth higher but resolves it now to C minor.

Identifying the moment the tonic becomes fixed may seem pedantic, but it is a guide for performance and explains the emotional power of these initial phrases. Beginning with a phrase which turns out not be on the tonic brings a sense of uncertainty, even to listeners who do not analyse the harmony – and no listeners do at a performance, not even professional musicians, except unconsciously; the uncertainty is only compounded when we finally realize in retrospect that the first chord was, in fact, the tonic. The second phrase is almost an exact replica of the first a third higher, but it has much greater intensity: it no longer starts tentatively, but in the tonic that has now been established. It is a beautiful effect when bar 8 returns to the harmony of C minor, which was the first chord we heard but which did not sound like the fundamental harmony of the movement, and which now turns out to be so, after all, as it is confirmed by the V/I resolution.

The next phrase (upbeat to bar 10) commences as if with new hope (in the major mode with a crescendo) but swiftly breaks off helplessly with a rapid diminuendo. It is followed, crescendo, by a climax of great despair (a series of dissonances insistently marked by *sforzandi*). The monophonic arabesque that climbs and outlines a diminished seventh on F# moves to establish G minor. The four detached thirty-second notes at the end of bar 14 direct a ritenuto, and enforce the dominant of G, now accepted as a tonic, first in the major and then in minor.

Bar 21 initiates a recapitulation (like so many slow movements of Mozart, this one is in cavatina form, i.e. exposition and recapitulation with no development), but it starts surprisingly at the subdominant (this is the only classical substitute for the tonic at the opening of a recapitulation, as any other harmony would demand resolution). Tovey remarks correctly that it is not until the end of the fourth bar that we realize that the recapitulation has started with the second phrase (bars 5–8) of the exposition, not the first. At the point that the exposition went towards the dominant (bar 11), the recapitulation does not continue symmetrically with what would now be the tonic, but remains at the subdominant. Beethoven temporarily withholds the presentation at the tonic of his material. The return is otherwise unchanged in structure, but both ornament and texture have become more powerful (bar 28 reaches towards the low E that Beethoven did not yet have – pianists have to decide whether the frustration of not granting the E is more effective than allowing it to appear).

After retracing the rest of the exposition at the subdominant, Beethoven returns at last to the first theme at the tonic. Here for the first time, the opening melody starts on C, the tonic note itself, now harmonized by a diminished ninth on the dominant. This dramatic dissonance implies an imminent cadence, promises closure. Instead, the motif rises, as if there were hope, confirmed as the bass rises to a B$\natural$ and resolves this to a B$\flat$, harmonized as the dominant seventh of the original tonic of E flat, while the motif continues to rise still higher and always *pianissimo*. On this dominant seventh chord, The Return (*Das Wiedersehn, Le Retour*) begins instantly with an explosion of joy.

After ten bars of introduction, consisting of virtuoso figuration on the dominant seventh chord, the principal theme gives the tone of the finale its extraordinary simplicity. Complexity of sentiment is left behind at least momentarily. The main theme is playful, and its counterpoint in bars 17 to 20 even more so. Transition to the dominant is simple: V7 of V for one beat at the end of bar 36. This is not quite enough, of course: four bars of pounding *fortissimo* on the notes of a G flat major sixth chord followed by a parallel effect on the dominant of the dominant establish the new harmony, and the whole passage is echoed playfully. Two new motifs, one in each hand, are ostentatiously childlike in their expression of happiness (bars 53–6). This is treated in double counterpoint at the octave in the development, by reversing the hands.

The development is astonishing in more than one respect, but above all in its dynamics. It is all quiet. This is an example of Beethoven's psychological penetration; he knew that there are forms of happiness too great at times for extrovert expression. The development begins by moving up a half step to B major (bars 81–101):

It is rare that a pianist will resist making a crescendo in bars 87–94, but the representation of happiness rests here on the absence of dynamics. The effect of an undiluted piano is exquisite, as if one were floating in an atmosphere of contentment and delight. The change from B major to G major is accomplished *pianissimo*. This leads to a three-voice stretto on fragments of the main theme, and the recapitulation begins apparently in the subdominant A flat, to be corrected swiftly after two bars back to the tonic. (This is an effect borrowed from Beethoven's teacher Haydn: the opening movement of the String Quartet in E flat major op. 50 no. 3 has a false reprise of four bars in A flat (bar 82), corrected at once to the proper E flat.)

The main theme (bar 110) is now played first in legato octaves in the right,* and then in powerful staccato octaves in the bass. Once again Beethoven gives individuality to each appearance of a motif not by ornamentation, but by a different touch and a new texture. The coda, in slower tempo at first, displays a new phrasing for a derivative of the theme (bars 181–90), and adds a touch of melancholy.

---

* The slur goes only over the first five notes of six in the bar, and the sixth note is marked by a stroke, indicating an accent (the first edition seems to have been printed with some care for the almost impossible task of distinguishing Beethoven's staccato dots from his strokes in the manuscript – either the engraver was unusually conscientious, or else Beethoven corrected the proofs with care). I think the legato should go to the sixth note: it is only the old convention that the last note under a slur is unaccented that ends the slur on the fifth note. Given the accuracy of the first printing, modern editors ought to refrain from normalizing the beams and stems, which may reproduce Beethoven's manuscript (the last two movements of which have disappeared). The stems and beams of bar 104 are different from the similar form of 106.

The greater articulation of 104 and the longer legato of 106 make a beautiful contrast. Further, there is no reason that the last note in the left hand of bar 129 should not have a separate stem as it does in the first edition instead of being beamed with the others.

The Years of Stress

From 1812 to 1817 were difficult years for Beethoven. It was the time of his law-suit with his sister-in-law over the custody of his nephew Karl, of the despairing letter to the Immortal Beloved, of his deafness that progressed to the point where he could no longer hear himself play the piano. He wrote only a few large works during this time. There were two relatively short sonatas, op. 90 and op. 101. A long time was spent on completing op. 106.

SONATA IN E MINOR, OPUS 90
COMPOSED IN 1814

The opening movement is lean. The first theme comes to a half close on the dominant after 16 bars, with a *ritardando* and a fermata; this articulation is harmonically necessary to define the tonic as the theme began by moving up at once to G major and then to B minor, and descending back through G major. A post-script of 8 bars, with an expressive motif that spectacularly drops almost two octaves in the middle of the phrase,* confirms the key with a full tonic close (bar 16), also ending with a *ritardando*. It would seem that Beethoven decided to use an old-fashioned form with a complete tonic close and a pause at the end of the main theme, a form he generally avoided, except in slow movements, in favour of one with greater continuity. Having chosen this type, however, he exaggerates the break at the cadence with the *ritardando* as if to isolate it, dramatizing the discontinuities in order to display as a virtue what was ordinarily an inconvenience that had to be covered up.

A modulation needs at least one note that is dissonant to the original key. In keeping with the stripped-down style of this movement, the dissonance is isolated, naked and quiet:

---

*Exactly the same huge downward leap of an octave and a seventh from E to F# is found in the principal theme of the finale of the Sonata in A major op. 2 no. 2.

The B♭s in both hands speak for themselves with great simplicity, a mysterious Neapolitan harmony to the subdominant transformed into A#, the leading tone of B minor. Similarly the closing theme (bar 67) repeats a dissonant G first in an inner voice with an *sfp* (bars 68 and 72) and then several times in the soprano (bars 69–70, 73–4, 75–6, 77–8): it takes this expressive G from the previous section, where it was also set in relief as a dissonance. It is first played with tremendous passion eleven times as the upper voice of a dominant minor ninth chord (bars 53–4), and then expressively sustained in bars 56, 59, 61, 63 and 65. The three final B minor chords of the exposition are laconic – *pianissimo* and short.

The rhythm of the three chords is instantly echoed by three sustained Bs. The development simply expands the first twelve bars of the opening theme over 50 bars. The first eight bars of the theme are engaged as the bass descends, juxtaposing the harmony of A minor, E flat major and minor, and the dominants successively of G major and C major. There is a halt on this last dominant, set in relief by bare descending and rising scales in the two hands. Then bars 9 to 12 of the principal theme appear first in the treble in C major, then in the tenor range in F major under a running arpeggio in the right hand, and finally in the bass in D minor, shifting at once to A minor. The motif of bar 11 is employed to build up the rising bass that has now become a trademark of Beethoven's technique, with accents on every second beat, mounting steadily from G# an octave and a third to B at the centre of the keyboard. B is the basic dominant, and normally Beethoven would sustain a dominant harmony to prepare the return of the tonic. He frustrates our expectations by a 6/4 tonic chord in one of his strangest passages.

From bar 130 to the return of theme at 144, Beethoven studiously avoids a dominant except by glancing gestures, passing tones in the melody. The underlying harmony of this passage is to be understood as a tonic chord throughout. (Since the B in the bass has never been resolved, one can hear this as an implied 6/4 tonic chord.) The return of the main theme and the tonic is paradoxically prepared by the tonic, as Beethoven had done many years before in the first movement of the Fourth Symphony. Here in the sonata the spare, indeed excessively lean, character of the movement achieves its extreme effect. Everything is reduced from *fortissimo* to *pianissimo*, to a two-voice canon, to the repetition of a single motif of five notes, and ultimately to the abridgement of five notes to three (a dogmatically simple scale descent (G F# E)), and even to the elimination of any rhythmic contour to the motif, which ends simply as three eighth notes. The canon itself has no contrapuntal interest, except, at one point (bars 140–1), to produce a forced dissonance of what are almost parallel seconds. (The most expressive moment comes when the composer directs a strictly unplayable swell on a sustained G to the F#.) On the contrary, the interest is focused almost entirely on the process of reduction, as the first three notes of the principal theme are gradually divested of all their intrinsic character until they become nothing more than a simple element of the tonality of E minor.

The recapitulation makes few changes to the exposition. The soft B♭s that were the agent of a modulation are replaced by a full major triad on F♮. Unison *pianissimo* octaves on B and E that introduced the dominant of C major in the exposition are replaced by G and C, perhaps a carry-over from the importance of C major in the development. The insistently reiterated dissonant G in the concluding theme, now of course a C, is given even greater emphasis, as Beethoven asks for an unrealizable crescendo and diminuendo on its final sustained appearance (bars 230–1). This introduces a drastic abridgement of the main theme (bar 232): the first four bars *pp* and *ritardando*. The sequence of those four bars is extended for two more, followed by a long pause. The eight-bar postscript to the theme closes the movement. This time the eight bars are *pianissimo*, and no *ritardando* is indicated. Perhaps none was intended or perhaps Beethoven assumed that the pianist would play one anyway. The last note is short and there is a fermata over the following pause.

E was an inconvenient tonality for Beethoven when he wrote this sonata, as the lowest note on his piano at the time was an F. Bar 214 clearly demands a low E that Beethoven could not yet write (he had the lower notes a year or so later), and there is no reason here except pedantry to withhold it.

The second and final movement is a rondo with the amiability of many Mozart finales and a much more up-to-date cantabile style. The direction is *Nicht zu geschwind und sehr singbar vorzutragen.** Its typical rondo theme repeats all its elements within itself: the first four-bar half-phrases differ only in their last two notes and by the fact that the second half-phrase is doubled at the higher octave. The second and third eight-bar phrases that follow are also identical, except for an octave doubling. Then the half-phrases 1 and 2 return, the second ornamented for two beats. Since the full melody is heard three and a half times (and there is even a further brief recall), some of the motifs become very familiar by the end. It is necessary for the theme to be extremely beautiful to support this.

As in another piece of fundamentally lyrical character, the first movement of

---

* For the tempo, see pp. 93–4.

op. 26, there is a frequent use of Beethoven's typical effect of *subito piano*: this can be found at the ends of the first three phrases (or phrases 1 and 2 and the repeat of 2), at bars 7, 15 and 23. It makes the *forte* at the end of the fourth phrase (the return of phrase 1) all the more telling. Beethoven insists upon transparency of texture in this piece, writing out all the rests after the short notes in the bass without using the conventional abbreviations, and emphasizes the lyricism as well: the return of the first phrase is marked "tenderly" (*teneramente*).

The first episode goes to the dominant. The second episode starts in the tonic minor, and then takes up in C major the 4-bar closing theme of the first episode, repeating it in C minor, C sharp minor, and C sharp major, which gives the section the air of a simple development. The complex harmonic excursion calls for an elaborate 10-bar dominant preparation of the return of the main theme. Then the first episode returns complete at the tonic: the end of it is the occasion for a long and mysterious contrapuntal development (bars 212–28). The main theme is now played with the melody at first in the left hand. It is almost fully presented, but at the repeat of its second phrase, it undergoes a considerable expansion of 24 bars leading back to the opening phrase. The last page is extraordinary in its manipulation of tempo, motif and expression:

The theme comes quickly to a full cadence (bar 283) as a long *ritardando* begins and the principal line goes from bass to tenor and alto, and then to soprano. A *crescendo* and *accelerando* begin together and continue over three and a half bars. With a *subito piano*, the original tempo returns for only a laconic 2½ beats. The last bar, *pianissimo*, is a variant and a diminution of the end of the first phrase, which was the subject of the development twenty bars before.

It is not clear to me whether the long *accelerando* after the long *ritardando* is intended simply to go back to the first tempo, or whether it should go slightly beyond, so that the *a tempo* pulls back to the opening pace. The *subito piano* following the *crescendo* at the beginning of the *a tempo* suggests that this moment is to be set in relief, in which case the second solution would be best, particularly if one expects a listener to be aware of exactly where the original tempo starts again. The first solution provides greater continuity, but is more difficult to make convincing. I do not think, however, that complete conviction was what Beethoven desired from his limited public for the effect of the last two bars. It would be enough if a listener could perceive both the poetry and the humour.

Played exactly as written, this ending would be a shock for modern audiences. The *a tempo* is so close to the end that there is no place for any slowing down, and so brief and so soft that it is difficult to grasp what is happening at a first hearing. Any *ritardando* at all, however, would be a vulgarization. The last note is very short. After the elaborate but delicate imagination of the last twenty-four bars, the final bar seems almost thrown away. For an intimate gathering, the effect would be subtle and exquisite, a touch of subdued humour in a lyrical context. Whether it works as it was conceived when it is performed in a large concert hall is another matter – but that is a question that Beethoven never had to ask himself.

SONATA IN A MAJOR, OPUS 101
COMPOSED IN 1816

Written at the same time as the two cello sonatas op. 102, this sonata resembles them in several ways, particularly the first in C major. Both op. 101 and op. 102 no. 1 have four movements, played *attacca*: the first a lyrical piece in 6/8; the second, a march in dotted rhythms; the third, an *Adagio* introduction to the finale with expressively ornamental lines, leading directly into a surprising recall of the opening bars of the first movement, and ending with a trill; the fourth, a vigorous *Allegro* in 2/4 of jocular character. The similarities are so striking, the form so eccentric, that it would seem as if Beethoven considered the structure an experimental one that he wanted to essay with two different kinds of material. I do not know of another example in his work of such a double trial.

The piano sonata begins not by establishing the tonic A major, but in the middle of the process of moving from A to the dominant, E major. A major is,

in fact, clearly established but by inference and largely by glances to the side. E
major, however, is well in place by bar 7. The tempo is *Etwas lebhaft und mit der
innigsten Empfindung* ("somewhat lively and with the most intimate sentiment"):
this is translated by Beethoven into Italian simply as *Allegretto ma non troppo*. The
long unbroken melodic line is not articulated into different themes; the few
motifs which have a semi-independent identity blend into the line, even at bar
16 where the melody moves to the tenor and back to the soprano. In bars 14, 16,
17 and 18, Beethoven's phrasing is very subtle:

The slurs over two notes in these bars do not mean that the second note is to be
detached from the third or in any way cut short: they indicate the most delicate
accents on the first note and a slight weight to the third note outside the slur.
This is confirmed by the three-note slur placed over the two-note slurs: it signifies a legato over all three notes, but the dot over the third note means that it is
to be slightly detached and, above all, lightly emphasized. In bars 19 and 21, the
melody is divided between tenor and soprano, and it must sound like two voices
and like one voice at the same time. An 8-bar concluding theme separates itself
from the basic texture, ending with syncopated chords on the third and sixth
beats of 6/8, which continue into the development.

This syncopated rhythm dominates three-quarters of the development, changing from tied notes on the weak beats to *sforzandi* at bar 47. The relative minor,
placed so often towards the end of a development, arrives very early and controls
the harmonic progress of the development. The return to the main theme and
the tonic major is achieved seamlessly through the other conventional harmony
of the classical development, the tonic minor. The fermata that arrived in the
exposition (bar 6) just before the dominant was completely confirmed is dis-
placed to the end of the development (bar 52) on a dominant of C sharp minor
(V of iii). The harmony of the dominant, E major, is only a step away from this.

The main theme is stated at the higher octave in the tonic minor (bars 55–6),
overlapping with an ascending line in the bass over an octave from E to E (bars

56–7), and the recapitulation starts, still in the higher octave with the first two bars of the main theme, omits bars 3 to 7 and moves without a pause down an octave to bar 8. The rest of the exposition returns without abridgement. The octave ascent in the bass sets the point of recapitulation in relief without any break in the texture or any disturbance of the sustained lyricism of the melody. This lyricism is emphasized (in bar 9 of the exposition and its later equivalent, bar 61) by a dynamic indication rare in Beethoven, *mezzo forte*, which almost always means a cantabile melody set strongly against a softer background in the accompanying voices.

The coda, like the development, continues the syncopated chords of the concluding theme, bringing them to a *fortissimo* climax with a thick texture of nine-note chords. After a sustained final chord, this climax does not so much return to, as dissolve into, the softer lyric mode; the syncopated chords are brought back, but now only one to a bar with a vibrant, pedalled sonority separated by pauses. A long *ritardando* of five bars brings both hands from the centre of the keyboard to the extremities.

The march follows at once (*Lebhaft. Marschmässig – Vivace alla Marcia*). The opening section is straightforward: 8 bars going from tonic to dominant, repeated. However, the repeat is followed by a 3-bar coda reiterating the preceding dominant cadence on the tonic. In the basic dance form, or minuet form, the first strain could end traditionally either on the dominant or the tonic without making much difference to the general conception of the form:* Beethoven was determined here to have it both ways. The second strain goes from the relative minor, D minor, starting with a crash on its dominant, to the tonic minor – standard procedure for preparing the return of the first strain in the tonic major. This is enlarged by Beethoven. He arrives at F minor somewhat deviously, as it is implied at bar 25, but he ends with a D♭ in the bass and pauses on it by tying it over to the next bar. This is the first break in the rhythm, the first bar that has no attack on its first beat, and it has a disquieting effect. F minor is confirmed in bars 28 and 29.

At this point, Beethoven interpolates four bars into the basic structure, returning to, and exploiting, the bass D♭. The passage is *piano, sempre ligato*, and with an unchanging pedal sustaining the low D♭; the end is *pianissimo*, and leads to a sustained dominant in the bass that lasts eight bars and prepares the return to F major. The long pedal gives a rich sonority to the D♭ interpolation. The return actually begins while still on the dominant (bar 40) with a contrapuntal stretto in three voices. A more settled F major arrives as a sudden *piano dolce* after a *fortissimo*. The first bars of the march do not return, but related motifs are substituted which act as cadences, and the original close of the first strain is used to conclude.

---

* See my *Sonata Forms*, pp. 112–14.

Beethoven put a repeat sign at the opening of the canonic trio, but forgot to enter the return sign at the end of bar 65. He should also have written a second ending with an E♮ instead of an F as the last note in the left hand (the F makes sense only to return to the opening of the trio). He writes the direction *dolce* three times, perhaps because the trio is one of his most extraordinary demonstrations of how to make something gracefully delicate out of contrapuntal combinations and motifs that almost anyone else would have considered intolerably awkward. This would later become an inspiration to Brahms, who, however, was rarely able to accomplish it with Beethoven's simplicity. Bars 65 to 72, in particular, are presented with the direction *dolce* repeated, as if to say that these arabesques that may seem angular and odd will be exquisite if they are played with sensitivity. There is a 10-bar dominant preparation of the return to the march with increasing excitement.

The slow movement is not an independent work, but one of the short introductions to a finale we first found in op. 53. It is marked *Langsam und Sehnsuchtsvoll* ("Slow and full of yearning"), translated by Beethoven as *Adagio ma non troppo con affetto*. It is to be played with the soft pedal held down throughout. Combining baroque ornamentation with the hymn-like texture for a slow movement that Beethoven had developed very early in his career from models by Haydn, this introduction clearly resulted from his study of Bach: in fact, bars 14 to 16 suggest an acquaintance with the *Chromatic Fantasy and Fugue*. The opening (a) is similar to the second theme of the slow movement of the Sonata for cello and piano op. 102 no. 2 (b), written at the same time:

a)

b)

Almost no pianist today is willing to follow Beethoven's directions for pedal in bars 9 to 16. He asks for it only on the last eighth notes of bars 14 to 16. We all want, however, to sustain the bass in all these bars and the preceding ones. It is evident that Beethoven thought the final chords of bars 14 to 16 need individual consideration. If we think it necessary to revise his pedal for the modern concert hall, these final chords should be singled out for a special sonority. It is even possible, however, to follow his directions for pedal literally, and to set the bass notes in relief by touch and by *rubato*: the grace notes must be played on the beat together with the right hand. It is interesting that when Beethoven is most influenced by Bach, he is apt to sound like Chopin.

A fermata *subito piano* on the dominant introduces a cadenza that starts slowly, quickens slightly and arpeggiates into the opening theme of the first movement. Marked *dolce* at first, this theme returns in fragments, like a memory difficult to recall with confidence. The technique was first worked out by Beethoven in the finale of the Sonata in G major op. 31 no. 1, where the main theme returns at the end, punctuated by pauses, and with some of the phrases at a very slow tempo. The technique reconstructs the effort of recalling something from the past. In op. 31 no. 1, the intention is partly humorous, in op. 101, purely poetic. Only the first four bars return. The concluding motif of the fourth bar is worked into a rising sequence *stringendo* to a *forte* on a dominant seventh chord, and a scale that sweeps down an octave as fast as possible (thirty-second notes *presto*) and diminishes to *piano*. As in the cello sonata op. 102 no. 1, after the brief return of the first movement, a trill on the dominant introduces the finale.

The main theme of the finale is designed so that it can be used for a fugue in the development, and is presented at once with imitation in the left hand. The counterstatement reverses this for a display of double counterpoint at the octave. The movement is an elaborate sonata form, and is not only a jocular piece but even bucolic, with yodel motifs in bars 44 to 48. The model is Mozartean, with a long opening section of the exposition in the tonic – more than forty bars, in fact. As in Mozart, there is a profusion of themes; the main theme itself is composed of two strongly contrasting elements: a boisterous two-bar motto, *forte*; and a softer running passage with a syncopated accompaniment; the rustic yodel motif follows; and then a final tonic theme with a sustained soprano line.*

---

* It seems to me there is a confusion in most editions, including the first. The four times repeated A in the upper voice in bars 66 , 67, 70 and 71 are quarter notes in the autograph, but eighth notes in the first edition in bars 66, 67 and 70 but not in bar 71. A long slur starts in bars 67 and 71. I think that Beethoven altered the A in bars 66 and 70 to eighth notes to distinguish them from the following notes which begin a long legato (six bars beginning in bar 71, but three bars from 67). It is, in fact, more graceful to release the notes in bars 66 and 70 to allow a greater cantabile to the following bars. The engraver made the mistake of altering bar 67 to an eighth note as well (this makes no sense since it is at the beginning of a slur), but the changes to 66 and 70 are correct. The corresponding place in the recapitulation should follow the same pattern (the engraver made only one correction there instead of two, just as he had made three instead of two in the exposition).

The move to the dominant is leisurely: five bars on V7 of V (bars 79 to 83) are enough, and the fact that they are all *forte* helps. A new theme, *dolce* and *piano*, leads to a half cadence on V of V, followed by an extraordinary effect of tone colour:

A *pianissimo* horn call with the pedal held throughout creates a blurred effect of a sonority at a distance, and there is a *secco* return of the jocular style. These are all pastoral matters.

As in Mozart, there are three concluding themes, the first one derived from the opening theme, the second an expansion of the first, and the third a staccato cadence ending *pianissimo*. The exposition is repeated, and then an eight-bar transition (Tovey correctly remarked on its Mozartean character[6]) leads to the fugue. First, it is necessary to change to the minor mode; an arpeggio on a tonic minor 6/4 dispatches this quickly. The first two notes of the fugue are played in octaves in both hands *fortissimo*, but the fugue starts *pianissimo* in the bass.

The fugue theme is distinguished by trills with comic afterbeats that often lead nowhere, generally followed by a rest. Afterbeats of a trill ought to resolve. Afterbeats that lead only to empty space not only do not resolve; they increase the tension with an effect of wit. This deforms the nature of the afterbeat: instead of being a conventional element of a cadence, it is now, isolated, a motif. Beethoven invents new meanings for the basic building blocks of the tonal system of his time.

The first answer in the fugue is not at the usual dominant but at the relative major, the third at the subdominant, and the fourth returns to the tonic. The fugue is Handelian in style with the character of a typical Beethoven development section. Fugal finales in string quartets had been written by Haydn and Gassmann to ennoble the genre; Mozart tried his hand at it, and Beethoven had followed them with op. 59 no. 3, but this is his first attempt at a fugal finale in a piano sonata, and it was not to be his last. Somewhat cautiously he incorporates the fugue as a development section (he was more daring in the contemporary Sonata for cello and piano in D major op. 102 no. 2, where it is the whole movement). The fugue does not stray far from the tonic minor. Opus 101 is the first sonata for which Beethoven had a piano with a low E, and he worked out an enormous climax on it at the end of the fugue, in which the limit of his instrument's capacity for volume of sound was tested.

The recapitulation abridges the tonic section of the exposition somewhat, and reserves the charming yodel theme for use in the coda. In place of the original counterstatement, the motto theme is presented softly for the first time, the melody deep in the bass with a new counterpoint in soprano and alto (bar 240): this is marked not only *dolce*, but also *poco espressivo* – that is, with a slight relaxation of the basic tempo. The last theme of the original tonic section is transposed to the subdominant. The "second group" is presented almost unchanged in the tonic.

The last bar of the recapitulation proper provides the stimulus for the coda and is echoed four times in the bass with a new motif in the right hand derived largely from the motto; this passage ends mysteriously with a fermata on the dominant of the subdominant, followed by the first two notes of the fugue in D major, *fortissimo* in octaves exactly as at the beginning of the development, except that the motif is now in the major mode. After a pause of two bars, this is softly corrected into the minor at a lower octave. Beethoven threatens to start the fugue all over again at the subdominant, and actually begins it two bars later. When the second voice enters after two bars to make parallel tenths with the bass, we realize that it was only a joke. The yodel theme returns, with the melody tossed back and forth from soprano to tenor, and then decorated with trills. The running theme (bars 9 to 12 of the *Allegro*) is developed with some flashy effects of crossing hands. Over a soft measured trill deep in the bass, a new variant of the opening theme is played, diminishing to *pianissimo*, and slowing down for the last four bars. Three final bars, *a tempo*, close the work *fortissimo*.

Sonata in B flat major, opus 106
Composed by 1818

This work has somewhat suffered from its reputation. Even the name of "Hammerklavier", which could just as easily have been given to op. 101, portrays it as massive. It has come to seem more like a monument to be admired than a work to be enjoyed. Some of the distress caused by Beethoven's metronome marks (the only one of his sonatas to be given them) is due to the unnatural reverence accorded the work.

The metronome marks are given at the beginning of a letter of 16 April 1819 to Ferdinand Ries,[7] who was correcting the page proofs for the original edition in London:

> Here, dear Ries ! Are the tempi of the sonata.
> First movement Allegro, but only Allegro; you must remove the Assai.
> Maelzel's metronome [half-note] = 138

The marks for the other movements follow.

We should observe first the change from *Allegro assai* or *Assai Allegro* to plain *Allegro*. Arguments go on about whether the qualifications made the tempo faster or slower. I should think that *Allegro assai* is probably faster, while *Assai Allegro* would tend to be slower, but there is no way of deciding these matters with certainty.

What is significant, however, is Beethoven's decision in favour of one of the *tempi ordinarii,* a standard tempo. This casts light on the nature of the piece. It was not Beethoven's intention here to assert the prerogative of genius and assign an individual tempo to this movement. And 138 would be more or less a normal Allegro of a work by Mozart, the kind of tempo that Beethoven would have accepted as standard in the 1780s. Of course, the texture of this work by Beethoven is more complex than most Mozart Allegros, and harder to play, but this is not a consideration that would have carried much weight with the composer.

Metronome marks are not sacred, and composers sometimes misjudge them, but there is no doubt that Beethoven wanted a fast tempo for this movement. Suggestions for revising 138 have ranged from Felix Weingartner's insanely slow 80 and Moscheles's 116, more reasonable but somewhat sedate, to Paul Badura-Skoda's proposed reduction of 10–15 per cent,[8] which would come out as 120 to 126.

If one considers that this movement has a much lighter character when played on one of Beethoven's instruments, 138 will not appear so unreasonable for many pages of it; it seems to me ideal for bars 39 to 63, for example. The fugato in the development section (bars 138ff.) becomes stodgy at too slow a tempo and benefits from at least 126 or faster. One must remember Beethoven's injunction as well that the metronome mark was only valid for the first bars since one cannot put a measure to sentiment.* In any case, I think we ought to abandon the view of this work as a kind of musical mammoth, or a construction comparable to the larger pyramids. High-minded pianists consider the very fast tempo vulgar, but that is not the criterion most relevant to Beethoven interpretation, much of which tends to suffer from excessive nobility. There is no reason to think that the first movement is majestic; that would go against the grain of most of it. It is not a commemorative work. More than anything else, it is an explosion of energy.

During the years following 1812, Beethoven struggled with various formal problems, creating forms that were either experimental, like *An die ferne Geliebte,* the two cello sonatas op. 102, and the piano sonata op. 101, or exercises in antique style, like the Overture *Die Weihe des Hauses.* The new sonata was an exercise in will power, his first four-movement piano sonata since op. 31 no. 3 – but it compares less easily with that lyrical work than with earlier ambitious sonatas in four movements like op. 2 no. 3 or op. 10 no. 3. In many respects, it marks a radical change in his style, but the price of that change was oddly an abandon of the experimental principles of the most recent works like op. 101 and

* See p. 45.

the song cycle. In many respects it is considerably less eccentric, more conventional, than the preceding sonatas. It appears more radical to us because of the
way Beethoven ruthlessly bends the tradition to his will. It was accomplished
partly by a return to earlier works, to those of Haydn and Mozart, or his own
Sonata in B flat major op. 22, and by an unprecedented expansion of the past
beyond anything imaginable before, a synthesis of his whole musical experience
with the innovations he had made over three decades.

I have pointed out elsewhere* that one of the most astonishing moments of the
opening *Allegro* from a formal point of view is the swift change to B major
towards the end of the development after setting up the completely conventional
D major half cadence on V of vi (the dominant of the relative minor), and that
is the same structure used by Haydn at the end of the development of his late and
most famous Sonata in E flat major, where he follows a massive half cadence on
a G major dominant of C minor with a shift to E major. That the
"Hammerklavier" does not sound in the least like Haydn is very much to the
point: I am not suggesting that Beethoven was attempting in any way to revive
an old-fashioned style. What he did was to reexamine and transform the principles by which he had been working throughout his whole career, including those
of the earliest years. A concomitant aspect of this project was his attempt to
rethink the principles of counterpoint that he had learned from Bach and Haydn
(and Fuchs – and later, Handel), and create a new form of counterpoint out of
the reconsideration. The introduction to the "Hammerklavier" fugue states this
clearly enough, and the fugue demonstrates it. The fugue may sound modern to
our ears, but it includes almost every traditional academic device of fugue: augmentation, cancrizans, inversion, combination with a second theme, *stretto* with
the original form of the theme and its inversion played together. The sonata was
not conceived as a classical monument or an act of piety, but as an act of violence that sought paradoxically to reconquer a tradition in a time of revolution by
making it radically new.

The opening is a set of expansions. The space from the lowest to the highest
region of keyboard is defined by a staccato and *fortissimo* fanfare with pedal as a
B flat triad, first an expanded third or seventeenth, and then an expanded fifth or
nineteenth from B♭ to F. The interval of a fifth from B♭ to F is lyrically redefined,
legato and *piano*, as an ascending scale within a smaller range, the spaces within
the triad filled in, so to speak, with the motif of the third still emphasized: essentially bars 5 to 8 repeat the opening fanfare, transforming it into an expressive
melody. The new lyrical form then expands the fifth to an octave (bars 9 to 17)
by an ascending scale, although the scale pauses insistently on F for four bars (11
to 15), to acknowledge the relation of the passage to the previous version at the
lower octave; the numerous articulations in the right hand are offset by the long

---

* *The Classical Style*, new ed., 1997. pp. 484–7.

7-bar slur in the left, which unifies the four-octave descent from F to F into the lowest region of the bass and synthesizes the whole phrase. The octave from B♭ to B♭ is defined once again (bars 17 to 27) as a scale progression, but more massively, with the motif of the third still in evidence:

The process is closed with classical integrity by a half cadence on the dominant.

The opening four bars are repeated, defining only the interval of the tenth from B♭ to D, and the last chord is changed to D major. This initiates a pedal on D of 24 bars (39–63), a dominant preparation of G major. We know we are in G major after only a few bars, but full confirmation or resolution is withheld until bar 63 with a new theme made up entirely of descending thirds or their complements, rising sixths.* The relation of B flat major to its submediant G major implies a clash between B♭ and B♮, and the rest of the work exploits that on a large scale. At the end of the exposition, Beethoven's method of modulating from G major back to B flat major is simply to play a B♭ *fortissimo*, to extend it with a third, B♭ and D, and then to start again with the *fortissimo* B♭ triad that opens the exposition. He knew that simple power, loud dynamics and repetition could replace more conventional arguments.

The fugal development (bars 138ff.), down a third to E flat major, concentrates single-mindedly on the structure of descending thirds. Larger harmonic areas are defined by slowing down the descending thirds from one or two to a bar down to one every two or four bars (bars 177ff.): B/G, E♭/C/A♭, F/D/B♭, G/E♭/C, A/F#/D. Reaching D in the bass, Beethoven arrests it there for 10 bars. It is evident that this is a dominant, not a tonic. The B major that follows is a lyrical interpolation: it interrupts the old and even outdated convention of going from V of vi (the dominant of G minor) back to the tonic, but it is an interpolation motivated by the clash between B♭ and B♮.

The classical recapitulation is governed by two principles: reducing the tension through a reference, however brief, to the subdominant area, and a playing at the tonic of important material from the exposition originally presented outside the tonic area. Using the submediant G major in the exposition instead of the dominant F major necessarily changes how these principles are to be applied; and the structure of the succeeding development section will also have its influence. The proper subdominant, E flat major, would not have enough power related to the course of events so far, but the subdominant or flat area represented by G flat major/F sharp major is exceedingly relevant to the prominence given B major. Accordingly, Beethoven goes through E flat major to E flat minor (bars 237 to 239), and then logically and decisively to G flat major for a long passage (bars 241 to 266) that transforms and replaces bars 11 to 34 of the exposition. This brings us to the point of greatest tension: the explosion of the opening theme on B minor, defused immediately through the descent by thirds in the bass to F, a dominant pedal, and the return of B flat major. In the original edition, the pedal on this explosion is sustained through the rest with a fermata that follows. This is often supposed to be a misprint, but I see no reason to accept an unnecessary assumption that this very extraordinary moment must be absolutely symmetrical with the earlier and less astonishing appearances of the theme.

The extensive coda brings a closing theme of the exposition back over a measured trill on C♭ and B♭ in the alto, and then over an unmeasured trill on B♭ and C♮ in a style approaching a cadenza. A final section overlays a measured trill on G♭ and F with fragments of the opening theme in sharp contrasts of *piano* and

---

* For a detailed account of the structure of descending thirds in op. 106, and of the clash between B♮ and B♭, see my *The Classical Style*, new ed., 1997, pp. 409–33.

forte, dying away to *ppp*, and then a brief *fortissimo* for a single chord and an octave unison.

The Scherzo, *Molto vivace*, is in a completely orthodox three-phrase minuet form, less eccentric than any minuet or scherzo in the sonatas until now. The only odd aspect is that the first phrase, ending on the dominant, is seven bars long (it could be described as a standard eight-bar phrase with the seventh bar missing). The repeat of the first phrase is written out an octave higher. The second and third phrases have together the more conventional length of 16 bars: to be more precise, the second phrase is eight bars long, and then the seven-bar third phrase starts with an empty bar at the opening, which evens it out to eight. The third phrase in this way corrects the eccentricity of the first. The repeated phrases 2 and 3 together are also written out an octave higher except for one bar which is transposed down.* The opening theme is a light-hearted, humorous parody of the main theme of the first movement (it clearly echoes the last page of the first movement), and descends in thirds like the second theme in G major. The clash between B♭ and B♮ is cleverly exploited throughout the second and third phrases.

The trio is in B flat minor, marked *semplice*. It is an ostentatiously simple binary form. Like the main theme of the first movement, the first phrase outlines the tonic triad. It ends in the relative major, and is repeated with the melody transferred to the left hand, and the right now following at the distance of a bar in canonic imitation. The second phrase begins by outlining the triad of the relative major, and ends back in the tonic minor. The repeat is rewritten in similar fashion. Each phrase begins and ends with an octave played twice, a motif heard at the end of the scherzo proper, a motto that will provide the material for a strange coda. The trio is characterized by a soft, rich, heavily pedalled sonority that contrasts with the drier scherzo.

The trio is completed at once by a second trio, *Presto*, a standard three-phrase form without repeats. The first phrase, in unharmonized detached notes, ends on the dominant minor. The second phrase largely repeats the first at the dominant, ends on the tonic, and places the melody in the left hand with an offbeat detached accompaniment in the right. The third phrase repeats the first back at the tonic, now harmonized and with broken octaves in the bass, and ends with a half cadence on F, the dominant. An F major scale, *prestissimo*, sweeps from bottom to top of the keyboard, followed by a three-beat measured tremolo on a dominant minor ninth, Beethoven's favourite chord for preparing a return (see op. 31 no. 1, op. 57, op. 53 (finale), etc.).

The scherzo, now marked *dolce*, returns with few changes except some octave transpositions, and, starting at the repeat of the first phrase, an extra note of rhythmic agitation added in a subsidiary voice, either alto or bass. The coda alternates the motif of a detached, unharmonized repeated octave, played first on a

---

* For consideration of the pedal indications in this part of the scherzo, see pp. 108–10.

B♭, then on a B♮, compressing into a small space with considerable violence the opposition of these two notes that was already laid out in the first movement:

With a *ritardando*, the opening motif of the scherzo is altered by an F# to suggest B minor in place of B flat major and diminishes to *pianissimo*. A sudden furious *Presto* plays the B♮ fifteen times rising to *fortissimo*, switching to B♭ at the last minute. The opening motif of the scherzo played three times rounds off the form ironically.

The first movement's profound opposition of B♭ and B♮ is extravagantly reworked on the surface as an ironic, even sardonic, comedy by the scherzo. For the irony to be apparent, it is important that the scherzo and the two trios all follow rigidly conventional eighteenth-century patterns. Beethoven's attempt to unify all the movements of a sonata, developed with great force starting with opus 27 and, above all, the "Appassionata", attains a new power with the "Hammerklavier", which will be applied with equal cogency to the last three sonatas.

The first bar of the *Adagio sostenuto*, which makes the opening conform to the initial motifs of the first and second movements, was added in proof by Beethoven: the two notes, A and C#, also sketch a modulation from B flat major to F sharp minor. The indication at the beginning is *Appassionato e con molto sentimento*, and this certainly applies to the entire movement. Underneath, between the staves, however, is the further direction *Una corda mezza voce*, which suggests that the full outpouring of sentiment is to be partially repressed on this opening page until the soft pedal is raised and *con grand' espressione* is directed 27 bars later. *Mezza voce* for Beethoven generally indicates a reserved and introvert tone (see the slow movement of the Sonata for Cello and piano in D major op. 102 no. 2, or the theme of the finale of op. 109). The metronome mark of ♪ = 92 has often seemed too fast for the movement, but if the sonority of the first page is held down, it is not so constraining. The next section demands the contrast of a more relaxed and free tempo, and it should not be spoiled by too expansive an opening page. I believe it is worth sacrificing some extrovert expression at the beginning in order to allow the succeeding cantilena its full power. It must be remembered that Beethoven's direction of *una corda* was capable of literal realization on one string on his instrument, while the modern piano has become so clumsy as to be unable to reduce to less than two. The sonority he had in mind for the first page was decidedly muffled and would be, indeed, ineffective in a large hall, but in its half-whispered sonority it must have been very moving for a small gathering. The intended performance of op. 106 was for a very intimate public. This may seem a curious paradox when one considers the spectacular brilliance of the opening and closing movements. Clearly, we must extend Schnabel's observation that a Beethoven sonata is greater than any of its interpretations: it also transcends any venue, any form of presentation, private, public or recorded.

The opening page of the slow movement ends with a firm cadence on the tonic from which the final chord has been withdrawn. Except for the dramatic elimination of the ultimate resolution, this falls within a late eighteenth-century tradition to which Beethoven remained faithful even late in life: the slow movement, unlike the opening movement, must have a melody complete in itself with a pause before going on to other matters. What follows, with the soft pedal raised, is a page of the greatest passion, expressed almost entirely through elaborate ornamentation over a detached accompaniment. The style of the decoration is fundamentally operatic, but the sonata offered Beethoven an intimacy that the public stage could not accommodate, and he achieved here an intensity greater than any operatic composer has ever imagined. The movement is a sonata form without repeats: the exposition descends a major third to D major.

Like the development of the first movement, the development section here descends through a long chain of thirds, alternating a full sonority with passages of *una corda*, and ending in the bass on the dominant C#, upon which Beethoven builds a dominant minor ninth chord. At the return, the main theme is no longer muffled but sings with the full resonance of the instrument, and also with a complex decoration. The style of the decoration at this place is not even remotely operatic, but derived from the variation technique of Haydn: a steady figuration that constantly changes pattern, responsive to the contour of the underlying melody. (Habitually, Beethoven's variation technique follows Mozart, for whom the figurative patterns of each variation generally remain relatively constant. This is the pattern that Beethoven uses in, for example, op. 111. He employs the technique found here in the "Hammerklavier" for the final variation in the slow movement of the Ninth Symphony.) The suppleness of this variation on the main theme and its pathos have won the admiration of composers: Brahms attempted a freely interpreted quotation in the slow movement of his First Piano Concerto. After a very long *ritardando*, the return of the more operatic ornamentation (bar 113) is given an even greater pathos by starting in the major (D major), and only later moving to the subdominant B minor (bar 118, *con grand' espressione*) before turning to the tonic major.

The coda uses the pathetic harmony of the Neapolitan, and rises to an expansive orchestral climax with a diminished seventh on B#. At the highest point, Beethoven uses the device called *Bebung*: repeating a note with a strong accent on a weak beat and the second playing on the strong beat a distant echo, a syncopated vocal effect like a sob. The tremendous sonority of this climax is followed immediately and with no pause by a drop into *una corda* – evidently a *subito pianissimo*, in which we hear the main theme once more with a long, exhausted *ritardando*. There is a brief recall of the texture of the second section *con grand' espressione*, a two-bar motif repeated with a decoration of extreme passion. Over a low bass figuration, rising F sharp major chords are played more and more softly with a slow rhythm of 5, 3, 3, 2, and 4 in eighth notes; the rhythmic pattern underneath is 6, 7 and 5: almost all sense of a basic beat is annulled. With the soft pedal down again, the first two bars of the main theme are heard one last time. A minor plagal cadence on F sharp major ends the movement: the soft pedal is raised for the final chord (this suggests that the finale should start without pause), but the dynamic is *ppp*.

The introduction to the finale may be called The Birth of Counterpoint, or The Creation of a Fugue. A sketch for this page in Princeton shows that Beethoven started by arpeggiating an F from the lowest part of the keyboard to the highest. On the next page, written large, the same arpeggio is applied to an A. These arpeggios will become the initial notes of the fugue theme.

The space between the F and the A is filled with a search while the bass, hesitantly accompanied by syncopated chords in the right hand, descends in thirds. First, F D♭ B♭ G♭. (The tempo is *Largo*, and must be played in relatively strict time, but there are no bar lines, and it is written to sound like an unmeasured improvisation.) This brings an extremely simple and slow three-voice imitative passage, an incipient but as yet inchoate fugue. The bass descends again: G♭ E♭ B♮. *Un poco più vivace*, we now have a slightly more brilliant two-voice imitative counterpoint. The hesitating descent begins once more: B G#. In G sharp minor the contrapuntal style of the early eighteenth century makes its appearance: a pastiche of a Bach fugue with an answer at the subdominant (the sketches for this movement show that Beethoven jotted down fragments of the *Well-Tempered Clavier,* perhaps to remind himself of the style); a third and fourth playing of the fugal motif very freely interpreted brings us to a four-voice texture. The first two interludes that had interrupted the descent in thirds died away gracefully, but this one rises to *forte* and breaks off brutally, as if to say *"Nicht diese Töne!"* The style of Bach is rejected: if there is to be counterpoint, it must be made new.

After a silence, the search and the descent recommence: G# E C# A. Like the F, all of the As on the piano are now sounded, and the sonority sustained while the dominant seventh of A major descends into the lower register ending with a trill on an E. Still very slow at the start, the descending thirds and the hesitating rhythm accelerate with increasing energy and excitement: A F# D B G E C A F D. (The sketch in Princeton shows that Beethoven intended the descent in thirds to go further, but he cuts it short to return to the A.) A final descent of a fourth brings us to *Prestissimo* and, once again, *fortissimo* back to A, with a full A major chord played five times in the right hand, seven times in the left. The chord is quickly eliminated, leaving only a repeating A in octaves, the tempo slows down, the dynamics descend to *pianissimo,* and the initial F is placed under the A, generating the theme of the fugue, which opens with a leap of a tenth, recalling the opening of the first movement.

The form of the fugue combines the rondo with a set of variations, both of these traditional forms for a finale. Each new variant of the theme descends a third, resembling in this the experimental Variations for piano on an original theme in F major op. 34.* The only exception to this scheme is an early presentation of the fugue theme starting on different beats. At bar 42 the theme begins not on the first beat but the third; at bar 55 it begins on the second beat. Both versions make for a curious alteration of accent. This first of these sections is in D flat major, the following one goes to its dominant, A flat.

An interlude based on an arpeggiated leap of a tenth is in G flat major. The augmentation of the theme is down a third to E flat minor. From a powerful climax on the lowest note of the contemporary piano, C, the bass rises as if each note were a dominant of the next (C F B♭ E♭) in a passage with trills of extraordinary ferocity, and finishes on A♭, where the interlude originally in G♭ is developed. (Beethoven did not have a low B♭ on his keyboard, and most editors add it in bars 104 and 105. The climax bar 106–7, however, is on the low C, and playing a whole step beneath it just before devalues its power and spoils the whole passage.)

The cancrizans, or retrograde, is in B minor with a new *cantabile* theme as a

---

* For a more detailed examination of the thirds structure of the fugue, see my *The Classical Style,* new ed., 1997, pp. 430–3.

countersubject. In this section, Beethoven tries for a strong opposition of touch.* The inversion goes down a third to G major and then to E flat major. A whirlwind of falling and rising tenths (bars 233–6) ends on an A major chord, the dominant of D minor, making the final drop of a third back to the tonic B flat possible. The *fortissimo* pause on A major recalls the similar climax at the end of the introduction to the fugue that just preceded the return to the tonic. Here the return is briefly suspended in a lyrical inspiration.

A new theme with a structure of descending thirds is in D major with the *una corda* throughout, *sempre dolce* and *cantabile*. The modulation back to the tonic (bars 267–70) is one of Beethoven's most magical inspirations. The new theme and fragments of the main theme are combined in the tonic in a transitional passage. The inversion and the original form are played in a traditional *stretto* at a distance of one beat, first at the dominant and then at the tonic. The quarter note D in all modern editions in the right hand of bar 287 is a C in the original. There is no reason to change it. The C is correct. Beethoven deforms the theme throughout this section to get the correct harmonies, and the dominant chord of F A C is what is wanted at this point.

The theme is fragmented continuously in a free fantasy of increasing agitation. Original form and inversion are played, not in *stretto*, but simultaneously in bar 335. A double pedal on both tonic and dominant underlies a playing of the theme on the Neapolitan C flat before a *Poco Adagio*, all of this with the improvisatory quality of a cadenza. At the end, the first four notes of the theme are played as if in 4/4 time, and even finally in 5/4. Beethoven has written out the *ritardando*, and the pianist need only play in strict time to achieve a slowing down that retains an extraordinary energy.

It has sometimes been claimed that Beethoven wished to change the order of the movements of the "Hammerklavier". That is based upon a letter to Ries of 20 March 1819, but a sensible reading will give a different interpretation:

> Should the sonata not be suitable for London, I could send another one; or you could also omit the Largo and begin straight away with the Fugue ... or you could use the first movement and then the Adagio, and then for the third movement the Scherzo – and omit entirely no. 4 with the Largo and Allegro risoluto. Or you could take just the first movement and the Scherzo and let them form the whole sonata. I leave it to you to do as you think best.... The sonata ought certainly to be published in London as soon as possible, for the Viennese publisher has really been kept waiting too long.[9]

It is evident that, since the sonata was to be printed properly soon in Vienna, Beethoven did not much care what the English thought about it, as long as they printed it without delay and he got his payment. The proposals to Ries have no musical interest; they concern only Beethoven's financial dealings.

* See pp. 35–6.

The Last Sonatas

At the end of his life, Beethoven declared that he found composition for the piano too limiting. The last three sonatas are his farewell to the genre.

The exceptionally long period of gestation of the "Hammerklavier", far from discouraging Beethoven, released the force of his creativity. He went to work on large projects; the *Missa Solemnis*, the Ninth Symphony, the Diabelli Variations, the last three sonatas. With the "Hammerklavier", he had, so to speak, abandoned the experimental forms of the last two cello sonatas and of the Sonata for piano op. 101: op. 106 is closer to the models of his early years, transformed and made almost unrecognizable by the will to create something new out of the old experience. The last sonatas are more radical, however, as if the writing of op. 106 had given Beethoven a new confidence. The experimental works of the preceding years shared some of the ideals of Beethoven's younger contemporaries; they were close to the music of the next generation, above all the works of Schumann and Mendelssohn. The increase in Beethoven's deafness made him withdraw into himself in greater isolation. The last piano sonatas needed a much longer time to enter into the mainstream of musical influence. Even the last quartets were easier for later composers to assimilate.

For all the consternation that the works of the middle period had aroused in critics and musicians, the Sonatas of op. 31, and the "Waldstein" and "Appassionata", revealed themselves fairly quickly to be respectable concert pieces. It took almost a century for the last sonatas to reach the same status with the public. They are deeply serious works, but they do not seem to have, at first hearing, the forthright moral earnestness of the sonatas from the "Pathétique" to "Les Adieux", largely because they make few concessions to the listener. Understanding them, taking pleasure in hearing them, requires an active participation from the listener never demanded before from the piano sonata. They have understandably inspired a good deal of pretentious interpretation in both writing and performance. This was inevitable: the composer clearly intended these works as exemplars of great spiritual experience. It is less evident that Beethoven's idea of transcendence is the same as ours.

SONATA IN E MAJOR, OPUS 109
COMPOSED IN 1820

The first movement, *Vivace ma non troppo. Sempre legato*, is remarkably compressed. To establish the tonic, to state the first theme, and to modulate to the dominant – all this takes approximately seven seconds. If we compare this with the leisurely and expansive first group of the finale of the Sonata in C minor op. 111, we have some idea of the range of Beethoven's sonata forms. No other composer comes close to such variety. After Beethoven's death, indeed, the mastery of the sonata became very limited. Brahms, for example, could handle only three or four ways of constructing an exposition, and was certainly incapable of dispatching a first group in seven seconds.

The difficulties of this opening theme (a) for the performer are multiple. The first is to convey tactfully that the first beat is an upbeat without too much of an accent at the bar line. Then it should be clear that the right hand is at one and the same time two voices and one voice, which needs subtle inflections within the *sempre legato* specified by Beethoven. In the left hand, the rest at the beginning of every beat must be respected. Only later, at the climax in bar 48 (b) that is the beginning of the recapitulation, does Beethoven allow a sustained line in the subsidiary voice with this figuration, and the effect there depends on the radical change of texture. It is also at bar 48 and the new legato texture in both hands that the bass is finally permitted to let us hear the simple descending scale from E to E which is its true line. The difference between the first presentation of the main theme (*piano*, transparent and unpretentious) and the powerful return is essential to the form:

The return is fused with the development: only the new firmness of the line in the left hand articulates the important structural junction.

The first and second themes are almost equally fused in spite of the startling change of tempo to *Adagio espressivo*. The upper line of the end of the *Vivace* is continued naturally and unaffectedly into the *Adagio*, and the arrival is efficiently prepared by the crescendo. Any break will be due to the misjudgement of the pianist. A comparison with the beginning of op. 31 no. 1 shows how important the continuity between two tempos has become to Beethoven, a preoccupation that will account for the mastery of the finale of op. 110. The transition from the second *Adagio* of op. 109 back to the *Vivace* is equally natural. The two-note slurs of the first edition at the end of bar 65 are omitted by some editors, perhaps because they are not in the autograph, but they were surely inserted by Beethoven, not the engraver, and ought to be followed. They add grace:

If one wishes to see the difference between Beethoven's ideas of exposition and recapitulation, one could not do better than to compare the way bars 9 to 11 are resumed in 12 to 14, with the more radical way the similar bars 58 to 60 are transformed into 61 to 63. The C major at bar 62 is the only *fortissimo* in the movement: it should sound exceptional.

The coda is deeply moving. The chord at the end of bar 77 belongs more with the detached chords in the previous bars 75–6 (which are an augmentation of bars 73–4), and less with the phrase that starts on 78. The surprisingly long eight-bar slur that starts on bar 78 defines a phrase that is independent both of what precedes and of what follows. It is difficult to make the last chord of the movement sound as if it came on a second beat, but worth the effort: allowing it to sound like a downbeat ruins the conception. The rhythm demands that it sound tentative, not final, and it is specifically linked by Beethoven's indication of pedal to the opening of the *Prestissimo*.

The descending scale in the bass from E to E that transformed the beginning of the recapitulation reappears at the opening of the *Prestissimo*, and unites the two opening movements. A variant of the same motif also provides the basis for the closing theme in the exposition of the *Prestissimo*. This theme is in double counterpoint at the octave. For four bars the right hand has a rising scale passage and the left hand an emphatic descending motif. The two hands start together in the centre of the keyboard and then go to the extreme treble and bass (bars 57–60). Right and left hands then exchange their phrases (bars 61–4); low bass and high treble are led back to the centre:

Double counterpoint at the octave is a common academic device, but nobody, as far as I know, ever employed it before Beethoven for a spectacular exploitation of the different registers of the keyboard. (He was evidently interested in the effect, as he repeats it with the third variation of the finale.)

At every point of this movement, Beethoven strangely refuses the low E that he had already employed in the first movement (and, indeed, in op. 101, after all). He even appears ostentatiously to avoid it in bars 68 and 161. It is curious that this one movement should seem to be conceived for the smaller instrument he had before 1815. As a result – or, perhaps, as a cause – the F# becomes the most important bass note, and it is the crux of a striking passage that used to pre-occupy theorists: the leap at the end of the development from a half-cadence *pianissimo* on an F sharp major chord to a *fortissimo* E minor as the main theme returns. Was this movement, certainly worked out specifically for op. 109, based on an earlier idea when the low E was not available?

The alternation of detached and legato touch dominates long sections of the exposition.* The development is compact. It begins over a dominant pedal with a strict canon in soprano and alto derived from the bass theme. With the *una corda* sustained until the return of the main theme, the rising bass that was so important to Beethoven proceeds over 12 bars (going up a sixth from C to A, after which, to continue rising, it must descend to B, rise through C D D#, and descend again to move up to F# with the following motif in the bass, transferred at once to the treble:

---

* See pp. 34–5. For the phrasing at bars 43ff. and 144ff., see pp. 32–4. For the interpretation of *espressivo* followed by *a tempo*, see pp. 97–8.

This is a variant of the motif of the descending scale in the bass with which the movement began. Immediately overlapping the return of the main theme, there is a restatement in double counterpoint at the octave, interchanging bass and treble, with the bass motif no longer in long sustained notes, but detached and hammered by the right hand. At the end of the movement, the scale motif in the left hand descends an octave and a fourth, from a B to the lowest F sharp. The last chords are a *secco* cut-off.

Beethoven had used the form of theme and variations for a finale in the "Eroica" Symphony and the Quartet in E flat major op. 74, but never before in a piano sonata; now he wrote one not only in op. 109 but also in op. 111, both slow movements. He was evidently concerned that all three sonatas should have deeply serious endings. As in the "Eroica" Symphony, the variations are continuous and without pause. No change of tempo should be made except when Beethoven demands one. The theme is marked *mezza voce* and the first variation *molto espressivo*, which implies the same tempo rendered more freely. The art lies in making the *espressivo* sound like the same tempo even as it measures out a little slower by the clock, occasionally held back by an excess of sentiment.

The *leggieramente* of the second variation is far more effective if it stays at the same slow tempo. Few pianists resist the temptation to make a crescendo in bars 41 to 44, but they are marked "tenderly" (*teneramente*), and the crescendo should be reserved for bar 47. The brilliance of the third variation, all in double counterpoint at the octave, sets the slower tempo of the fourth into relief. Bars 69 to 72 are bars 65 to 68 with the bass and treble interchanged. Bars 73 to 80 repeat bars 65 to 72 with the two lines varied. Bars 89 to 96 similarly interchange the treble and bass of bars 81 to 88.

The fourth variation, one of the composer's most extraordinary inspirations, is worked out in great detail. To be played more slowly than the first tempo ("less andante – that is, more adagio – than the theme" is how Beethoven spells it out), expressive arabesques weave intricately through a four-voice texture of transparent grace. At the end of the first bar – and at other places – there is both a dotted quarter note and a quarter note with an eighth rest struck simultaneously – in bar 1 simultaneously by the same hand, indeed. Beethoven exploits here the novel effect of sounds that continue to sing briefly while others die away. The quarter note must be released early enough before the dotted quarter has lost all of its cantabile resonance. In the first four bars, none of the notes in the bass line is longer than two beats of the 9/8 signature, and in each bar the bass line disappears for just a brief moment against the movement of tenor, alto and soprano. In the fifth bar, however, the bass becomes the principal voice, and the long melody note is now sustained for four beats. The complex texture should remain transparent, not made richer and thicker than notated. A heavier, more overtly expressive, sonority comes at last with bars 106 to 109. In bar 107, the original edition displaces the accents in the autograph to the weakest beats. I like to think that this is a revision made at the proof stage by the composer.

The polyphonic intricacy of a fifth variation sets the opening simplicity of the sixth variation into relief. It is a common mistake at the opening of this final variation to bring out the melody in the alto: the important voice is the soprano, generally neglected by performers as uninteresting because it repeats only one note, the dominant B (the alto can take care of itself and is always audible at this point). This repeated dominant is itself the essence of the variation: for twelve bars it steadily accelerates from quarter notes to eighth notes, to triplet eighths,* sixteenths, and finally becoming a measured trill in thirty-second notes. This trill shifts briefly at a few points to the tonic, always returning to the dominant, and speeds up still further against triplet eighths playing a decorated form of the melody. It is finally transferred to the bass over which the ultimate and most passionate decoration of the melody rages in thirty-second notes,† and then to the treble with the flow of thirty-seconds underneath and the theme played in syncopated form above. The different levels of sonority generate tremendous tension (this page had a great influence on the piano music of Liszt). The principal difficulty on the modern piano is to keep the trill in the bass from drowning the rest of the texture. In the final bars of the variation, the melody descends a dominant seventh over a tonic ostinato and over and under a dominant trill in the treble as the dynamic descends to *pianissimo*. Without pause (the pedal is to be held down until the first note of the melody returns), we hear the theme once again in its original form, no longer marked *mezza voce* but a more overt *cantabile* and with the bass doubled in bars 5 to 8 of the theme at the lower octave for greater resonance. The end is signified with no other change than a *ritardando* and pedal on the last chord: this suggests that the last chord is to be held beyond its written value.

Perhaps the most unusual aspect of the sonata is how unassuming on the surface are the opening of the first movement and the end of the last, how apparently modest, and yet how much they demand and reward meditation.

---

* The theory that the 9/8 bars are not to be interpreted as triplets gives an effect that is too odd to be convincing and pays no dividends.

† The rhythm of the change to thirty-second notes is hard to control: most pianists play the trill against the triplet eighths as twelve notes to the quarter, and reducing from 12 to 8 often results in too fast a tempo.

SONATA IN A FLAT MAJOR, OPUS 110
COMPOSED IN 1821

No sonata of Beethoven is more tightly unified by the recurrence of the same or similar motifs throughout the work, and by the clear desire of the composer that the movements succeed each other without pause. At the same time, no work has movements of such disparate emotional character. The first movement begins *con amabilità*, and never completely loses that quality. The scherzo is humorous, folksy, sometimes brutal, and even sardonic. The finale starts with a scena and recitative full of pain, continues with a lament that is, when it returns, literally choked with despair, goes through a condition close to death and ends with a triumphant return of life.

One might imagine that there is a programme connected with this work, and that is certainly possible. Nevertheless, one must distinguish a programme which renders a work of music more intelligible from a programme which is only an inspiration for the composer and is no help to an understanding of the music. The first case may be found in music as different as J. S. Bach's *Capriccio on the Departure of a Beloved Brother* and Richard Strauss's *Don Quixote*. The scenario of the first is given by the titles of the various numbers: at the end, for example, we can recognize the coachman's post horn. Knowing the Cervantes novel helps us to identify the sheep and the windmills in Strauss, passages that would otherwise seem weirdly unprovoked. The second case would be the Chopin ballades, often said to be based on poems by Mieckiewicz, but which the composer refused to identify or even confirm, and which would be irrelevant to an appreciation of the music, or the relation of the Orpheus legend to the slow movement of Beethoven's Fourth Piano Concerto: anyone who needed to be told that the latter work pictured a pleading individual against an angry group, a gradual appeasement and reconciliation of the group, and the unhappiness and despair of the individual, has not been listening to the piece (whether Beethoven had the Orpheus legend in mind may interest the biographer, but for an understanding of the music the point is strictly moot). There is a scenario to op. 110, but whether it refers to any real event or literary inspiration we do not know, and it would not help us either to play the piece or listen to it if we could find out.

The sonata is based on two kinds of motifs: ascending or descending parallel fourths, and rising or falling sixths in scale motion. The first type may be found in the main theme of the first movement, the popular theme in the scherzo (bars 17 to 24), the trio of the scherzo, and the main theme of the fugue. The second type is found in the rising sixths of the first movement (bars 28–31), the main theme, descending, of the scherzo, and the main theme, similarly descending, of the finale's *Arioso dolente*. The contrast of these two kinds of musical material is important in establishing the variety of textures within the work. To what extent it is a help to listening to recognize these recurrences – that is, to what extent they are references – is not easy to determine. Most pianists have recognized the kinship of the fugue theme with the opening of the first movement, and the similarity of bars 162 to 165 of the second fugue with the folk theme of the scherzo has escaped few musicians. Perceiving that the main theme of the scherzo and of the *Arioso dolente* are so much alike, however, may be found to be merely a distraction. What is important is that the fugue theme and the *Arioso* theme are created out of such different material, but this can affect us, and should, without any analytical awareness coming into play. Becoming aware of it, nevertheless, allows us to understand how Beethoven works upon our sensibilities and our emotions. Finding out if there was an occasion for the scenario of the sonata would only tell us how reality acted upon Beethoven (more or less how it acts upon anyone else, we would almost certainly discover), not how Beethoven acts upon us, his listeners and his interpreters.

The exposition of the first movement, *Moderato cantabile molto espressivo*, follows a tripartite Haydnesque model with some original features. It opens with a four-bar motto theme of rising parallel fourths, rounded off with a fermata and trill on a dominant seventh chord, resolved gracefully to the tonic; this is followed by an eight-bar lyrical extension ending with a contour similar to the opening phrase, and closed with the beginning of a new section, a kind of ritornello, light arpeggios delicately accented every four notes. The arpeggios lead directly to the dominant, and to a variety of expressive motifs linked continuously together. A decisive cadence on the dominant is found, without a break in continuity, at bar 28, and another, with a brief moment of space, at bar 34. At the latter point, there is a very short closing section, a brief new cadential theme, marked *dolce*, that rounds off the exposition formally. The unbroken line of melodic progression is what is most striking.

Two of the conventions of Beethoven's formative years appear, not only fulfilled, but magnified on a grand scale in the opening movement of op. 110. The first is the use of the relative minor to end the development section: here Beethoven actually starts in the relative minor and never really leaves it for the entire development. In a strict sense, there is no development, but only a retransition back to the tonic. The whole section is radically simple: the motif of bars 1 to 2 is played eight times in a descending sequence. The left hand is made up of two voices, tenor and bass, which alternate antiphonally. The voices should be clearly distinguished and not run together (Beethoven made a great point of changing the beaming for the entrance of a new voice here, not always correctly followed by the engraver of the first edition). The tenor line has no dynamic indications whatever, the bass always has an expressive swell. This leads eventually back into A flat major and the motto theme, now combined with the thirty-second note *ritornello* arpeggios in a grand sonority.

The second convention is the introduction of subdominant harmony after the opening of the recapitulation. This is memorably exploited by Beethoven. The lyrical extension of the motto is played at the subdominant, and then pushed further in the flat direction, continuing eloquently in the subdominant minor, notated as C sharp minor, and returning to the thirty-second-note arpeggios in E major. The prolongation of D flat minor/C sharp minor by this means adds extraordinary harmonic tension to the recapitulation, and the return from E major to the tonic A flat major at the end of bar 77 is properly ambiguous and mysterious. Opus 110 stands out from any other work of Beethoven or of his predecessors: the most remote harmonic region is placed in the recapitulation, and yet this is achieved simply by the expansion of the most conventional procedure of late eighteenth-century style.

The closing theme is extended in a long sustained climax. The arpeggios return for six bars, the motto appears once more in the left hand, and the final cadence is resolved by two soft, short chords, clearly at once an ending and yet sufficiently indecisive that we expect an immediate continuation. The scherzo starts with the same note in the treble as the previous cadence, as if it had been prepared by the first movement.

There used to be arguments about the accent of the bars of the scherzo:

Are the strong bars the odd-numbered or the even-numbered ones? It is evident that the question is badly put. The strong bars are 1 and 4, and 5 and 8. Beethoven opts for a complex accent system. This implies that there is a contradiction in the rhythm that works itself out later in the scherzo. In the trio the two hands are out of phase: the strong bars in the right hand are 40 and 48, in the left hand 41 and 49. (Beethoven carefully distinguishes with which hand the *ff* is supposed to go.)

The scherzo returns with both halves repeated again. The simple coda works out the rhythmic ambiguity in a simple manner. To understand it, we must look at the last bars of the scherzo:

The *ritardando* in bars 136–8 changes the interpretation of the accent. It is all *piano,* and the *fortissimo* is sudden. In the tiny coda, if one plays the half notes with *sforzandi* as downbeats, it sounds like one bar is missing. This gives the odd conclusion that the downbeats are all missing, that is, they all take place in a bar of rest. That is because the two beats of bar 138, no longer slurred legato as in bar 137, but portamento – detached, slower, and both beats accented – count as if each one were a whole bar. The sudden *fortissimo* of bar 139 is a downbeat and 142 is an upbeat. The second ending, bar 143, is a downbeat, the beginning of a four-bar phrase. There are two more four bar phrases, both beginning with blank bars, the second phrase with a *diminuendo.* The last phrase, also four bars, begins with the *piano poco ritardando* in bar 155. In playing this coda, one must make bar 143 at the second ending sound like the downbeat of a four-bar phrase. It should therefore be interpreted as still *fortissimo* and played percussively. The half-note chord in the next bar must follow metronomically, and that will make it appear to be a syncopation. And all the following chords will sound like syncopations if the rhythm remains absolutely strict until the *poco ritardando,* which sets the rhythm straight and prepares the opening of the finale.

With the *Adagio ma non troppo,* we leave the humour of the scherzo far behind. This is an operatic scena, beginning with three bars of orchestral introduction and a recitative, *più Adagio.* The tempo changes several times. The *Andante* and the *meno Adagio* should be considerably faster than the opening tempo. The *Bebung* we found in the slow movement of op. 106, the representation of a cry of pain by pairs of notes, first struck firmly and then delicately echoed, is the climax of the recitative. A bar-and-a-half-long imitation of the pulsating accompaniment of a string orchestra, crescendo – and with a sudden diminuendo at the end – precedes the entrance of the soprano in the *Arioso dolente* (a lamenting arioso). An arioso is not quite a full aria, but a combination of aria and accompanied recitative – in other words, half *cantabile,* half *parlando.* The *Adagio ma non troppo* in 12/16 is followed by a fugue in 6/8, *Allegro ma non troppo.* Its movement is flowing, tranquil and grand.

This is not an adagio introduction to a fugue, however. The two are indissoluble. The *Adagio* returns, and clearly continues the motion of the fugue:

The tempo of the *Adagio* is consequently a free expressive version of the tempo of the fugue, with its sixteenth notes not mathematically but phenomenologically equal to the eighth notes of the fugue.* The return of the *Adagio ma non troppo*, marked *Perdendo le forze, dolente (Ermattet, klagend* – 'Exhausted, lamenting"), may be compared to the cavatina of the Quartet in B flat major, op. 130, in which the violin solo of the central section is marked *beklemmt* ("choked"), as if excess of sorrow and despair were making it difficult to breathe or to sustain expression for more than a few notes. Harmonically, this effect is reinforced: the return is not in A flat minor, but in the unprecedented key of the leading tone, G minor. We do not need either perfect pitch or key symbolism to hear this as flat, dissonant and depressed.

The end of the return of the *Arioso* has Beethoven's most astonishing effect of tone colour: a series of heavy offbeat chords, crescendo but with the soft pedal held down, and continued to be held down for 30 bars of the return of the fugue. As the return of the fugue specifies *poi a poi di nuovo vivente* (little by little

---

*For a more detailed discussion of these tempos and of this finale in general, see my *The Classical Style*, new ed., 1997, pp. 498–507. When Schindler reported that Beethoven said that there must be several changes of tempo in the *Largo* slow movement of op. 10 no. 3, he also reported that Beethoven added that only connoisseurs should be aware of the change. It is difficult to take anything that Schindler had to say as an authentic or authoritative account, but there is no reason here to think that this misrepresents Beethoven's aesthetics of performance. The first fugue and the second *Adagio* and fugue should appear to be continuing the previous tempo, although an effective performance demands an adjustment. In any case, since the *Arioso* is in 12/16 and the fugue in 6/8, the bars of the *Arioso* will be felt as twice as long, the fugue as having a strong accent twice as often.

coming back to life), we may take these soft, stifled but heavy sonorities as representing the imminence of death. Still veiled by the soft pedal, an arpeggio ascends from the deepest bass to the centre of the piano to recommence the fugue.

Beethoven does not simply symbolize or represent the return to life for us, but persuades us physically of the process. To do this he employs the dryest and most academic devices of counterpoint that all young musicians were forced to learn as soon as they finished going through their species exercises: these are the inversion of the fugue theme, the augmentation (playing it slower) and the diminution (playing it faster). Contrapuntal ingenuity consists of combining these various devices together, and it is usually a purely academic exercise. For the first time in the history of music, however, these hackneyed devices have become the elements of a dramatic scenario.

The original fugue theme ascends: its inversion descends – no longer aspiring but declining, and performed *pianissimo* with the *una corda*, it sounds exhausted. The diminution (the theme played right side up three times as fast) sounds like the stirring of new life. The return to life "little by little" is represented by taking the augmentation of the theme, starting twice as slow, and accelerating it back into the original tempo. The diminution increasing in speed at the same time produces in the end a texture of much greater agitation and energy than the original texture of the fugue. For twenty-four bars there is a *pianissimo* with the soft pedal and no indications of dynamics. Everything is in suspense. Finally a long crescendo begins.

There is, however, one notational problem. If Beethoven simply took the fugue theme twice as slow and accelerated it into double speed back to the original tempo, and did this little by little with the continuity he demanded throughout the second fugue, he would end up with the notation of the fugue in notes twice as long as the original notation but with the tempo twice as fast. He preferred to end up with the original notation and the original tempo so that the beginning and the end would both sound and look the same. This means that halfway through the process he had to change to a faster notation and a slower tempo so that doubling the tempo of the augmentation would finish with exactly the same notation as the original. He did this in bar 168, changing from eighth notes to sixteenths but telling the pianist to play more slowly (*Meno Allegro*). The listener should not know that there has been a change of notation, but experience what happens as part of the continuous process. Every indication is "little by little": *poi a poi di nuovo vivente* (*nach und nach wieder auflebend* – little by little with new life); the crescendo in bar 160 has dots continuing it for eight bars; then, in bar 165, we find *poi a poi tutte le corde* (little by little lift the soft pedal [from one to two to three strings]); in bar 171, *poi a poi più moto* (*nach und nach wieder geschwinder* – little by little faster again). There must be no break in the process of returning to life, of coming back to the original tempo.

Nevertheless, one rhythmic problem remained: the original fugue theme had eight beats of dotted quarters in 6/8, and the diminution is three times as fast. Eight beats are inconvenient in 6/8. So Beethoven lopped off two notes of the rising parallel fourths, making a six-beat motif. This abridgement adds to the acceleration. He does this at the point that he changes the notation from eighths to sixteenths at the *Meno Allegro*. However, in order to represent the agitation of new life, and to make the change from an eight-note theme to a six-note theme convincing, the augmentation in the left hand and the diminution in the right have become out of phase. The right hand is consistently one beat ahead of the left, starting in bar 161. It takes Beethoven a bar and a half of the *Meno Allegro* to bring the two rhythms back in phase, and to correct the accent of the diminution in bar 170. This increases the excitement of the process:

In bars 165 to 170, the diminution in the right hand should be understood in
the following form:

The goal of the original tempo is reached precisely with the return to A flat major
and the main theme in octaves in the bass (bar 174), so that the traditional sense
of the sonata recapitulation is now applied to tempo as well as to theme and
tonality.* In this finale, Beethoven reconceived tempo as if it were an element of
classical form and a part of tonality.

   The notation may have set a complex problem (the manuscript at the *Meno
Allegro* contains mistakes, with rests of the wrong value, some, but not all, corrected by Beethoven), but the basic idea is a simple and dramatic one. The work-
ing-out is a triumph: the return to life is gloriously ecstatic. Of the last three
sonatas, this is the only one with a brilliant final page.

SONATA IN C MINOR, OPUS 111
COMPOSED BY 1822

Combining fugue and sonata was a great classical preoccupation. The fugue was
a learned technique and it gave prestige to the more sociable form of the sonata.
We must not, however, ascribe the introduction of fugal texture only to crass
social ambition, as if court musicians wished to assert their qualifications for
being admitted to an academy. Fugue allowed for an intensity of sentiment and
a richness of texture threatened by the *galant* style of the late eighteenth century.
Putting a fugato in a development section was a common recourse of many composers, but full-fledged fugues were reserved by Haydn for an occasional quartet
finale. Polyphonically more complex than the average first movement of a sonata,
a fugue was generally harmonically simpler and less ambiguous. It was therefore

---

*The end of the first playing of the theme in octaves in the bass is a short unaccented note
before a rest, bar 178, and must be played shorter than written with no pedal, or the entrance
of the theme in the alto will not be heard; the *forte* certainly applies here only to the alto E♭.

best placed as a last movement, which had traditionally less harmonic tension than the first. Mozart made a considerable advance in the ambitious use of fugue by combining the fugue with a sonata structure in the finale of the first of his String Quartets dedicated to Haydn, the one in G major K. 387, and also with overture form in *The Magic Flute*. (He made extensive use, as well, of canon and stretto and other contrapuntal devices in works like the finale of the "Jupiter" Symphony and the first movement of the Sonata for Piano in D major K. 576, but this evaded the problem of combining fugue and sonata.) Otherwise, fugue writing was better indulged in liturgical works.

In his last five piano sonatas, Beethoven grappled with the problem four times. Opus 101 was the easiest solution, incorporating fugal texture in a development section, although the fugue here is considerably more formal, longer, and more impressive than the occasional indulgence in a little bit of fugue in a development (as in the finale of Beethoven's Third Piano Concerto). Opus 106 outdid anybody else's finale as a fugue, including Beethoven's own String Quartet in C major op. 59 no. 3. Opus 110 was a conception far more profound, a rethinking and humanization of all the most basic devices of fugue in order to create a scenario of dramatic power. With op. 111, Beethoven now attacked the problem that only Mozart had been able to solve, and then only with a finale: combining sonata and fugue textures, and accomplishing this with a first movement. The finale of Mozart's G major Quartet was courtly: Beethoven's fugue-sonata was to be tragic, and this is announced with the opening gesture of the *Maestoso* introduction.

The *Maestoso* is not an adagio, and it should certainly be quicker than the *Grave* that opens the Sonata Pathétique. The opening harmony is a diminished seventh chord on F#: the three possible diminished seventh chords (on F#, B and E, with their inversions) govern the first movement, and are presented always in the order that they occur in the introduction.* The main theme of the *Allegro con brio ed appassionato* is stated without accompaniment, as if it were the beginning of a fugue, but doubled at the octave. The monophonic presentation, however, continues surprisingly for 9 bars with continuously changing tone colour distinguished by slight changes of tempo (staccato, *portamento*, and detached sixteenth notes), followed by a counterstatement no longer monophonic but with a homophonic accompaniment, also with three different touches (staccato, *portamento*, and legato).[†]

At the end of the counterstatement, a third statement (bar 35) moves first to the relative major and then to the submediant A flat major. This time the texture is that of a double fugue with a countertheme: the fugal writing here as in the

---

* For the tempo see pp. 99–100. For the role of the diminished seventh chords, see my *The Classical Style*, new ed., 1997, pp. 442–4.

[†] For changes of touch in this work, see p. 39.

"Hammerklavier" is characterized by heroic virtuosity. A two-bar motif (bar 48) that leaps from treble to bass and back to treble on a diminished seventh chord introduces an expressive new theme in a dotted rhythm, which is repeated with an elaborate decoration (twelve-note, sextuplet and quintuplet arabesques) in a continuously slowing tempo, ending with the briefest of adagios. A cascade of descending broken thirds on a diminished seventh chord, followed by an ascending scale with a non legato touch, leads to a powerful, concluding military march theme (bar 58), returning at the end to the monophonic texture, brutally punctuated by a *sforzando* on every beat, and ending with unharmonized A flat octaves. The exposition is repeated.

The development moves to the dominant G minor in the most laconic and efficient fashion: a soft, offbeat octave G, a pause, and a brusque offbeat chord of the dominant of the dominant are all that is necessary. The rest of the development is another short double fugue with a new countertheme (based on the dominant sevenths of the introduction and on an augmented reference to the shape of the beginning of the principal theme):

The motifs in Beethoven may often be related by simple contour or shape, and not precisely by pitch or rhythm. The fugal texture is succeeded by a dominant pedal of six bars preparing the return of the main theme. In fact, the transition overlaps with the return as its last two bars (90 and 91) already contain the complete theme at the tonic, although with the dominant still in the bass. This kind of overlapping at a recapitulation was an inspiration to Brahms.

The statement of the main theme at the return introduces a new element in the repertoire of touch and tone colour, detached octaves in both hands, but with the right hand on the beat and the left hand following a sixteenth note late. The recapitulation then moves to the subdominant traditional at this place, with the texture of a double fugue. This lasts for nine bars, at which point a variant of the monophonic texture takes its place, five bars in steady parallel tenths (changing to sixths and thirds when it rises beyond the range of the keyboard). Throughout this whole passage the bass moves up mostly bar by bar: F (bars 100–1), G (102), A♮ (103), B♭ (104–6), C (107), D♭ (108–9), E♭ (110), F (111), G (112). There is then a jump from the dominant G back to the tonic (bar 119). The effect is one of enormous excitement, and the virtuosity is essential to create the tension.

On the return of the motif that leaps into the bass and back to the treble (bars 114–15), it has often been suggested that the high C in bar 121 should be an E♭, and I agree that the E♭ makes more sense (it is possible that Beethoven miscounted ledger lines, and put only five instead of six). The expressive theme in a dotted rhythm with a retarding tempo is considerably extended, and comes back a second time in the subdominant (bar 124). Its quintuplet decorative turn is employed to create a rising and accelerating sequence back into the original tempo. The broken thirds that descend on two diminished seventh chords in bars 132–3 are a more brilliant version of a similar passage in Mozart's Sonata in A minor K. 310:

The figuration is paradoxically both commonplace in character and infrequent. Both examples are found at precisely the same structural point, at the end of the recapitulation preceding a closing theme of military character with a dotted rhythm (the two bars in Beethoven dramatically expand a single bar in the exposition, but the Mozart is an impressive interruption of the original pattern which must have been as striking to the young Beethoven as it is to musicians today). In his last sonata, in spite of the extraordinary transformations that he had effected in style, it is remarkable that he still consciously or unconsciously recalled the models in Mozart's work that he had studied more than thirty years before.

A coda presents the outline of the main theme *fortissimo* with offbeat staccato chords separated by pauses, first marked by *sforzandi* and then diminishing. Nine bars of quiet minor plagal cadences on C major with the sixteenth note motion that characterized so much of the piece steadily present in the left hand close the *Allegro*. The ending in C major clearly prepares the second and final movement.

The slow movement is called an *Arietta*, and the tempo – *Adagio molto semplice e cantabile* – is *molto semplice* not *adagio molto*. As I have said, it is hard to resist the temptation to play this profound work too slowly, as that is a way of convincing a docile public that it is listening to something spiritual and sublime, and the movement can be very effective dragged out if it is done by a master. A very slow tempo, however, gets in the way of the direction *molto semplice*: with too long a time between one note and the next, it is impossible to avoid a certain amount of unneeded fuss as the melody proceeds.

The contour of the theme, as musicians have often observed, resembles in many respects the waltz that Diabelli sent to so many Central European composers in 1819, asking each of them to contribute one variation for a charity publication. It would not be unfair to say that Beethoven profoundly reshaped Diabelli's theme for his sonata:

The *Arietta* is more concentrated than the waltz: Beethoven's first two bars do the work of Diabelli's first eight. But the resemblance is clear: even the timid harmonic excursion of the *Arietta* at the beginning of its second half (vi to V, A minor to G major) is foreshadowed by the end of the first half of the waltz. Yet Beethoven's first reaction to Diabelli's tune was that it was trash, and we all feel that the *Arietta* is sublime.

The kinship of Beethoven's sublime with trash or junk reveals an essential aspect of his art. Eventually Beethoven was won over to Diabelli's unprepossess-

ing waltz: he saw that it had possibilities, and wrote not one but thirty-three variations that can lay claim to being his greatest work for piano – at least it is the
work that allows us best to grasp almost all the facets of his genius. Nevertheless,
his initial reaction was right, the waltz is indeed trash. It displays in the crudest
fashion the simplest elements of tonality – tonic, dominant, relative minor, and
subdominant – and does nothing with them but present them in the right order
with disconcertingly commonplace motifs.

It would be only a slight exaggeration to say that this is what Beethoven himself
does on so many occasions. What the exaggeration hides is crucial: Beethoven
knew how to strip naked the simplest elements of tonality in order to release their
full power, to use the commonplace to reveal what made it so irresistible. Diabelli
is complacent; he does no more than use the commonplace – he does not, like
Beethoven, insist upon it obsessively until it releases its full potential. Beethoven's
crudeness was provocative, never fortuitous or thoughtless, and it could be juxta-
posed to, and even combined with, a sophistication of extreme refinement and
delicacy. His art was never innocent, but it often deliberately skirts the edge of the
artless. The *molto semplice* of the *Arietta* is a direction to the performer, not a
description of the piece, but simplicity is necessary to bring out what is already
there. Almost every bar of the theme, considered separately, is commonplace, there
are no eccentric harmonies or turns of phrase: the art lies in the controlled and sustained rise to the sixth bar and the swift fall back to the opening. Bar 3 leaps a sixth
from G to E, but the E is part of a simple compact line that springs from the C and
D of the opening. We have to wait for it, but that only makes it more expressive.

To comprehend the craft of Beethoven, no detail is more cogent than bar 13:
after the insistence on the harmony of the relative minor for four bars, the dominant in root position arrives, and all harmonic motion ceases for a moment. As
we listen to it, we become aware that the dominant alone, simply sustained and
repeated, can be more expressive than any more exotic harmony. And from here
to the end of the theme every chord is in simple root position, and bar 15 intensifies bar 13 only by repeating the dominant three times and raising the melody
to the high point it had reached at the end of the first part. The crescendo and the
final *sforzando* make us grasp the power of this excessively commonplace chord.

Unless we think that the extraordinary resemblance of the *Arietta* to Diabelli's waltz is entirely coincidental – and this is unlikely since he worked at both of them around the same time – we must admit that not only did Beethoven realize that he could create a grand work with Diabelli's trashy tune, but he also, perhaps unconsciously, rethought the principal elements of the tune into a melody of great beauty.

Each variation increases the speed of the previous one: with the first variation, the dotted eighths of the theme triple to sixteenths; in a complex move, variation 2 doubles the three sixteenths to two groups of one sixteenth and one thirty-second; variation 3 makes a second doubling to four times one thirty-second and one sixty-fourth, *sempre forte*, and with eighteen offbeat *sforzandi*: this transformation has always impressed with its jazzy energy. Variation 4 divides these last sets by nine even notes in a perpetual motion *sempre pp* (the agitation is heightened by steady and systematic disruption, as a shadow of the melody in the right hand is placed only on a weak beat with the first beat always void).

A coda starts with six bars of crescendo which seems to be leading to a simple tonic cadence finished by the traditional trill – except that it is not finished and the trill on D that should close in C major, suddenly metamorphoses into a triple trill on the dominant seventh of E flat major. What should have been the ultimate cadence in C major ends up dramatically as the first departure from C major in the movement, and the banal structural device of the final trill becomes the most original juncture of the form.

As a young pianist Beethoven was famous for his triple trills, which he displayed several times in his concerto cadenzas and in op. 2 no. 3, and he returns to his youthful accomplishment in the virtuosity of his last sonata. The trill is the limit of the gradual acceleration of the movement, an unmeasured velocity: with it, the process of acceleration comes to an end. The trill rises in the soprano to close on a high E♭, but the melody rises still further as if played by a violin and then descends rapidly into a long diatonic circle of fifths.* Harmonically this does not move but merely revolves. All forward motion is suspended as we wait for the sequence to be halted. The theme returns in the middle of the preparation for the return to the tonic: most pianists like to set the re-entrance in relief, but I think it would be more in conformity with the structure to allow the listener to become gradually aware that the theme has already returned. (There is no break in texture when the theme begins: the new texture has already been introduced towards the end of the preceding process.)

The final variation (like the end of the "Eroica" variations or the last variation of the slow movement of the "Appassionata", partly a return of the original theme) combines the slowest and the fastest motion, the theme and variation

---

* For a more detailed consideration of this page, see *The Classical Style*, new ed., 1997, pp. 446–8.

four, then adds to it the third and faster speed of the trill. The last page is almost entirely *pianissimo* with a sonority of diaphanous delicacy and refinement, most of it in the highest register. Three bars before the end it rises briefly to *forte*, with fragments of the theme reduced to its simplest elements, and then falls back rapidly to *pianissimo*. The last note is short, an eighth note followed by a sixteenth rest. The modesty of the final chord is significant.

Endnotes

PART I

[1] From "Journées de Lecture", pp. 162–3, in *Contre Sainte-Beuve (précédé de Pastiches et mélanges)*, Gallimard, Paris, 1971.

[2] *School of Clavier Playing*, translated with introduction and notes by Raymond H. Haggh, University of Nebraska Press: Lincoln and London, 1982, p. 345.

[3] Türk, p. 345. For consistency with the terms used so far here, I have altered the translator's "detached" to "staccato".

[4] Quoted from Emily Anderson's translation, *The Letters of Beethoven*, London, 1961, vol. II, p. 743.

[5] Trans. Emily Anderson, *The Letters of Beethoven*, London, 1961, vol. III, p. 1325.

[6] *Thayer's Life of Beethoven*, ed. Elliot Forbes, Princeton, 1964, vol. II, pp. 687–8.

[7] Anderson, *Letters of Beethoven*, vol. II, p. 727.

[8] Rudolf Kolisch, "Tempo and Character in Beethoven's Music", *Musical Quarterly*, vol. 77, nos 1 and 2, 1993.

[9] See *The New Grove*, "Allegretto".

[10] *The Letters of Mozart and his Family*, trans. Emily Anderson, 2nd ed. by A. Hyatt King and Monica Carolan, London and New York, 1966, vol. II, p. 930.

[11] Quoted by William Newman, *Beethoven on Beethoven*, New York, 1988, p. 94.

[12] In his edition for The Associated Board of the Royal Schools of Music.

[13] W. de Lenz, *Beethoven et ses trois styles*, Paris, 1855, p. 190.

PART II

[1] *A Companion to Beethoven's Pianoforte Sonatas*, Associated Board, London, 1935, p. 48.

[2] Ibid., p. 134.

[3] Cited by W. de Lenz, p. 159.

[4] *On the Proper Performance of all Beethoven's Works for the Piano*, ed. Paul Badura Skoda, Universal, Vienna, 1970, p. 49.

[5] Review of Beethoven's Symphony no. 5, *Schriften zur Musik*, Winkler, Munich, 1963, p. 50.

[6] In his Associated Board edition, vol. III, p. 115.

[7] *The Letters of Beethoven*, trans. Emily Anderson, London, 1961, vol. II, p. 806.

[8] *On the Proper Performance*, Commentary, p. 6.

[9] *The Letters of Beethoven*, trans. Emily Anderson, vol. II, pp. 804–5.

Index

All Sonatas are for piano unless otherwise indicated; key signatures are major unless specified as minor.

Allegretto, classical   48–79
Allegretto finales   82–95
Allegro, conventions of   96–7
"authenticity"   47, 76 n.

Bach, Johann Sebastian   10, 33, 199, 216,
  220, 227
  *Capriccio on the Departure of a Beloved
    Brother*   235
  Chromatic Fantasy and Fugue   215
  Partita no. 4 in D   118–19
  Toccata, Adagio and Fugue in C   23
  Two-part Inventions   76
  Well-Tempered Clavier   4, 138
Bach, Philip Emanuel   35–6
Badura-Skoda, Paul   88, 93 n., 219
Beethoven, Ludwig van
  accents   20–2
  Adagios, tempi of   105–6
  Allegretto, classical, use of   80–95
  Allegretto finales   64–9, 80, 82–95,
    133–4, 149, 159, 168, 171–3, 186–8,
    190–91
  Allegros, tempi of   95–104
  "Andante favori"   136
  An die ferne Geliebte   219
  autographs   16, 24–6, 32, 43, 192
  barcarolle   202
  cavatina   170–1
  C minor, symbolic use of   134
  Diabelli Variations   229, 246–9
  finales   12, 69
  fingering   36–8, 125
  fugue finales   217–18, 226–8, 243

Great Fugue   26
legato, non legato, staccato   34–42
Mass in C major   64–5
metronome marks   44–8, 55, 81–2, 92,
  96–7, 98–9, 218–19, 225
minuet form   11–12
Missa Solemnis   55, 204, 229
"Nord oder Süd"   42–3
pedal, use of   107–14, 156–7
perpetuum mobile   171–3, 196–7
phrasing   13–42
Piano Concerto no. 3   78–9, 117, 148
Piano Concerto no. 4   78, 235
Piano Concerto no. 5 ("The Emperor")
  97
phrasing   13–42
pianos   38–9, 105–6, 117–20, 139,
  156–7, 185
piano sonatas *see below*
piano sonatas, home and concert
  performance of   3–7
Quartet op. 18 no. 1 in F   128
Quartet op. 59 no. 1 in F   87
Quartet op. 59 no. 3 in C   87, 96, 243
Quartet op. 74 in E flat   85, 86, 233
Quartet op. 95 in F minor   85–6, 102
Quartet op. 130 in B flat   239
Quartet op. 131 in C sharp minor
  46–7
Quartet op. 135 in F   92–3, 95–6
Rondo finales   12, 128, 133–4, 140–1,
  144, 145–6, 149, 152, 162–3, 168,
  186–7, 200–1, 210–12
rubato   21–2, 97–9, 164–6

Septet op. 20 in E flat   179
short endings   23–8
slurs   13–20
Sonata op. 30 no. 1 in A for violin and piano   85
Sonata op. 69 for cello and piano in A   186
Sonata op. 96 for violin and piano   94–5
Sonata op. 102 no. 1 in C for cello and piano   104, 186
Sonata op. 102 no. 2 in D for cello and piano   96, 215, 225
sonata form   9–12
sonatas, piano   *see below*
spianato, cultivation of effect of   33
symphonies, metronome marks   55
Symphony no. 3 ("Eroica")   79, 96, 134, 233
Symphony no. 4   81–2, 209
Symphony no. 5   89
Symphony no. 6 ("Pastoral")   55, 87, 96–7
Symphony no. 7   55, 83, 85, 86, 95, 190 n.
Symphony no. 8   12, 55, 85, 89, 92
Symphony no. 9   11, 81, 101–2, 226
tarantella   177–8
tempi   43–8, 80–106, 218–19
terminology, conventional Italian, use of   45, 213, 215
theme and variations as finale   233–4, 238–11
trills   114–17, 248
Trio op. 70 no. 1 in D ("Ghost")   104–5
Trio op. 70 no. 2 in E flat   86–7, 190 n.
Trio op. 97 in B flat ("Archduke")   97, 186
Viennese tradition, transformation of   96, 149
Weihe des Hauses, Die   219
Beethoven, Ludwig van, piano sonatas
op. 2, nos 1–3   123–30
op. 2 no. 1 in F minor   123–5, 143, 194
op. 2 no. 2 in A   6, 23, 25–7, 78, 80, 125–8
op. 2 no. 3 in C   12, 28–9, 128–30
op. 7 in E flat   29–30, 80, 130–4

op. 10, nos 1–3   134–43
op. 10 no. 1 in C minor   17, 134–7
op. 10 no. 2 in F   137–8
op. 10 no. 3 in D   11, 23, 24, 89, 117, 138–41
op. 13 ("Pathétique")   3, 15–16, 83, 141–4
op. 14 no. 1 in E   144–6
op. 14 no. 2 in G   146–7
op. 22 in B flat   80, 147–9, 190 n., 220
op. 26 in A flat   16, 150–2, 209–10
op. 27 no. 1 in E flat (Sonata quasi una Fantasia)   39–42, 153–6
op. 27 no. 2 in E flat ("Moonlight")   24, 107–8, 156–9
op. 28 in D ("Pastoral")   10, 30–2, 79, 160–3
op. 31   6, 111, 164–78, 229
op. 31 no. 1 in G   10, 37, 82–3, 104, 111, 164–8, 184, 216
op. 31 no. 2 in D minor   117–18, 119, 168–73, 194
op. 31 no. 3 in E flat   10, 11, 12, 89, 93, 96, 173–8
op. 49, nos 1 and 2   178–9
op. 53 in C ("Waldstein")   10, 91–2, 111–14, 114–15, 136, 144, 166, 167, 180–8, 229
op. 54 in F   87–8, 90–2, 119, 189–92
op. 57 in F minor ("Appassionata")   91–2, 97, 111–12, 186, 192–201, 224, 226
op. 78 in F sharp   197–201
op. 79 in G   5–6, 201–2
op. 81a ("Les Adieux")   10, 11, 12, 186, 202–7
op. 90 in E minor   21–2, 93–4, 208–12
op. 101 in A   110–11, 186, 212–18
op. 106 in B flat ("Hammerklavier")   6, 12, 35, 78, 80, 81, 96, 99, 104, 108–10, 116, 119–20, 147, 172, 218–28
op. 109 in E   12, 32–5, 36, 97–8, 151, 225, 230–4
op. 110 in A flat   12, 19–20, 20–1, 22, 235–42
op. 111 in C minor   12, 19, 22, 39, 98, 99–100, 142, 242–9
Berlioz, Hector   156, 157

Brahms, Johannes   215, 230
  Piano Concerto no. 1 in D minor   226
  Piano Concerto no. 2 in B flat   55, 89,
    102–3
Breitkopf & Härtel, Beethoven's works,
  critical edition   35

Chopin, Frédéric   7, 18, 21, 28, 33, 81,
    142, 150, 194–5, 216, 235
  Etude in E flat minor op. 10 no. 6   88,
    90
Clementi, Muzio   79, 80
Cone, Edward T.   84 n.
Constable, John   162
Czerny, Carl   6, 28, 36, 46, 69, 80, 82,
    85, 86, 88, 90, 91, 93, 107, 125, 141,
    144, 159

Debussy, Claude   43
Dussek, Jan Ladislav   79

fugue, and sonata   242–4

Haydn, Joseph   5, 9, 10, 11–12, 41–2,
    46, 48, 77–9, 123, 125, 126, 126 n.,
    127, 132, 172, 199, 201, 206, 215,
    217, 220, 242
  Quartet op. 33 no. 6 in D   77
  Quartet op. 50 no. 3 in E flat   11, 206
  Quartet op. 55 no. 2 in F minor   77, 78
  The Seasons   78
  Sonata in A flat, Hob. XVI/46   11
  Sonata in C minor, Hob. XVI/20   11
  Symphony no. 85 in C   78
  Symphony no. 94 in G ("Surprise")   78
  Symphony no. 100 in C ("Military")
    77
Handel, tempi of age of   44
Henle, Urtext edition   17, 185
Hoffmann, E. T. A.   9 n., 181
Hummel, Johann Nepomuk   46, 136

Jean-Paul   167

Koch, Heinrich Christoph   9 n., 124
Kolisch, Rudolf   46–7, 96

Larsen, Jens Peter   9
legato, non legato and staccato   34–9
Lenz, Wilhelm von   90–1, 141
Leschetizky, Theodor   4

Levin, Robert   76 n.
Liszt, Franz   6, 133, 234

Mackerras, Sir Charles   27, 69, 88
Mahler, Gustav   69
Mälzel metronome   45, 46, 48
Marshall, Robert L.   44, note
Marty, Jean-Pierre   48
Mendelssohn, Felix   176, 229
minuet form   11–12
Moscheles, Ignaz   219
Mosel, Ignaz Franz, Edler von   45
Mozart, Leopold   55
Mozart, Wolfgang Amadeus   5, 9, 10, 17,
    28, 33, 46, 48, 49–54, 56–64, 65–78,
    97, 123, 126, 127, 128, 130, 133,
    164, 166, 174, 204, 210, 216, 217,
    219, 242, 246
  Concerto K. 271 in E flat   14
  Concerto K. 414 in A   76
  Concerto K. 453 in G   49–54, 55, 57
  Concerto K. 491 in C minor   66–9
  Concerto K. 503 in C   69–71
  Così fan tutte   77 n.
  Don Giovanni   27
  Fantasia K. 475 in C minor   153
  Marriage of Figaro, Act 3, Allegretto
    finale   58–63, 76
  Quartet K. 465 for strings in C   64 n.
  Quartet K. 493 for piano and strings in E
    flat   72
  Quartet K. 575 for strings in D   72
  Quintet K. 452 for piano and winds in E
    flat   72
  Quintet K. 581 for clarinet and strings in
    A   72
  Rondo K. 494 for piano in F   64
  Rondo K. 511 for piano in A minor
    153 n.
  Sonata K. 306 for violin and piano   57
  Sonata K. 310 in A minor   139, 197,
    245
  Sonata K. 330 in C   65
  Sonata K. 331 in A   20, 76 n.
  Sonata K. 333 in B flat   5, 65–6
  Sonata K. 376 for violin and piano in F
    58
  Sonata K. 379 for violin and piano in G
    58
  Sonata K. 454 in B flat for violin and
    piano   56, 57

Sonata K. 457 in C minor 153
Sonata K. 481 for violin and piano in E
   flat 57
Sonata K. 533 in F 64
Sonata K. 545 in C 11
Sonata K. 570 in B flat 18, 74
Sonata K. 576 in D 73–7
Symphony K. 550 in G minor 88–9,
   90, 123
Trio K. 496 for piano and strings in G
   72
Trio K. 498 for piano, clarinet and viola
   in E flat 72, 95
Trio K. 502 for piano and strings in B
   flat 72
Trio K. 542 for piano and strings in E
   72–3
Viola quintet K. 593 in D 143
Zauberflöte, Die 77 n., 243

Nägeli edition (1803), Sonata op. 31 no. 1
   in G 37, 38
Newman, William S. 14
Nottebohm, Gustav 82

performing practice 6–7, 43–4, 69,
   105–6, 108, 110–11, 114, 139, 212
pianos, modern cf Beethoven's 105–6,
   117–20, 157
Pollini, Maurizio 88
Prokofiev, Sergey 166
Proust, Marcel 3–4
Puchberg, Michael 74

Ries, Ferdinand 218, 228
Rondo finales 186–7, 200–1, 210–12
rubato 21–2, 97–9, 164–6
Rudolph, Archduke of Austria 5, 202

Scarlatti, Domenico 115, 125

Schindler, Anton 82–3, 239 n.
Schnabel, Artur 4, 6, 13, 88, 225
Schoenberg, Arnold 43
Schott, Bernard, & Sons, Beethoven letter
   to 44, 47
Schubert, Franz 11, 79, 85, 199
   Sonata in A 84
   Sonata in B flat 132
   Symphony in C 100–1
Schumann, Clara 90
Schumann, Robert 7, 33, 229
   Humoreske 148
   Toccata for piano op. 7 90
Serkin, Rudolf 142
Simrock edition (1803), Sonata op. 31 no.
   1 in G 37, 38
slurs 13–20
sonata form 9–11
Stravinsky, Igor 81 n.
Strauss, Richard, *Don Quixote* 235

tempi ordinarii 44–8, 48–79, 219
tempo 43–106
Tchaikovsky, Peter Ilyitch 69
Tovey, Donald Francis 11, 13, 83, 91,
   135, 143 n., 151 n., 189, 205, 217
Tyson, Alan 77 n.
Triest, Johann Karl Friederich 6
Türk, Daniel Gottlob 15, 35–6

Vienna
   Hausmusik in 4–5
   standard tempi 46–8, 96

Webster, James 42 n.
Weingartner, Felix 80

Zaslaw, Neil 96 n.